WOODWORKING PROJECTS II

50 Easy-to-Make Projects from HANDS ON Magazine

A Shopsmith®/Rodale Press Publication

Shopsmith®, Inc.
6640 Poe Avenue
Dayton, Ohio 45414

Rodale Press, Inc.
33 East Minor Street
Emmaus, Pennsylvania 18049

Preface

This book contains fifty woodworking project plans from back issues of *HANDS ON,* The Home Workshop Magazine published by Shopsmith, Inc. These easy-to-make wooden projects are sure to provide any woodworker, from beginner to expert, with hours of fun and enjoyment in the shop. The projects are ideal gifts for friends or family, and they're suitable for many occasions—Christmas, birthdays, weddings, etc.

A word of appreciation is addressed to the dozens of *HANDS ON* readers who have contributed their project ideas to the magazine over the years. Their ideas continue to provide success and enjoyment for many other woodworkers.

A final note: As you undertake these (and any other) woodworking projects, keep safety your top priority. Use the recommended tools and procedures. Also, remember to plan your work before you begin. Be sure to study every project plan thoroughly, including the diagrams and list of materials, before making any cuts.

LC 85-29792
ISBN 0-87857-619-3 hardcover
ISBN 0-87857-616-9 paperback

Printed in the United States of America on recycled paper containing a high percentage of de-inked fiber.

Rodale Press Edition

1986
10 9 8 7 6 5 4 Hardcover
10 9 Paperback

Publisher: Shopsmith®, Inc./Rodale Press, Inc.
Design: Kearns Design Studio
Text Preparation: Scharff Associates, Ltd.
Cover Photography: Dan Gabriel

Contents

FURNITURE

ACCESSORIES

HOME IMPROVEMENT

Furniture

Not only will you gain a sense of accomplishment after completing these projects, but you'll also end up with very practical, beautiful furniture pieces. This section contains fourteen projects from which to choose. Select the one that fits your needs or fancy most, and get started. Once you see the results of your work, you'll probably be back to start in on your next choice.

SIMPLE TABLES

From *HANDS ON* Sept/Oct 83

One of the simplest pieces of furniture you can make is a table. Basically there are only nine parts—four legs, four rails, and a top. And, if you know how to rip, crosscut, dowel, and glue—you can make any table, any size.

But, simple doesn't mean plain. By using woodworking techniques such as shaping, molding, and turning, you'll easily add elegance to a simple project.

Four simple end tables illustrate this point. You can make the table you want using the various techniques illustrated.

The basic end table measures 18″ wide × 24″ long × 22″ high. Here's how to make one in ten easy steps.

1. Select your stock. To save time and frustration, first select stock that's properly dried, straight, and free of knots and defects.

Alternate the end grain on the boards for the top. This will reduce the effects of any warping that may take place.

2. Prepare the stock. First, rip stock to the proper width, then crosscut it to approximate length. Allow an extra 8″ on the legs (A) and rails (B,C) and 2″ for the top (D) pieces.

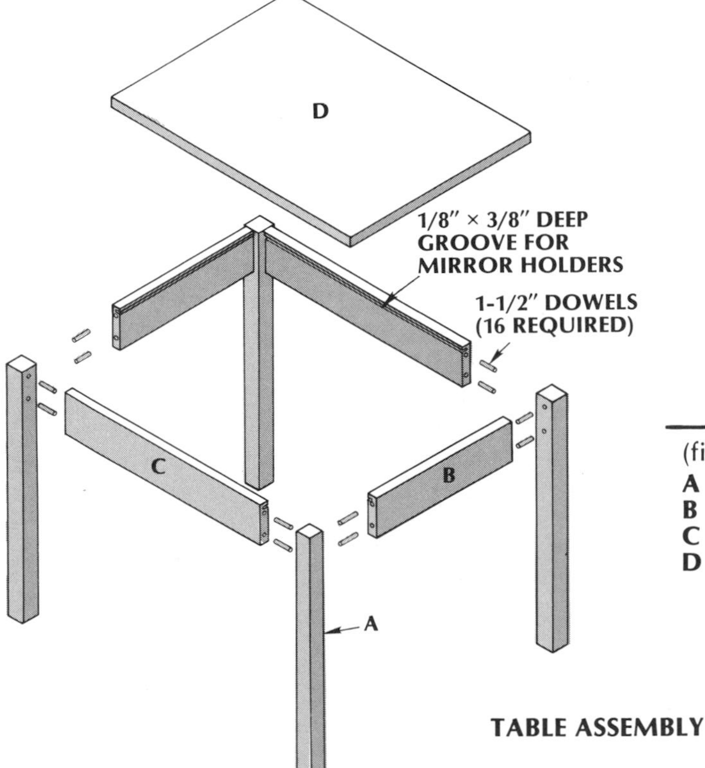

TABLE ASSEMBLY

LIST OF MATERIALS

(finished dimensions in inches)

A	Legs (4)	1-1/2 × 1-1/2 × 21-1/4
B	End rails (2)	3/4 × 3-1/2 × 13-1/2
C	Side rails (2)	3/4 × 3-1/2 × 19-1/2
D	Top	3/4 × 18 × 24
	Dowel pins (16)	3/8 dia. × 1-1/2
	Mirror holders (6)	

3. Prepare legs (A) and rails (B,C). Use a disc sander to get the finished length on the legs and rails. With a good combination square, check the ends of these pieces for squareness as you go. Arrange the legs and rails, and then mark them for their location on the finished project.

4. Assemble the top. Arrange the boards for the top so end grain alternates, then mark the boards in order to keep track of this arrangement. To glue up, joint the edges of each board. For added strength and easier alignment, dowel the edges by using horizontal boring. Apply an aliphatic resin (yellow) glue evenly to facing edges and clamp using bar clamps.

After the glue has dried, remove the clamps and scrape off any excess glue with a cabinet scraper.

Cut the top to size by first jointing one edge. Then, clamp a straight guide board perpendicular to the jointed edge and trim one end of the top. You now have two square edges as guides to obtain final width and length.

5. Mounting the top. There are many effective ways to secure the top to the frame, one of which is to use at least two screw pockets per side. Using mirror holders is another good method for mounting tabletops. Screwed to the underside of the top, these holders project into a saw kerf on the rail. Use six holders for this table—one for each end and two for each side. Whichever method is chosen, it is necessary to perform the operations on the rails before proceeding further.

6. Joinery. Among the several different ways to join legs to rails, one of the most common methods is by using dowel joints. They're simple to make and very strong when properly glued and clamped. Using a square, carefully mark the location of dowel holes on the legs. Allow an extra 1/16" depth on each dowel hole for glue. From the location of the dowel holes on the legs, mark the location of the matching holes on the rails. (Dowel center finders make this easy.) Bore the holes in the rails using horizontal boring.

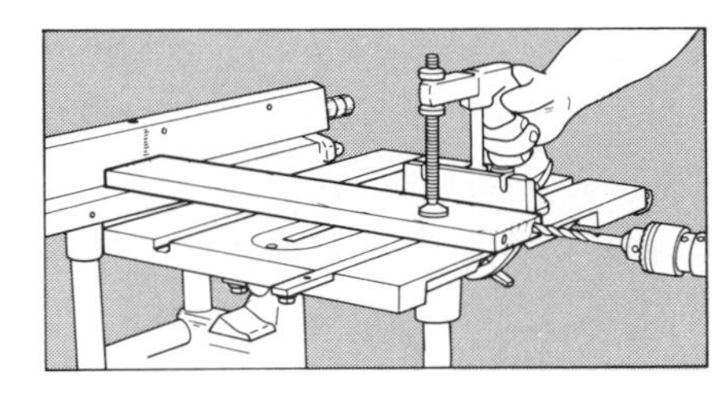

Boring dowel pin holes in the end of a rail with horizontal boring. The rip fence and miter gauge are used to position the stock.

7. Customize the table. At this point, special operations should be used on the table components. Check out the variations provided or use your own to create a really unique piece of furniture.

At this stage, finish-sand all the components.

8. Assemble the frame. Glue and clamp the side rails and legs together. Check for squareness as you proceed. Scrub off any excess glue. (This will raise the grain around the joints slightly but a little touch-up sanding will remedy that.)

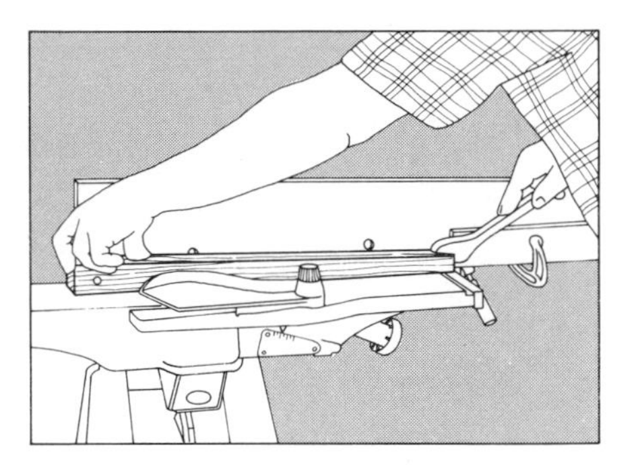

Set jointer at 3/16" depth-of-cut and make two passes on each side. Note use of stop block and safety push stick.

After these two assemblies have dried, glue them to the end rails and clamp.

9. Attach the top. Flip the top upside down and center the frame on it. If you use the mirror holders, locate and drill holes for the mounting screws and secure the top in place. If you made screw pockets, drill pilot holes into the tabletop and secure the top with #8 × 1" roundhead wood screws.

10. Finishing touches: Before applying any finish, go over the entire project with a tack rag to remove dust. Select the stain and/or finish of your choice and apply.

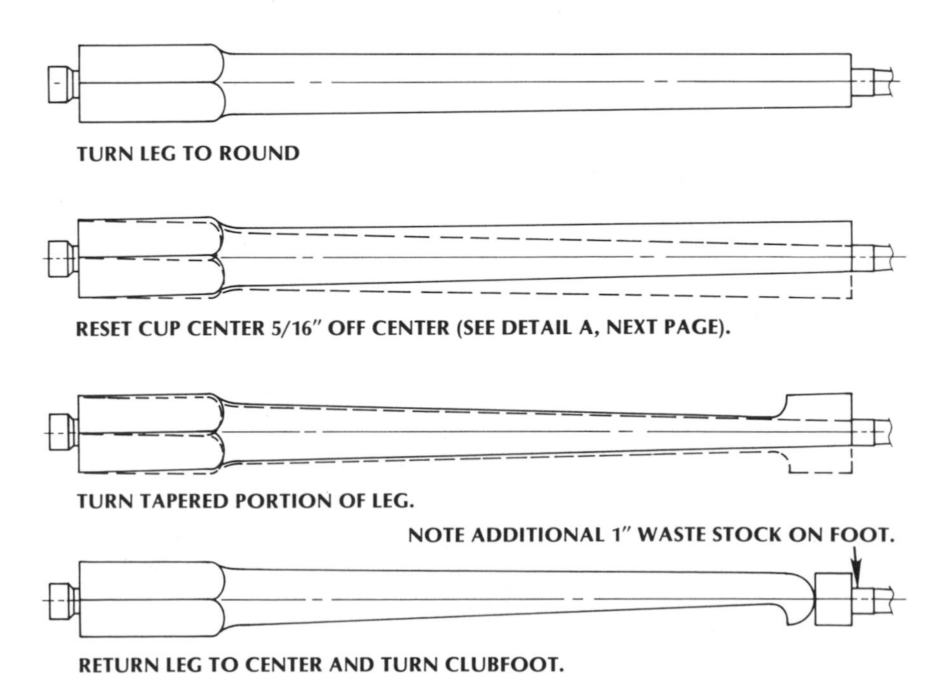

Turning a clubfoot leg.

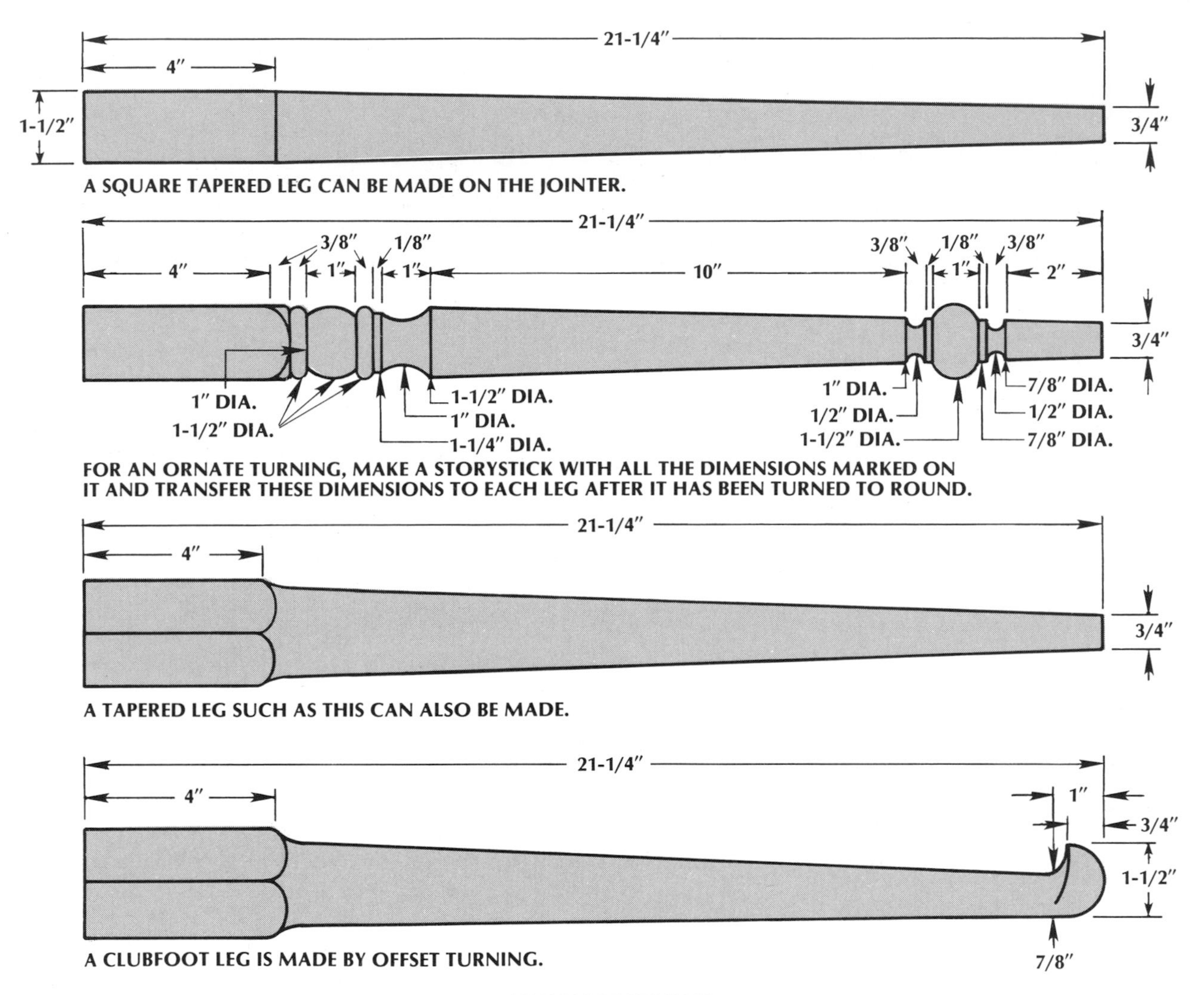

LEG VARIATIONS

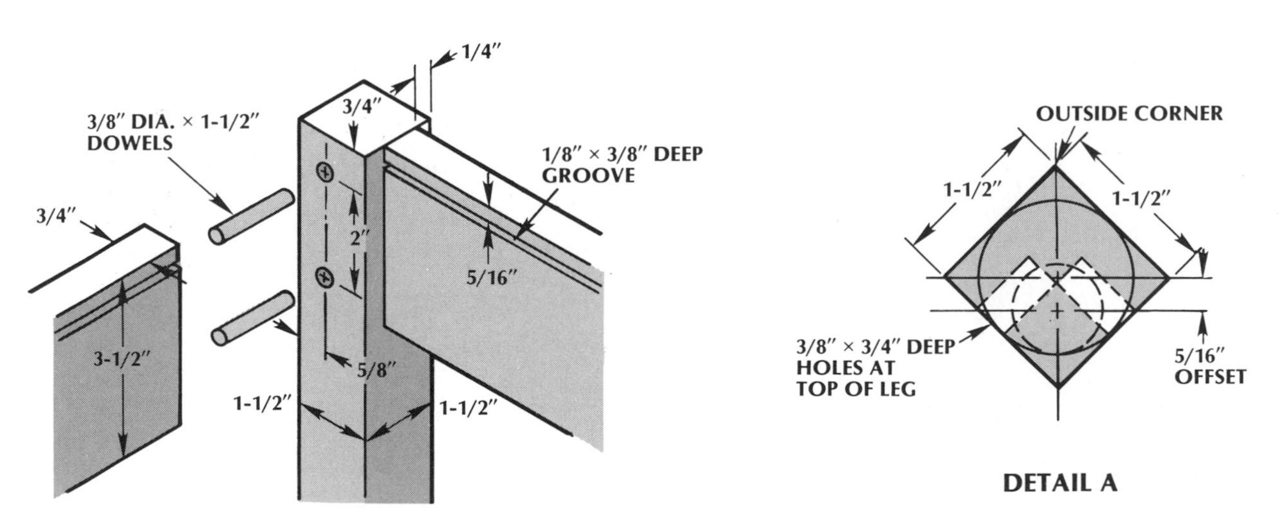

LEG TO RAIL CONSTRUCTION DETAIL

DETAIL A

The square tapered legs of this Mission-style oak table were all done on the jointer. The shaper with the V-cutter was used to chamfer the top.

Simple, turned tapered legs, a rounded table edge, and partial shaping of the rails combine to give this walnut table a warm look.

This Early American-type table made of cherry features turned legs with a series of beads and coves. The rails were formed on the bandsaw. The ogee edge on the top was done on the shaper.

This mahogany Dutch Colonial-type table has clubfoot legs turned on the lathe. The rails have molded bead on the bottom edge. The bead-and-step edge on the tabletop was done on the shaper.

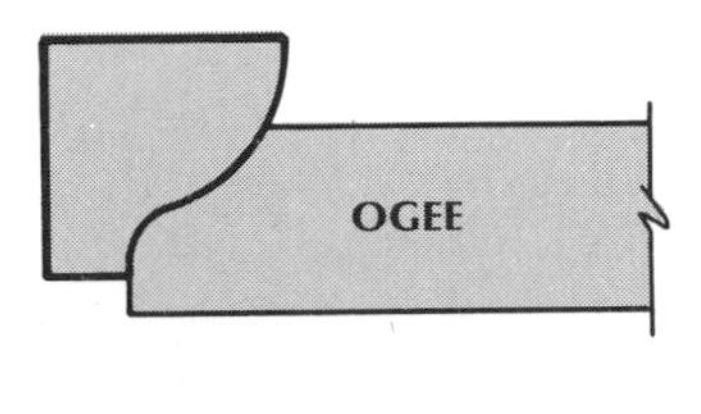

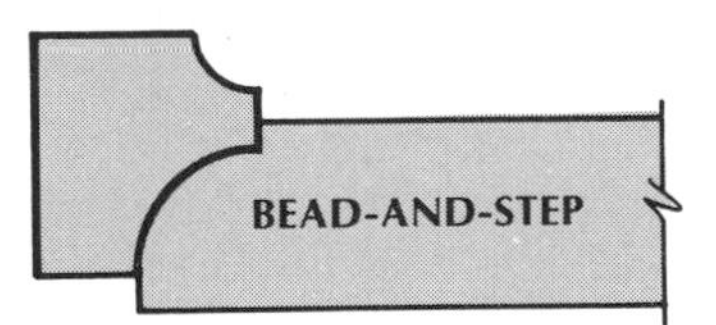

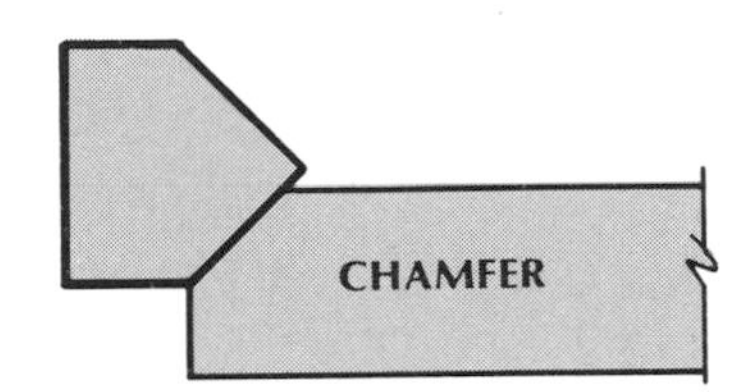

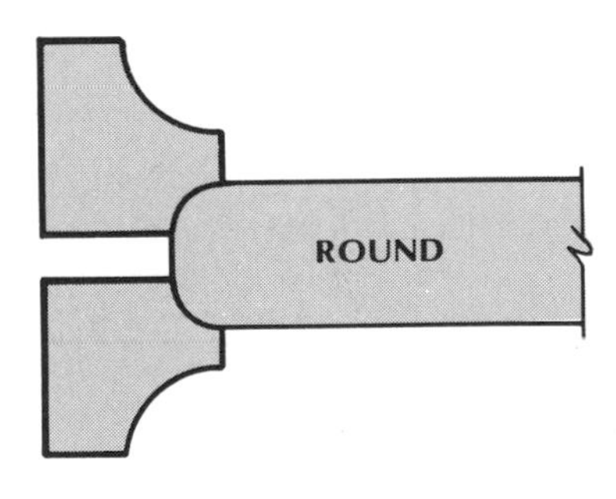

TABLETOP EDGE VARIATIONS

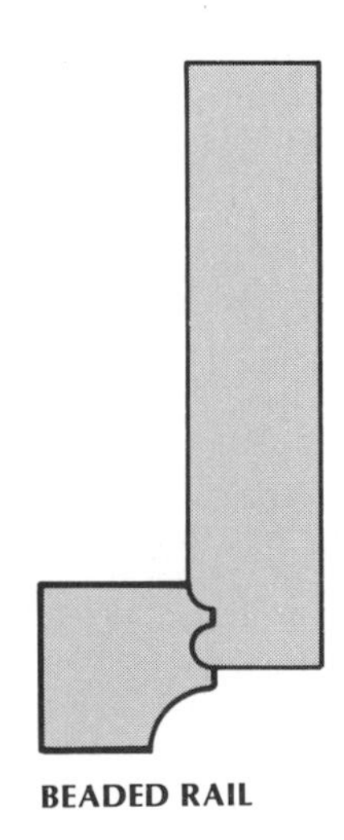

BEADED RAIL

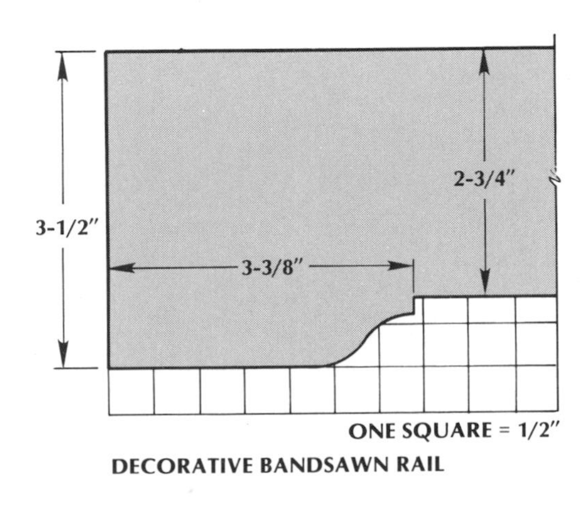

DECORATIVE BANDSAWN RAIL

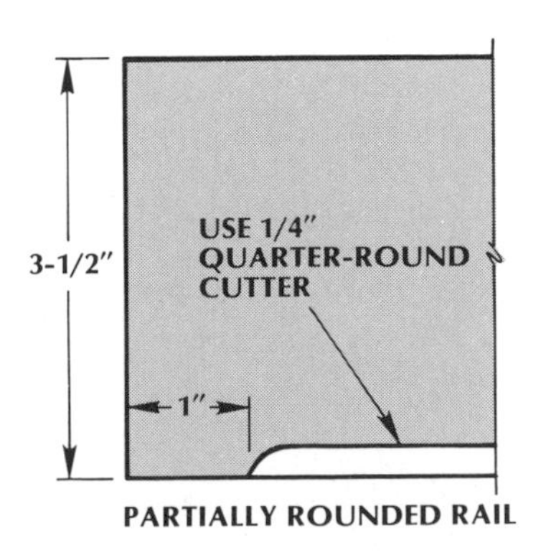

PARTIALLY ROUNDED RAIL

RAIL VARIATIONS

THE QUILT RACK

From *HANDS ON* Jan/Feb 82

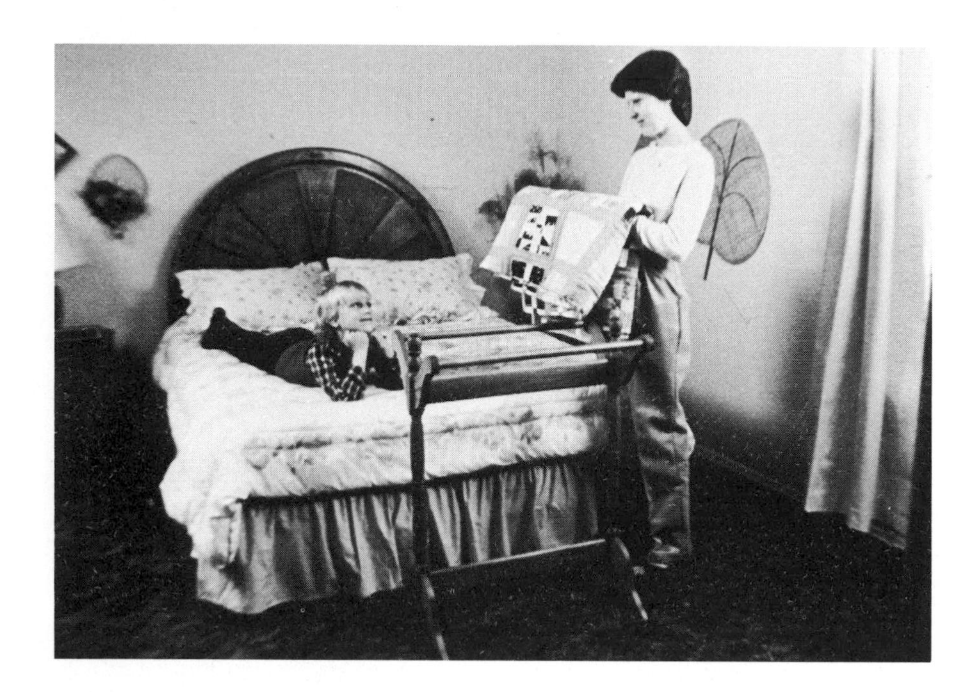

To save on your heating bill it makes sense to crank down the furnace thermostat each night; then, to help you stay cozy and warm in bed it makes sense to add a nice thick quilt or a colorful wool blanket.

When you're making up the bed, it's nice to have just the right place—like this quilt rack—to store those extra blankets and quilts.

Choose the stock you wish to use. We used mahogany. Keep in mind that stock for the spindles must be as straight and true as possible.

You'll make two spindles, and they don't have to be absolutely identical. You'll form one spindle, and then before sanding it, you'll form the other. Use calipers or a cardboard template to help duplicate the design. Then you can sand and finish both spindles.

No one is going to be disappointed if you don't follow the dimensioned drawing for the spindles right down to the smallest detail. The joy of lathe work is that it allows you the freedom to craft what *you* think looks good.

Whatever your design, mark out its pattern with a pencil on the stock *before* you begin to turn it.

Sand on the lathe carefully. Sandpaper acts as hundreds of tiny little scraping tools, and you can take off more stock than you might think. A neat little trick is to tear out a half-moon in the edge of the sandpaper to make it easier to use in the coves and over the large beads.

To assemble, you can clamp it by attaching hand clamps to the legs, drawing a cord tightly around them, and wedging them tightly.

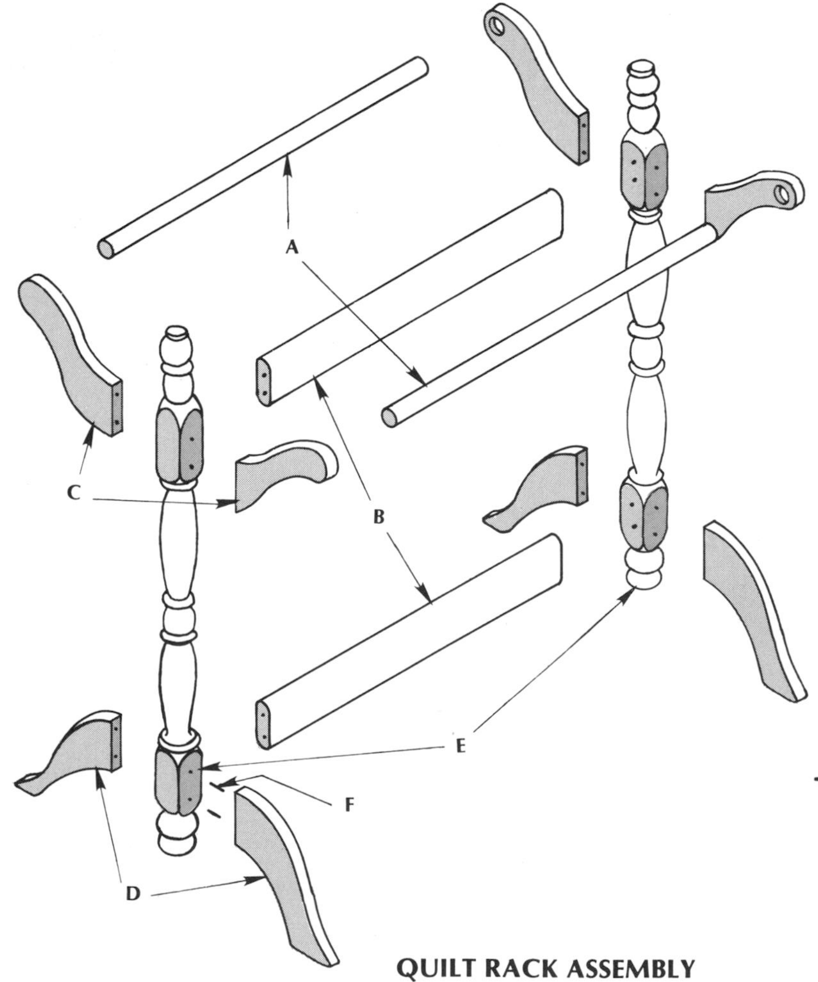

QUILT RACK ASSEMBLY

LIST OF MATERIALS

(finished dimensions in inches)

A	Rods (2)	7/8 dia. × 24-1/4
B	Spreaders (2)	3/4 × 3 × 22-1/4
C	Supports (4)	3/4 × 3-1/2 × 9-1/2
D	Legs (4)	3/4 × 3-1/2 × 10-3/4
E	Spindles (2)	2 × 2 × 33-1/4
F	Dowels (24)	3/8 dia. × 2

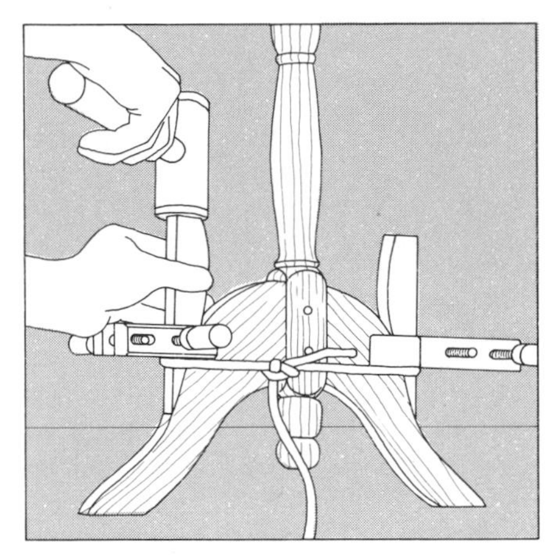

Clamping legs to spindles. Scrap wood wedges draw rope tight. Clamps keep rope in place.

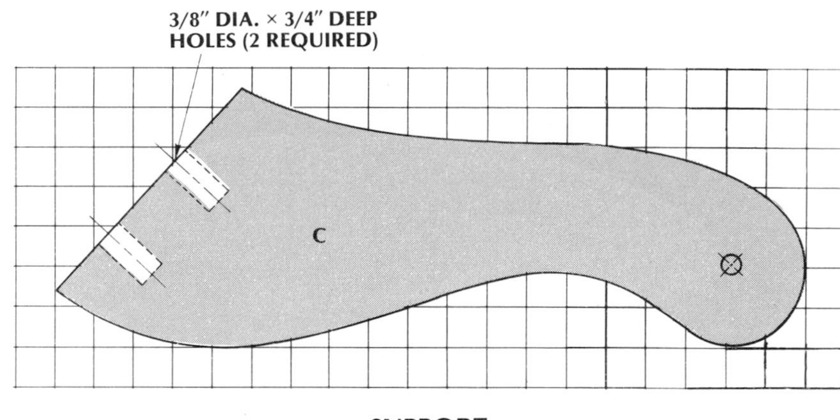

SUPPORT

ONE SQUARE = 1/2"

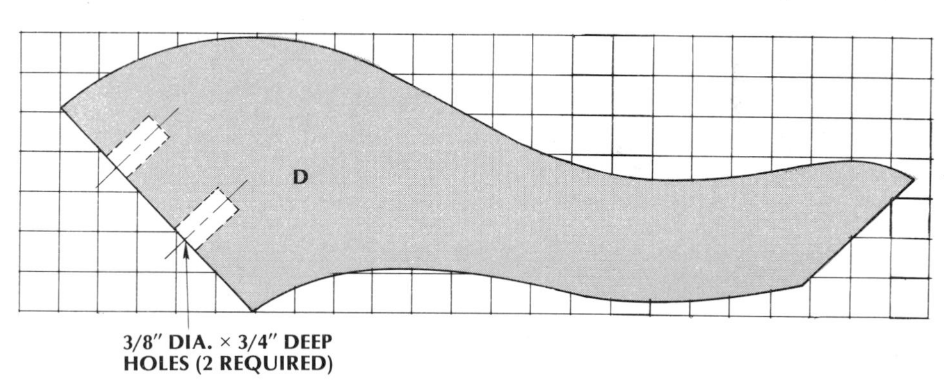

LEG

1-1/4" DIA.
2" DIA.
3/8"
1/2"
1-1/2"
2-3/8"
4-1/2"
1/4"
7-1/4"
33-1/4"
5/8"
2"
7-1/8"
5/8"
4-3/8"
1-1/2"
1"

SPINDLE PROFILE

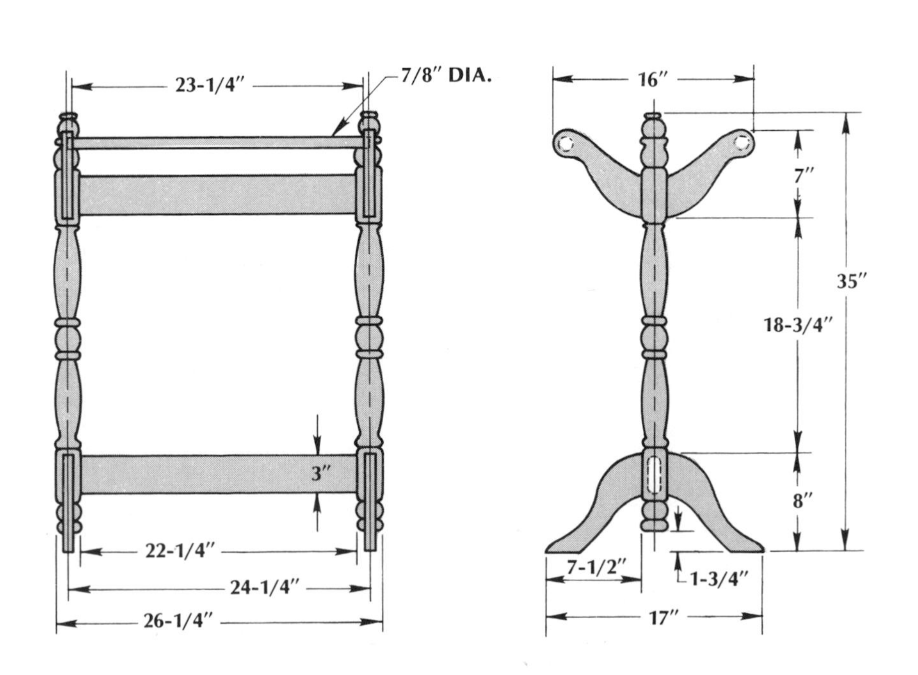

QUILT RACK LAYOUT

GATELEG TABLE

From *HANDS ON* Jan/Feb/Mar 83

The plans for this gateleg table are based on those from a small antique shop in London, England. The table there was of mahogany; this one is from walnut. You can build your own version by following the steps outlined below.

1. Prepare turning stock by cutting wood to 1-1/4" square and 1" longer than finished length. To obtain square finished turning stock, joint one side of each turning blank on the jointer. Then, place the jointed side against the fence and joint the second side square to the first. Mark these two sides. You can plane the two remaining sides to proper thickness on the thickness planer—1-1/8" for parts (A,B,C) and 1" for part (D). Or, rip stock to 1/16" oversize and joint to square final dimension on the jointer. All stock must be true and straight.

2. Prepare remaining stock. You will need 3/4" stock for the main stretcher (E) and 5/8" stock for the remaining pieces (see List of Materials).

3. Glue up tabletop (L) and set aside. In this version, the adjacent edges are simply prepared on the jointer and then glued together. The battens (K) provide added strength.

4. Cut mortises in parts (A,B,D,G) for stretchers. Mark off the square sections then the mortises on the turning stock. (Remember: The turning stock has 1/2" waste on each end.) Use a mortising accessory, a router accessory, or a drill. All mortises are 1/16" deeper than the lengths of the tenons to allow for glue. You can then chisel the mortises square or round off the tenons.

5. Cut stretchers (F,G,H,J) to size. Cut the tenons on these parts using the dado accessory. *Note:* All tenons are 1/8" smaller in width and height than the stock except for the tenons on the upper stretchers (F,H). Take an extra 1/4" off the tops of these tenons (3/8" total). This will prevent the tenon from splitting the tops of the turned legs since they are so close to the end.

6. Turn parts (A,B,C,D). Accurately mark the centers on the ends of each piece. Seat the lathe centers with a soft mallet.

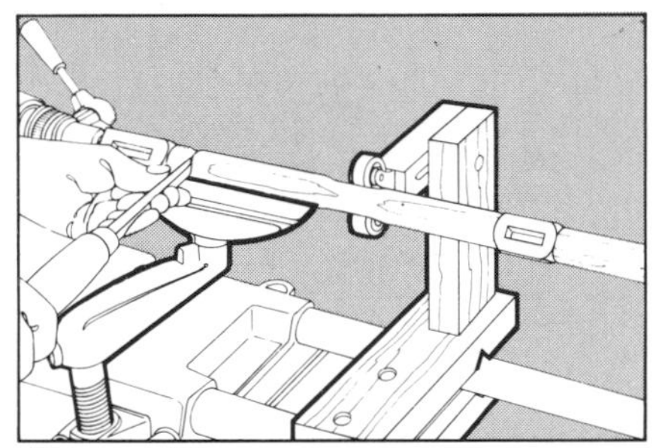

Turn a 2" section in the middle of the tapered section and mount a steady rest to prevent whip.

Start turning by roughing to round a 2" long section at the center of what will be the long tapered section. Sand lightly and then install a steady rest.

Cut the shoulders, then round the turned sections. Form the design by turning next to the squares and work your way toward the center. Turn the feet as required on parts (A,B). Remove the steady rest and complete the turning making light passes to reduce chatter. Sand turning while still on lathe.

7. Cut off excess at top end of each turning and sand square on the disc sander. See drawings for accuracy.

8. Cut and sand to length the opposite ends using the disc sander, quill feed, and the extension table with the fence.

9. Mark and cut the notches in the main stretcher (E) for the legs (A). Use the bandsaw or jigsaw to cut the notches for the gatelegs (B).

10. Drill 1/4" diameter × 1/2" deep dowel holes in the ends of the main stretcher (E) and legs (A). Drill countersunk holes for #8 × 1-1/2″ flathead screws in (E) and (C) for the gateleg pivots (D).

11. Dry-assemble all leg assemblies and check for fit and squareness. Disassemble, then assemble with glue.

12. Cut tabletop (L) into the three parts. Joint the adjacent edges of the leaves, then clamp all three parts back together. Mark and cut the mortises for the hinges with a hand chisel or hand-held router. Mount the hinges.

13. Draw an ellipse on the bottom of the tabletop. Secure a temporary batten on the underside to hold the table rigid, then cut the ellipse on the bandsaw or jigsaw. Sand the sawn edges.

14. Shape the tabletop edge with the shaper. Use a 1″ collar and the bead and cove cutter. Cut from below in at least two passes. Make sure that at least 1/8″ of the top is riding on the collar during the final pass. Put a prop under the table for added support. Remove the temporary batten after you have formed the edge.

15. Install the battens (K) on the underside of the leaves with #6 × 1″ flathead screws. Be sure that the battens are a minimum of 1″ from the inside edge so that they will clear the main stretcher (E) when the leaves are down.

16. Finish-sand and apply the finish of your choice. Assemble the gatelegs and tabletop to the frame with screws.

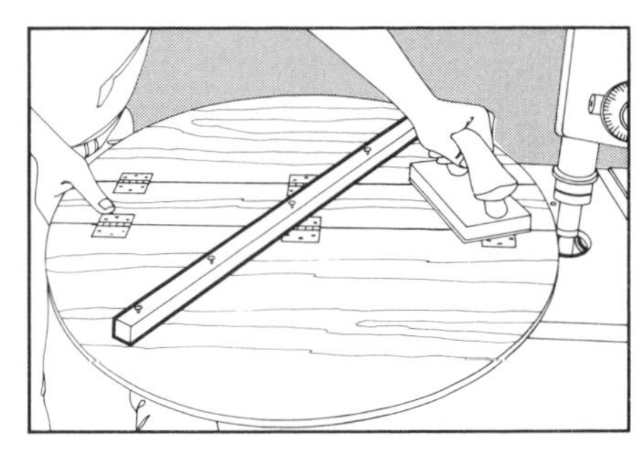

Cutting the decorative edge of the tabletop on the shaper. Use starter pin for this operation.

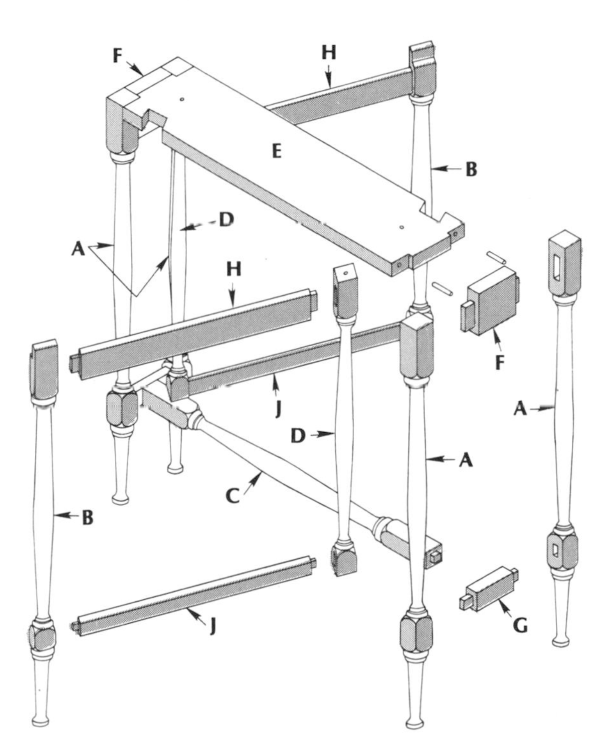

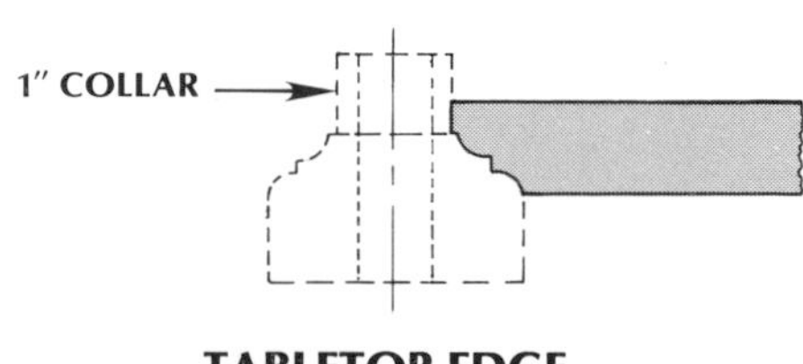

LIST OF MATERIALS

(finished dimensions in inches)

A	Main legs (4)	1-1/8 × 1-1/8 × 23-1/2
B	Gatelegs (2)	1-1/8 × 1-1/8 × 23-1/2
C	Lower turned spindle	1-1/8 × 1-1/8 × 19-1/2
D	Gateleg pivots (2)	1 × 1 × 17-1/8
E	Main stretcher	3/4 × 4-3/4 × 19
F	Upper stretchers (2)	5/8 × 2-1/2 × 3-1/2
G	Lower stretchers (2)	5/8 × 1-1/8 × 3-1/2
H	Upper gateleg stretchers (2)	5/8 × 1-5/8 × 15
J	Lower gateleg stretchers (2)	5/8 × 1-1/8 × 15
K	Battens (2)	5/8 × 1-1/2 × 14-3/4
L	Tabletop	5/8 × 24 × 36
	Hinges (6)	1-1/2 × 2
	Flathead wood screws (4)	#8 × 1-1/2
	Flathead wood screws (14)	#6 × 1
	Dowels (4)	1/4 dia. × 1

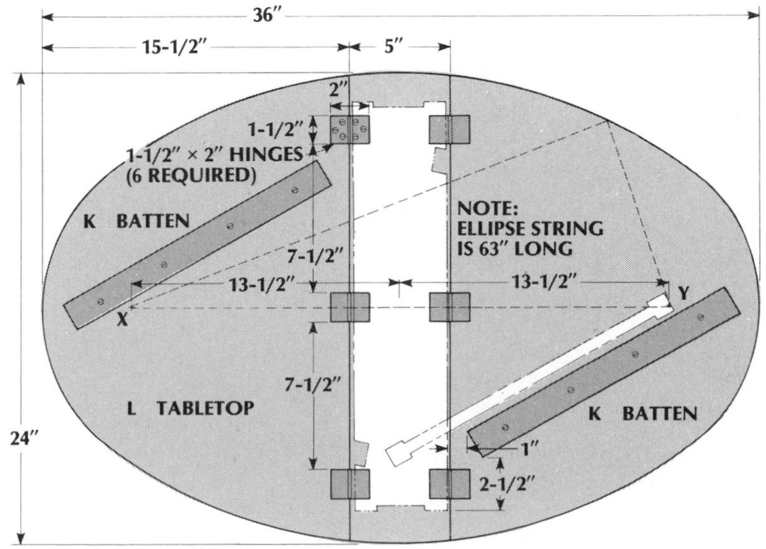

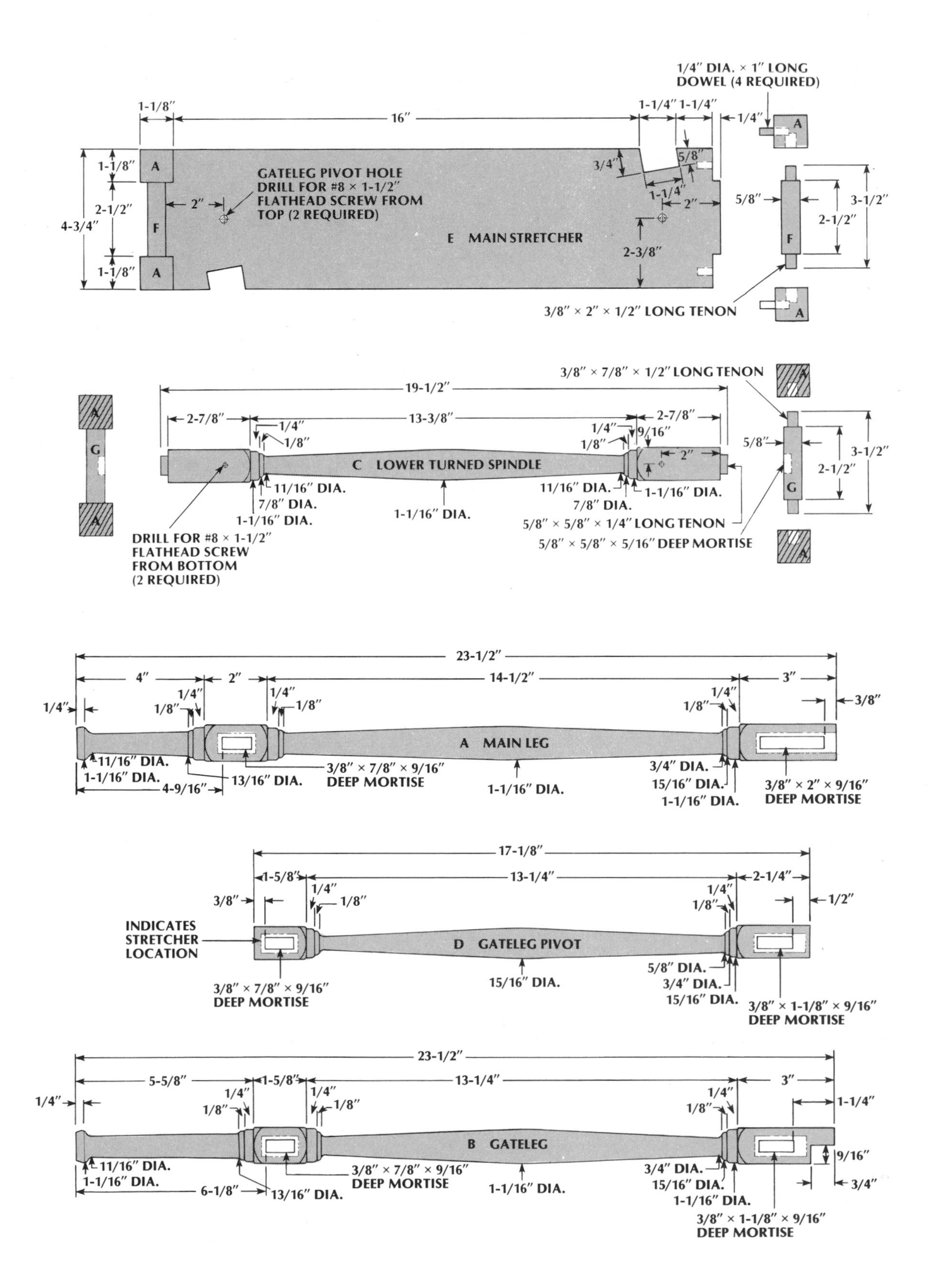
1/4" DIA. × 1" LONG DOWEL (4 REQUIRED)
1-1/8"
16"
1-1/4" 1-1/4"
1/4"
A
5/8"
3/4"
1-1/8"
GATELEG PIVOT HOLE DRILL FOR #8 × 1-1/2" FLATHEAD SCREW FROM TOP (2 REQUIRED)
2"
1-1/4"
2"
5/8"
3-1/2"
2-1/2"
4-3/4"
F
E MAIN STRETCHER
2-3/8"
3/8" × 2" × 1/2" LONG TENON
3/8" × 7/8" × 1/2" LONG TENON
19-1/2"
2-7/8"
13-3/8"
2-7/8"
1/4"
1/8"
9/16"
C LOWER TURNED SPINDLE
G
11/16" DIA.
7/8" DIA.
1-1/16" DIA.
1-1/16" DIA.
11/16" DIA.
1-1/16" DIA.
7/8" DIA.
5/8" × 5/8" × 1/4" LONG TENON
5/8" × 5/8" × 5/16" DEEP MORTISE
DRILL FOR #8 × 1-1/2" FLATHEAD SCREW FROM BOTTOM (2 REQUIRED)
23-1/2"
4"
2"
14-1/2"
3"
3/8"
A MAIN LEG
11/16" DIA.
1-1/16" DIA.
4-9/16"
13/16" DIA.
3/8" × 7/8" × 9/16" DEEP MORTISE
1-1/16" DIA.
3/4" DIA.
15/16" DIA.
1-1/16" DIA.
3/8" × 2" × 9/16" DEEP MORTISE
17-1/8"
1-5/8"
13-1/4"
2-1/4"
1/2"
INDICATES STRETCHER LOCATION
D GATELEG PIVOT
3/8" × 7/8" × 9/16" DEEP MORTISE
15/16" DIA.
5/8" DIA.
3/4" DIA.
15/16" DIA.
3/8" × 1-1/8" × 9/16" DEEP MORTISE
5-5/8"
1-1/4"
B GATELEG
9/16"
3/4"
6-1/8"
13/16" DIA.
3/8" × 7/8" × 9/16" DEEP MORTISE
1-1/16" DIA.
3/4" DIA.
15/16" DIA.
1-1/16" DIA.
3/8" × 1-1/8" × 9/16" DEEP MORTISE

From *HANDS ON* Jan/Feb 84

Why is it that some projects take only a few hours and others take many hours to complete? Part of the answer is found in the care with which a project is approached. Think of each board as an individual project; then the hours spent on one piece of furniture represent the putting together of many projects. While you could dedicate an evening to producing a cutting board or a trivet, you may balk at giving that much time to one side of a cabinet or a piece of molding.

This wall-mounted curio cabinet is a project that will take more than one evening or one day if properly approached. Slow down, enjoy the wood, measure carefully, and take your time; then reap the rewards of your efforts.

1. Take the time necessary to select good, properly cured, straight stock. Good stock results in fewer problems throughout the entire project. Select the best pieces for the sides, face frame, and doors. Make your selection based not only on the quality of the wood but also the grain configuration.

2. Rip all stock to the proper width according to the List of Materials. Remember to joint one edge first, rip to width plus 1/32", then joint the other edge, removing that extra 1/32".

3. Crosscut all the stock to length except for the door parts (G,H) and the molding (J,K). Allow an extra 1/8" of length on each board for careful trimming later.

4. Crosscut the sides to final length and mark the locations of the rabbets and dadoes. Transfer the bottom contour from the drawing to the sides.

5. To form the rabbets for the back, set up the dado attachment and attach a wooden auxiliary fence to the rip fence. Cut the 3/8" × 3/8" rabbets on the sides (A) and top (B). Be sure to use push blocks and a feather board.

Remove the fence and cut the dadoes in the sides (A) for the bottom and shelves (C). Then form the rabbets on the ends of the sides for the top.

6. Cut the contours on the bottom of the sides with the bandsaw or jigsaw. When cutting, leave the line. Next, sand the contours with the drum sander.

7. Assemble the cabinet case (sides, top, bottom, and shelves) with aliphatic resin glue and #8 × 1" flathead wood screws or 6d finishing nails. Countersink the screws (or nails).

8. The face frame pieces (D,E,F) are cut to fit. Starting with the stiles (D), mark the correct length and cut on the bandsaw leaving the line. Disc sand the stiles to exact length. Measure the width of the assembled case and subtract the widths of the stiles to obtain the length of the rails. Cut and sand the rails to length. Transfer the contour for the bottom rail, then cut it out with the bandsaw or jigsaw and sand.

Locate the dowel holes 5/8" from the edges then drill the dowel holes by utilizing horizontal boring. Glue and assemble the face frame. After the glue has dried, attach the frame to the case with #8 × 1-1/2" screws or 6d nails.

9. The door frames for this cabinet can be made by selecting the desired design of shaper molding knives. The actual length of the rails will depend on the cutter you use. Whichever cutter is used, form the ends of the rails first then mold or shape the edges of the stiles and rails. Use scrap pieces for testing. Assemble the frames with glue and check for squareness.

10. Sand the entire project. Start with #80 grit paper and work your way up through #220 grit paper. Slightly round off all edges to prevent any splintering.

11. Cut the 3/8" plywood back to exact size and apply a stain or matching hardwood veneer. Attach the back with 4d nails.
12. Form the molding for the top on one piece of stock. Since this molding projects 45° from the cabinet surface, it can be mitered by setting the miter gauge at 56-1/2° and the table at 30°. Hold the trim flat to the table and cut all three pieces to length. Take the actual measurements from the cabinet.
13. Mark the locations of the hinges and mortise the face frame and door frames with a chisel.
14. Apply the finish of your choice. After the final coat has dried, install the glass in the doors and then mount the doors on the cabinet.

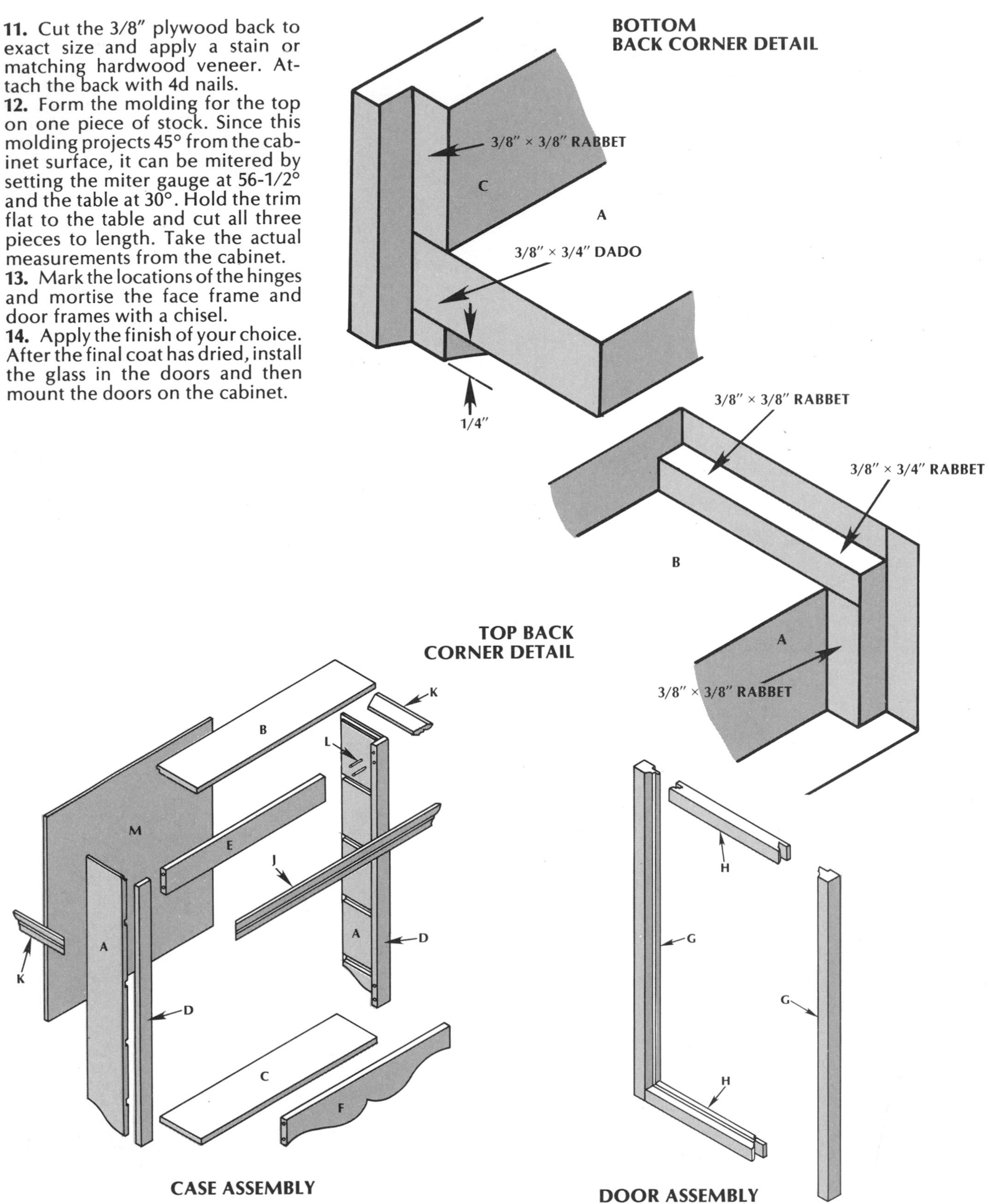

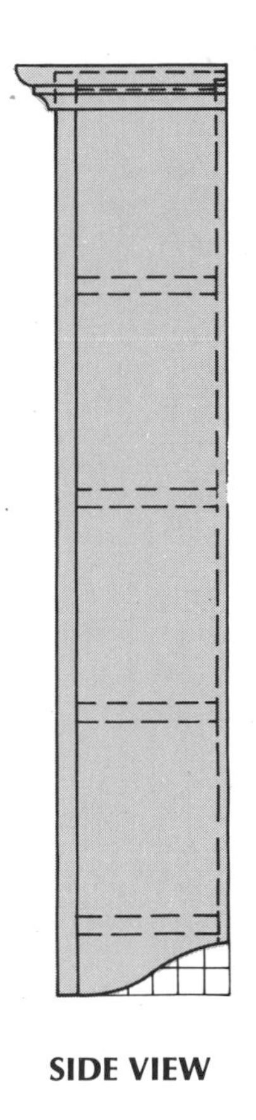
SIDE VIEW

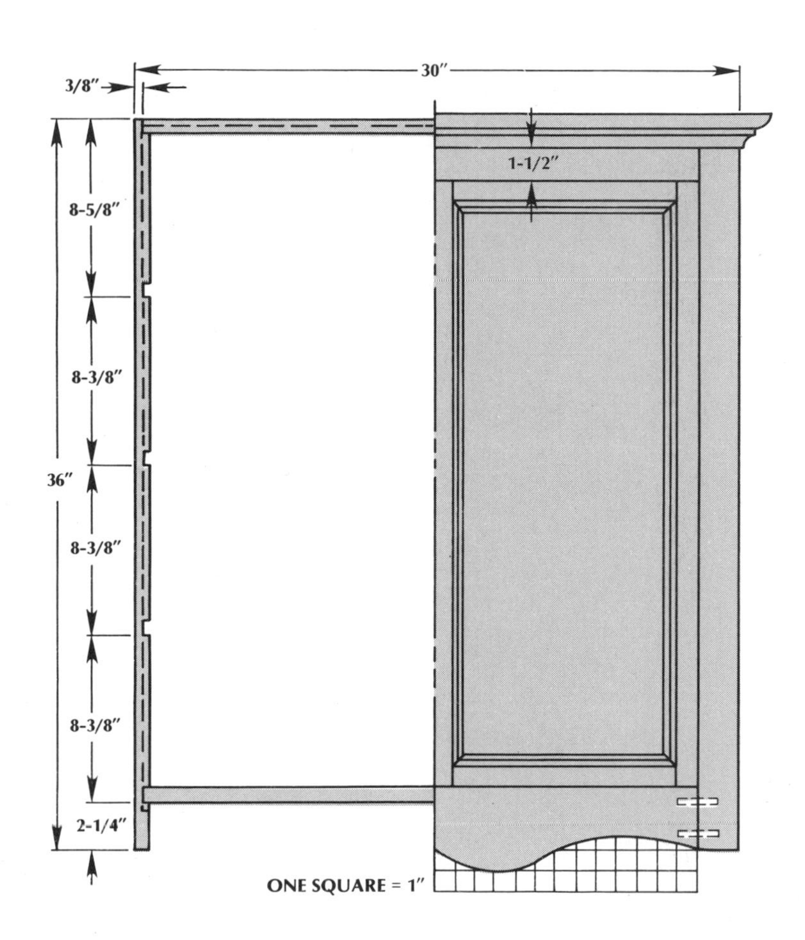

FRONT VIEW

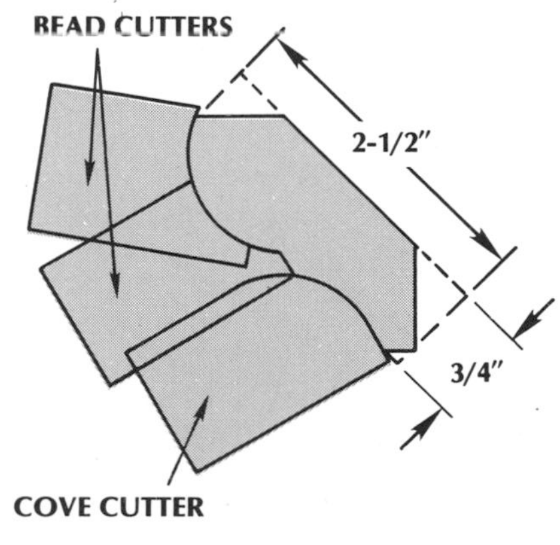

MOLDING DETAIL

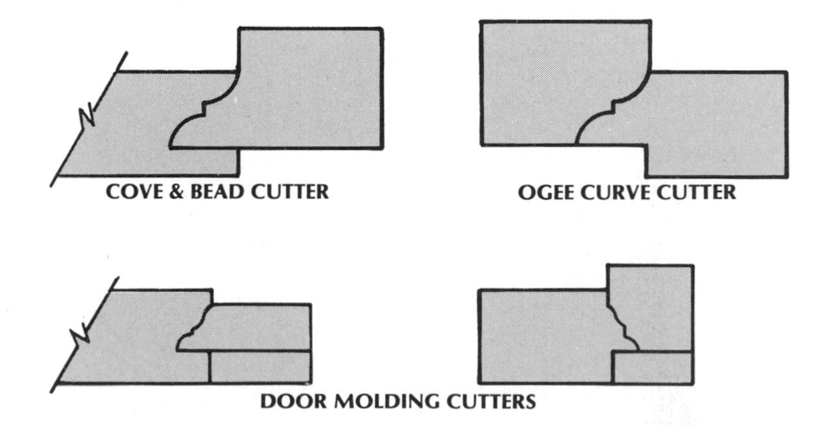

DOOR FRAME DETAILS

BOOKSHELVES

From *HANDS ON* Apr/May/June 83

LIST OF MATERIALS

(finished dimensions in inches)

A	Sides (2)	3/4 × 11 × 60
B	Shelves (5)	3/4 × 10-1/2 × 34-1/2
C	Top	3/4 × 10-3/4 × 34-1/2
D	Top rail	3/4 × 2 × 34-1/2
E	Bottom rail	3/4 × 3 × 34-1/2
F	Back	1/4 × 35-1/4 × 59-1/2
G	Dowel pins (16)	1/4 dia. × 1-1/4

Here's a project that you can put together in a few hours. The cost for materials is little more than a tank of gas in the family sedan. The woodworking on these basic adjustable bookshelves is simple—just a matter of crosscutting, ripping, forming a rabbet in the back, and drilling some holes up the sides.

We selected two 6′ and two 8′ pieces of #2 common 1 × 12 shelving stock at the local lumberyard for this project. A piece of scrap stock was used for the rails and a leftover piece of 1/4″ plywood for the back. The boards were as straight as we could find and the knots were tight. The only problem we encountered was that the edges were a little nicked up. We couldn't complain since the price was reduced. To solve the problem we ripped all the stock twice—once to shave off one edge and then the second time to cut to width.

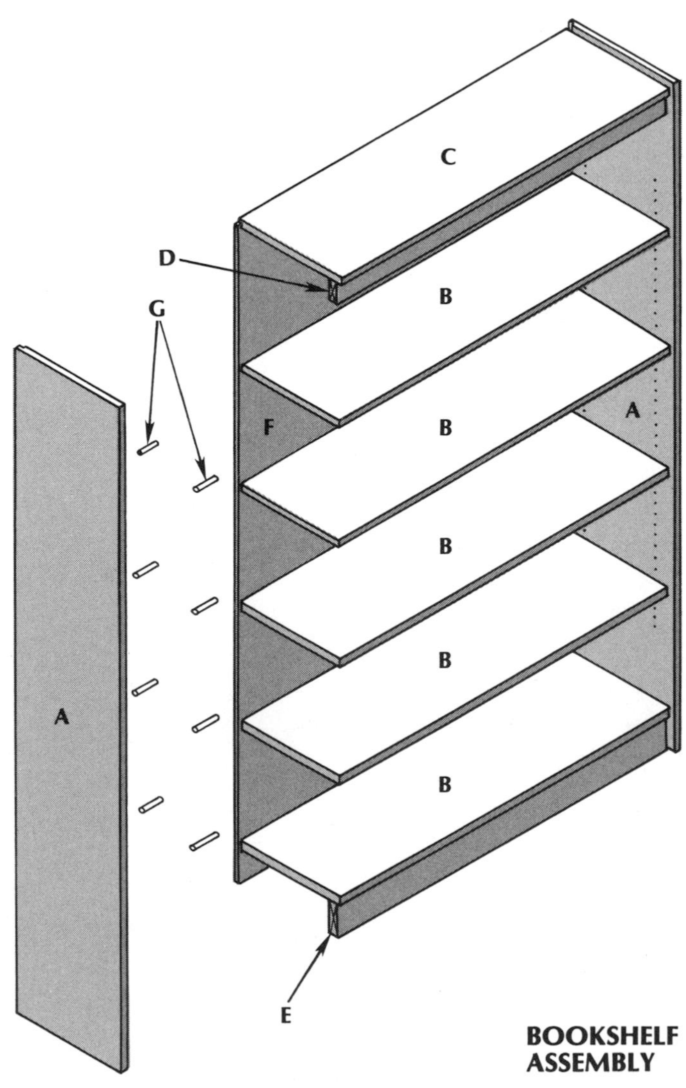

BOOKSHELF ASSEMBLY

1. Prepare your stock. Use the saw or jointer to clean up the edges of the boards. Crosscut the boards to length according to the List of Materials. Rip the boards to finished width. Don't cut out the plywood back yet.

2. Cut the rabbets. Cut a 3/8" wide × 1/4" deep rabbet in the back inside edges of the sides (A) and in the top (C).

3. Drill the shelf adjustment holes. Mark off the adjustment holes on the insides of the two sides (A). Use a storystick (a board with marks every inch or two depending on your spacing) to ensure all the holes are evenly spaced. Set the rip fence 2" from the center of your drill bit and drill the holes 1/2" deep. Skip this step if you want to permanently mount the shelves.

Sand the faces of all the boards before you start the next step.

4. Assemble the case. Attach the rails (D,E) to the top (C) and bottom shelf (B). Then, attach these assemblies to one side and then the other. Check for squareness as you progress. Measure the back and cut it out. Attach this with 4d finish nails or #6 × 1" flathead wood screws and no glue.

5. Cut the dowel pins (G). The shelves are supported by 1-1/4" lengths of 1/4" dowel pins. Cut these pins on the bandsaw if you have one but, if you don't, use a miter box and a handsaw. Hold them with pliers and chamfer the ends with the disc sander.

6. Finishing touches: Countersink the nails and fill the holes with putty. If you used wood screws, you will need to fill these holes with plugs.

Apply the stain and finish of your choice.

60"

36"

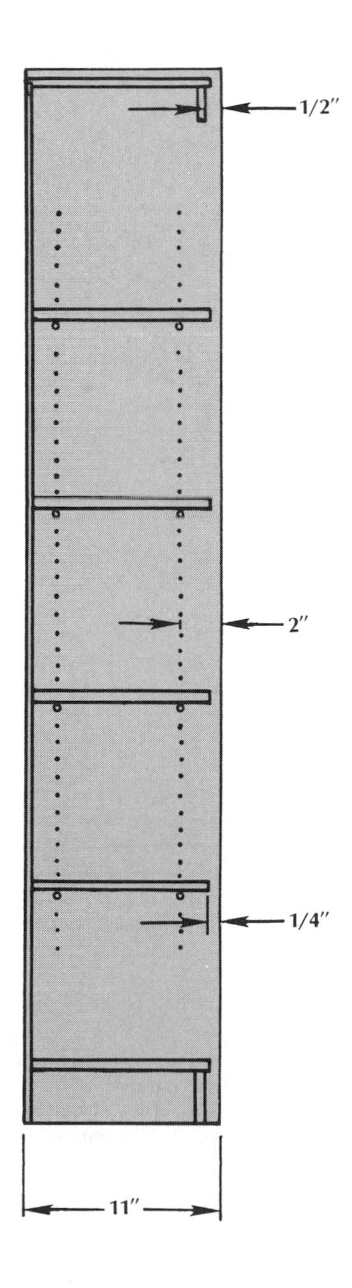

CANDLE STAND

From *HANDS ON* Jan/Feb 82

Simple and functional—those are the hallmarks of Shaker furniture. This graceful pedestal table is a faithful copy of an original Shaker design, and it's a perfect project for the lathe.

Start with gluing up stock for the top, using 1/4" dowels to strengthen the edge joints. Allow this to set up and dry for at least 24 hours. Locate the center, then cut the stock to a rough circle with the bandsaw or jigsaw.

Make the tabletop brace. You'll want to mount it so that its grain runs perpendicular to the grain of the top. The Shakers used this method to prevent the top from cupping and warping.

Now mount the brace temporarily to the top. Attach them both to the large faceplate. Use slow speed to turn the edge first, then scrape the recessed top surface. Finish-sand before you remove it from the lathe.

Next, glue up the stock for the spindle, again allowing plenty of time for the glue to dry. Turn the spindle and final-sand it on the lathe.

WEDGE TO FIT SLOT
A
B
RUN AT 90° TO TOP GRAIN
C
D
E
F

CANDLE STAND ASSEMBLY

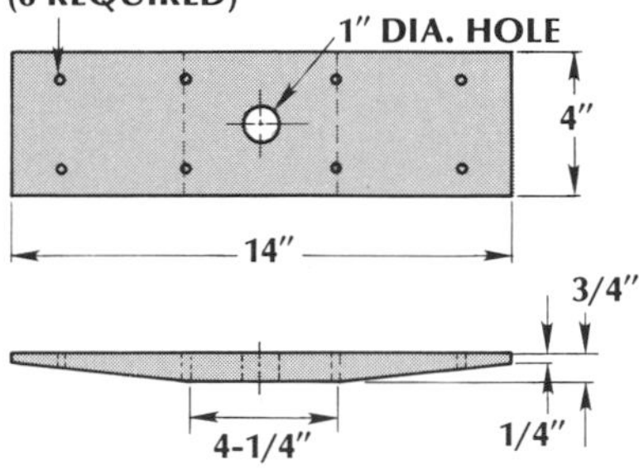

BRACE LAYOUT

LIST OF MATERIALS

(finished dimensions in inches)

A	Top	16-3/8 dia. × 3/4
B	Brace	3/4 × 4 × 14
C	Spindle	2-1/4 dia. × 19-1/2
D	Legs (3)	3/4 × 4 × 12-1/2
E	Dowels (3)	3/8 dia. × 7/8
F	Dowels (6)	3/8 dia. × 1-1/2
	Flathead wood screws (4)	#6 × 1
	Flathead wood screws (4)	#6 × 1-1/4

Make a pattern for the legs (see drawing). Lay out the pattern on the stock so that the grain runs lengthwise from the top to the bottom. This is a necessity for strength. Use the bandsaw or jigsaw to cut them, then sand the contours with the drum sander. To round the top edges, use the shaper or router, or do it by hand. To finish the concave radii on the legs where they join the pedestal/spindle, use a 1-1/2" × 1-1/2" drum sander.

Drill the dowel holes in the pedestal for mounting the legs. Use dowel center finders to locate the holes you'll drill in the legs. Use care not to drill through the legs!

Saw a kerf in the top of the spindle; remove the brace from the tabletop and mount it to the spindle, tapping in a small wedge to lock the pieces together.

Attach the legs with dowels and glue. Cut up an old rubber inner tube and wrap it tightly around the pieces to clamp them all equally.

Screw on the top and apply the finish of your choice.

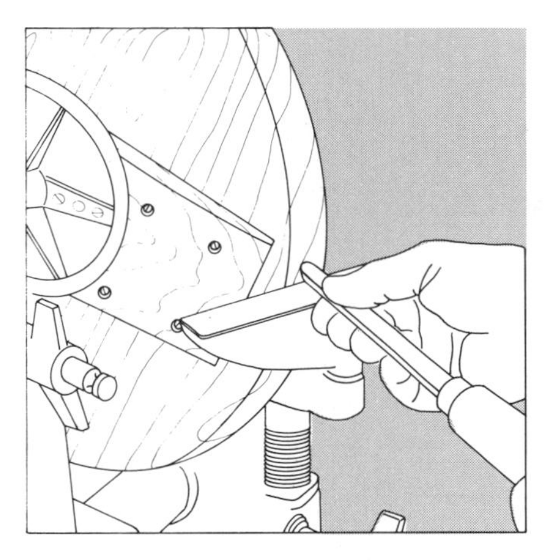

Slow speed turning of tabletop. Note position of toolrest.

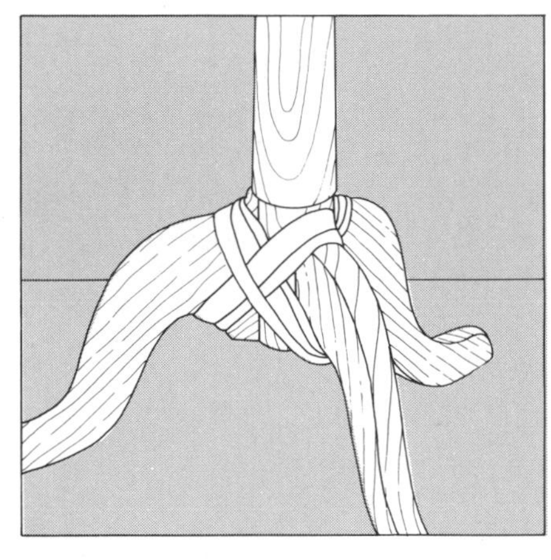

Rubber from old inner tube interwoven around legs to grip and clamp equally.

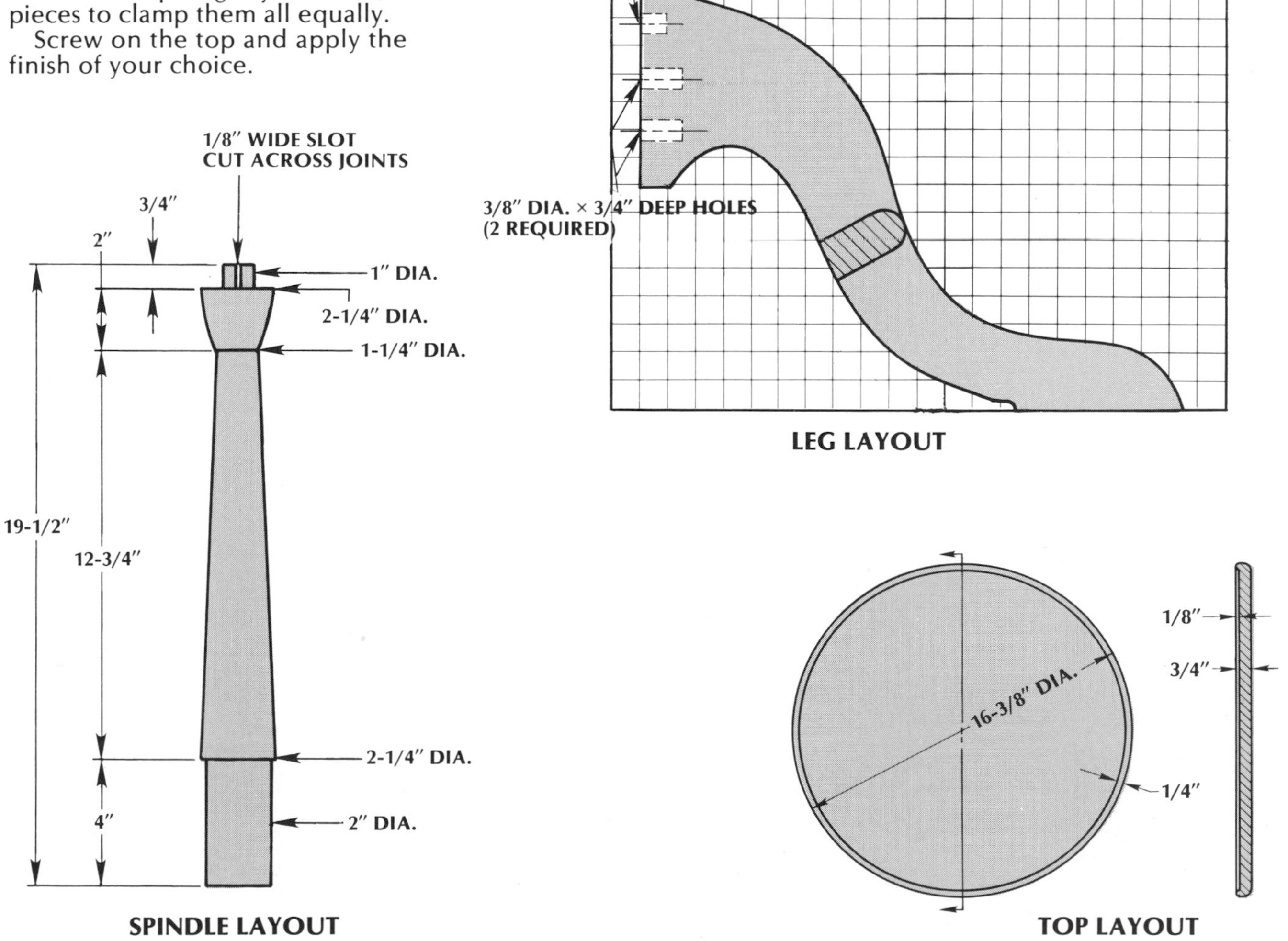

ENTERTAINMENT CENTER

From *HANDS ON* Mar/Apr 82

Your living room is the new frontier for all sorts of electronic audio-visual gadgetry, and you can organize it in this beautiful, simple project.

Use two sheets of 1/2" plywood, double-faced birch veneer. Check the size of your components and television. Dimensions given here are only suggestions, based partly on the standard 19" wide stereo component.

Build the project on its back. First dry-assemble the parts, using utility or flathead wood screws with a pilot hole and countersink.

To assemble, attach face strips (D) to shelves (B). Next, attach bottom partition (E) to the two bottom shelves (B), then attach this assembly to the right-hand side (A).

In the middle section, attach shelves (G,L) to the center partition (F) and then fasten this assembly to

LIST OF MATERIALS

(finished dimensions in inches)

A	Sides (2)	18 × 56
B	Shelves (3)	17-1/2 × 40
C	Shelf	18 × 40
D	Face strip	2-1/2 × 40
E	Bottom partition	14-1/2 × 18
F	Middle partition	18 × 27-1/2
G	Shelf	15-1/2 × 18
H	Upper partition	9 × 18
J	Door	5-1/2 × 15-1/2
K	Door	12-1/2 × 13
L	Shelf	15-1/2 × 17-1/2
	Hinges (2)	1" × 2"
	Magnetic catches (2 pr.)	
	Knobs (2)	
	Screw plugs (64)	3/8" dia.
	Light chain	20" (approx.)
	Flathead pivot screws (2)	#6 × 1"
	Utility screws (64)	#8 × 1"
	Edge stripping	480" (40')

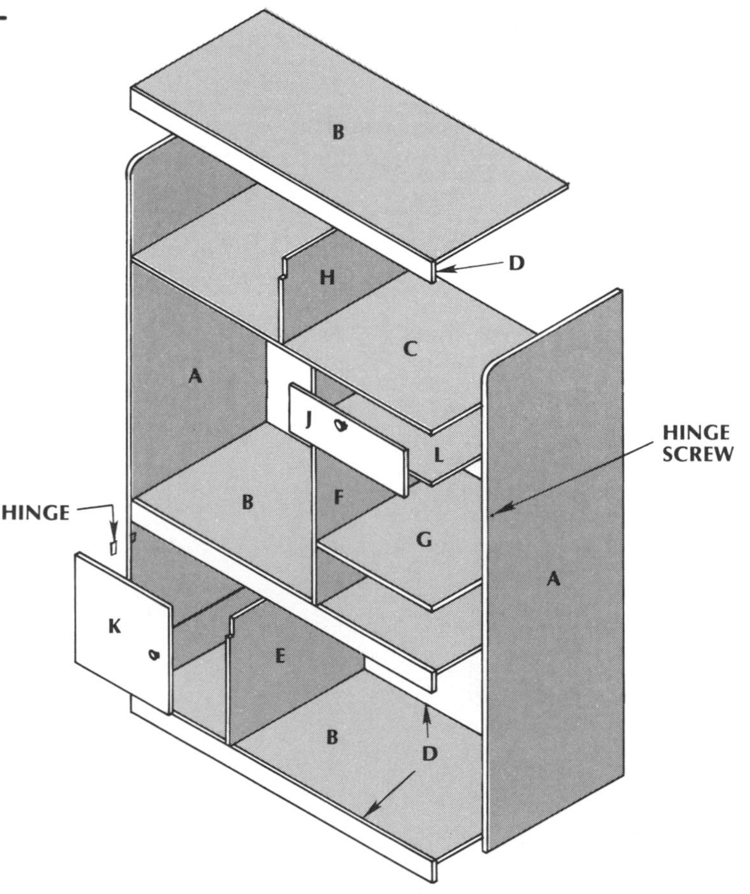

the right-hand side assembly. Attach part (H) to shelf (C) and fasten this to the rest of the assembly. Finally, add top shelf (B) and the left-hand side (A).

The next step is to disassemble the entire project and apply veneer strips to all exposed edges. Once applied, reassemble the project with screws and glue. Use dowels to plug the countersunk screws.

Mount the hinges to the lower door (K) and pivot screws for the small door (J). Round over the lower inside edge of this door to allow for movement. Using screw pivots instead of hinges on this small door eliminates a "step" between the door and the shelf. Lightweight chain keeps the door from folding down too far. Apply the finish of your choice, and start organizing all that fancy equipment.

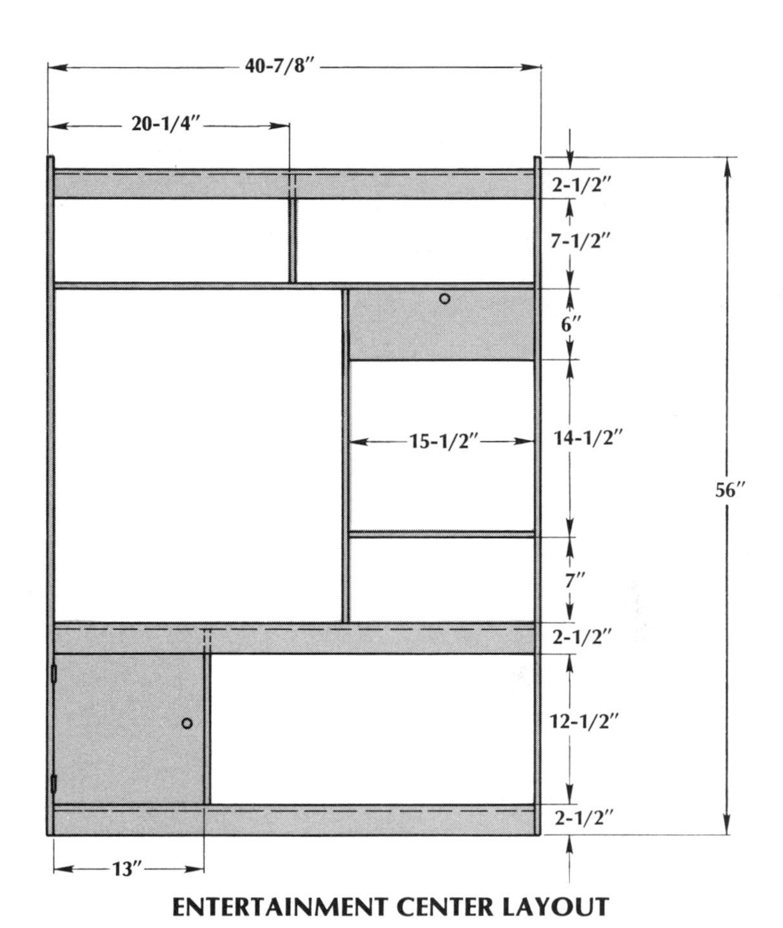

ENTERTAINMENT CENTER LAYOUT

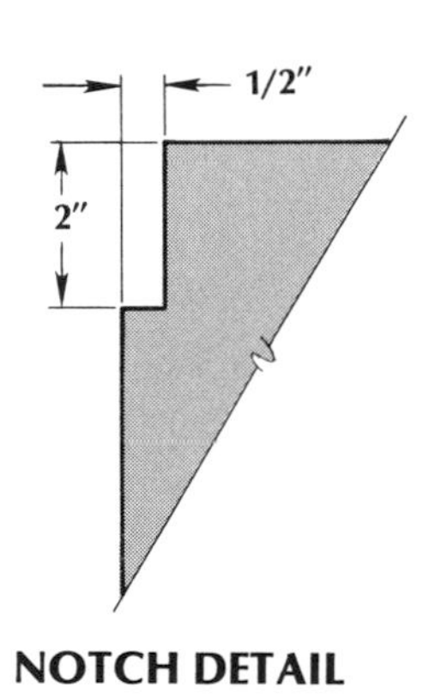

NOTCH DETAIL

CUTTING LAYOUT

STACKABLE DRESSER DRAWERS

From *HANDS ON* Nov/Dec 81

The idea of traditional joinery was partly to encourage the illusion that furniture looked like it was carved from a single, thick slab of wood. The better the joinery was hidden, the better the piece.

In contemporary design, however, the joinery isn't at all bashful. In fact, modern craftsmen flaunt perfectly fitted, exquisite joints.

Once assembled, this contemporary, stackable chest of drawers shows locking dovetails on the sides that align to look like the units are held together with butterfly joints. It goes beyond beauty though; its interchangeable units lock together and you can make as many as you want or as few as you need.

In choosing the wood for this project, go ahead and revel in the unique compatibility of different woods joined together. We built the chest of contrasting poplar and walnut.

When gluing up stock for the sides and drawer fronts, the specialty glue joint helps align each piece.

The secret to making these joints identical to one another is to mark off the dovetail pins on both ends of one spreader, then use this master spreader to mark all the others.

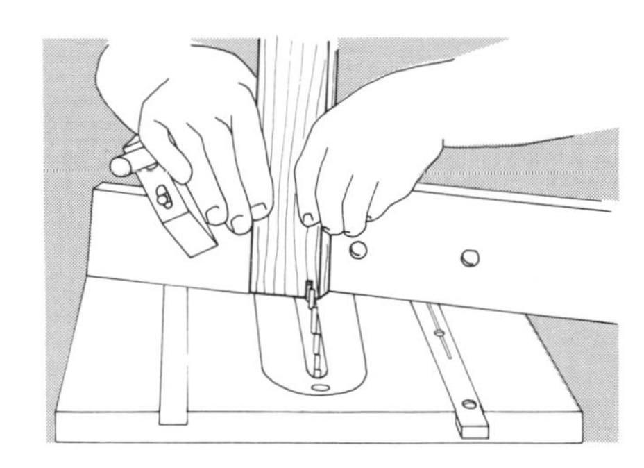

Cut for dovetail pin. Miter gauge set at 15°.

Set up the saw table at 90°; set the miter gauge with extension and stop block clamped onto it at 15° to the saw blade and cut the first side of the pin. Using stop blocks assures that each spreader pin will be identical to all others.

For the opposite side of the pin, move the miter gauge to cut 15° in the other direction.

To finish the pin, set the table and miter gauge to cut at 90°. Adjust the height of the blade to cut no more than 7/16" deep. This cut removes 80% of the waste stock and opens the face of each pin's shoulder. Finish the pin with your hand chisel.

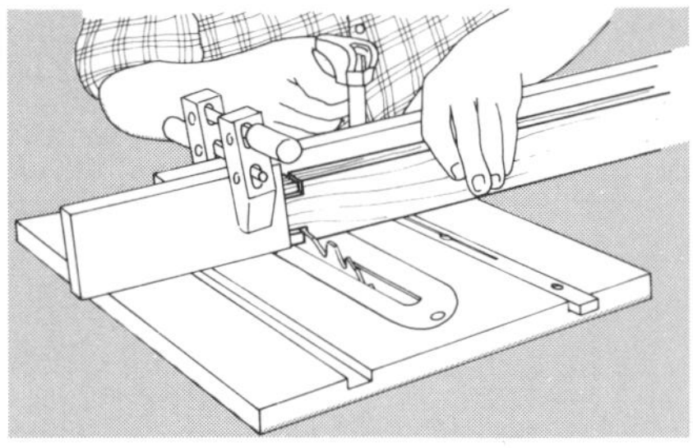

Making rough cut of dovetail pin shoulder.

Use the existing dovetail pins on the master spreader to trace onto the sides for positioning the dovetail slots. Tilt the table 15° to the right with the fence on the left side of the blade. Cut one side of the slot on the front, back, top, and bottom of all sides.

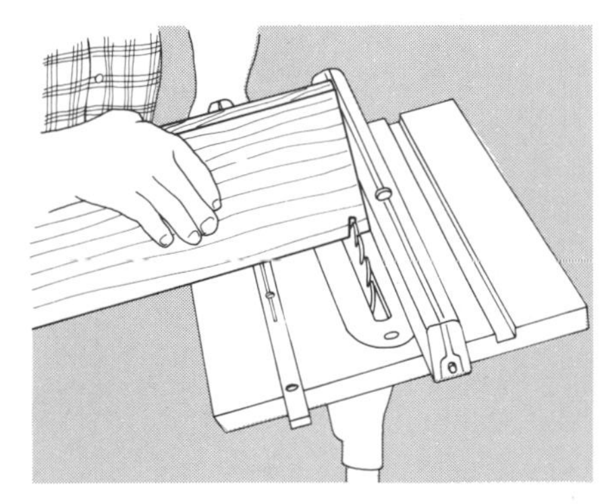

First cut: dovetail slot. Fence on left side.

Now set the fence on the right side of the blade for cutting the second side of the slot in all sides, front, top and bottom. Finish the slot on a bandsaw or jigsaw.

Use a chisel or knife to gain final fit of the pin into the slot. Number each joint for final assembly, but don't assemble them yet.

Make the 1/4" rabbet in the back pieces with a dado blade.

Locate and drill the aligning holes through each spreader for the 3/8" dowels that lock the units together.

The drawers rest within a three-element, self-aligning assembly: the blind dado, the guide, and the dovetailed slot in the drawer side. This allows for easy sliding.

Cut the blind dado in the carcase side. For correct distance, experiment with scrap, then clamp a stop block onto the fence extension. To position this slot accurately on each piece, measure from the top of the side and cut with the top against the fence.

Cut the plywood backs; glue the carcase together. Check the squareness of each carcase as you clamp it.

Glue the wood to make the drawer stock, then cut the pieces to size, allowing 1/16" on each side for total drawer clearance.

Cut the lock joints into the pieces. Rout or dado the 1/4" groove for the drawer bottom.

Cut the dovetail slot in the drawer sides that will accept the guide. Mark the sides according to the drawer guide blind dado already cut into the carcase side. Dado the main portion of this, and finish forming it with a dovetail cutter router bit.

From straight stock at least 3" wide, cut dovetails on the edges of both sides. A wider board makes this easier to control and then it's a simple matter to rip the portion you need from this stock.

Use the disc sander to fit the guide to the blind dado. Then glue and screw these guides into the slot.

Cut the plywood bottom and glue up the drawers.

LIST OF MATERIALS

(finished dimensions in inches)

	10" Unit	
A	Sides (2)	3/4 × 10 × 16-3/4
B	Spreaders (4)	3/4 × 2-1/4 × 36
C	Back	1/4 × 9-1/4 × 35-1/4
D	Drawer front	3/4 × 9-1/4 × 35-1/4
E	Drawer sides (2)	3/4 × 8-3/8 × 16-1/4
F	Drawer back	3/4 × 7-7/8 × 33-5/8
G	Drawer bottom	1/4 × 16-1/8 × 33-3/8
H	Drawer guides (2)	3/4 × 3/4 × 15-1/4
	6" Unit (not shown in dimensioned plans)	
	Sides (2)	3/4 × 6 × 16-3/4
	Spreaders (4)	3/4 × 2-1/4 × 36
	Back	1/4 × 5-1/4 × 35-1/4
	Drawer front	3/4 × 5-1/4 × 35-1/4
	Drawer sides (2)	3/4 × 4-3/8 × 16-1/4
	Drawer back	3/4 × 3-7/8 × 33-5/8
	Drawer bottom	1/4 × 16-1/8 × 33-3/8
	Drawer guides (2)	3/4 × 3/4 × 15-1/4
	Top Unit	
B	Spreaders (2)	3/4 × 2-1/4 × 36
J	Top	3/4 × 17-3/4 × 38
K	Sides (2)	3/4 × 1 × 16-3/4
	Base Unit	
B	Spreaders (2)	3/4 × 2-1/4 × 36
L	Front	3/4 × 3-1/4 × 34-1/2
M	Sides	3/4 × 4 × 16-3/4
	Miscellaneous	
N	Dowels (4 per unit)	3/8 dia. × 1-1/2
	Drawer pulls	3/4 × 1-1/2 × 5-3/4
	Flathead wood screws (4 per unit)	#9 × 1-1/4
	Flathead wood screws (4 per unit)	#6 × 1

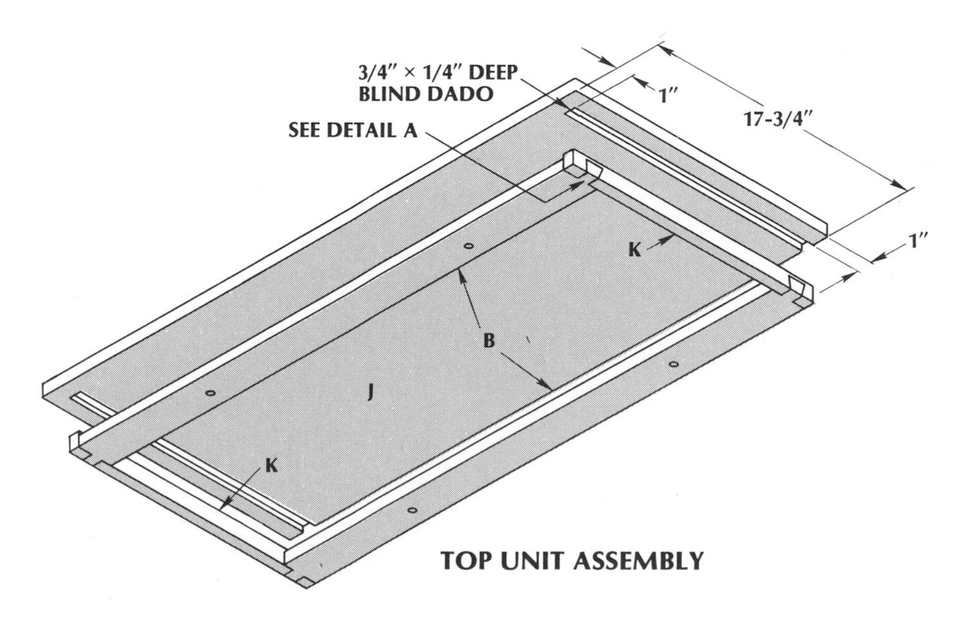

TOP UNIT ASSEMBLY

Cut the wood to make the top. Into the bottom of the top, cut a blind dado which will lock in the small side pieces (use a chisel to square up the end of the dado). Then glue in the top's sides and spreaders. Cut the pieces for the bottom unit, then glue and screw them together.

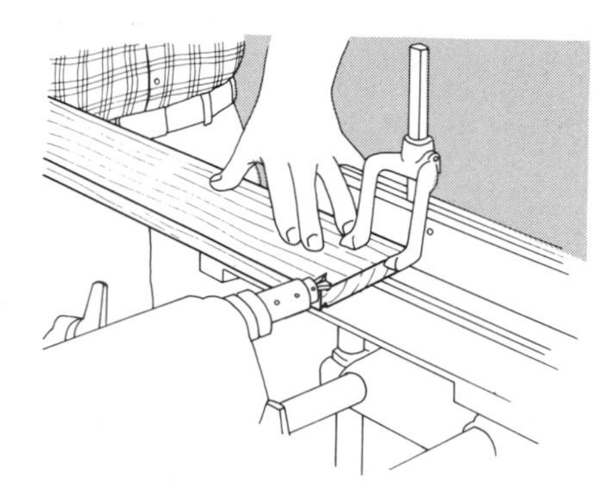

Forming dovetail guides.

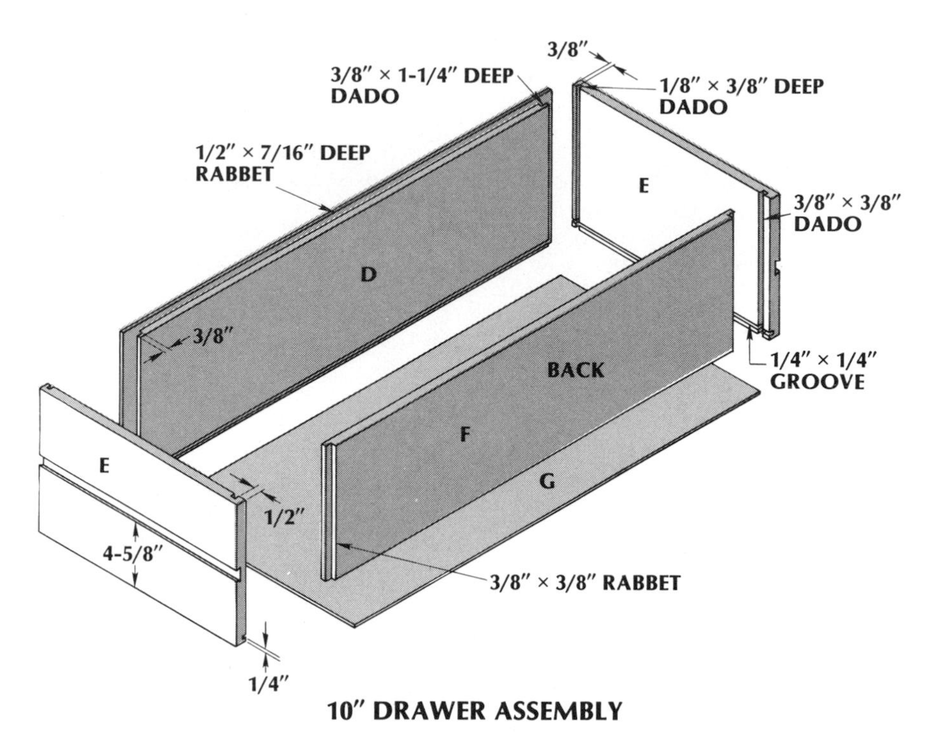

10" DRAWER ASSEMBLY

Place dowels in the spreaders and assemble the units on top of one another. Finish-sand.

Lay out and cut parts for the drawer pulls (see Drawer Pull Layout) using the bandsaw set at 20°. Disc sand the outside of the pulls with a sander set at approximately 20°. Glue the halves of the pulls together, sand the inside surface on the drum sander, and mount them with wood screws from the inside of the drawer front.

Stain and seal the project inside and out, wax the drawer guides, then move it into your bedroom—and breathe a sigh of relief that you finally have all the drawer space you need!

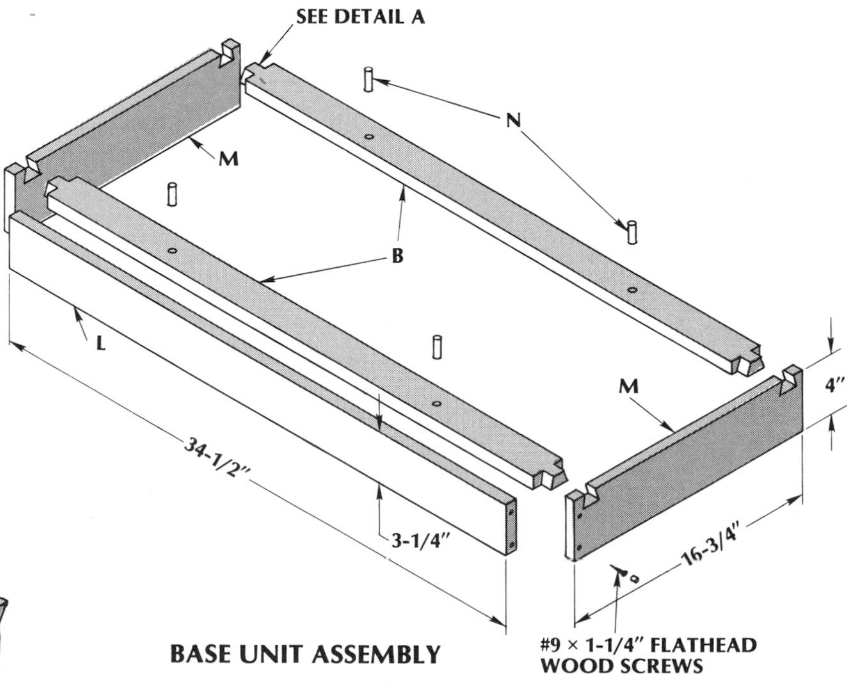

BASE UNIT ASSEMBLY

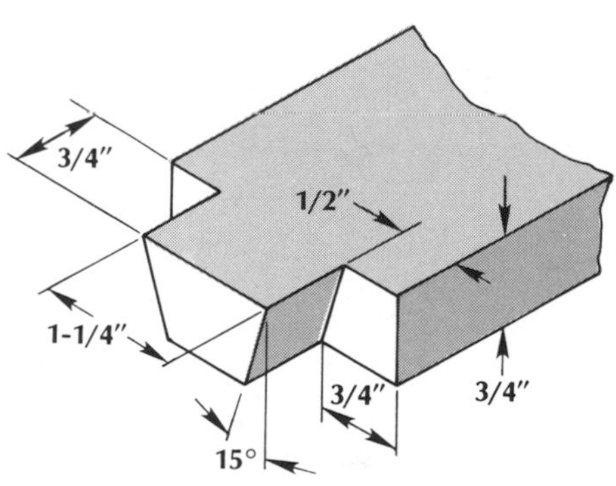

DETAIL A

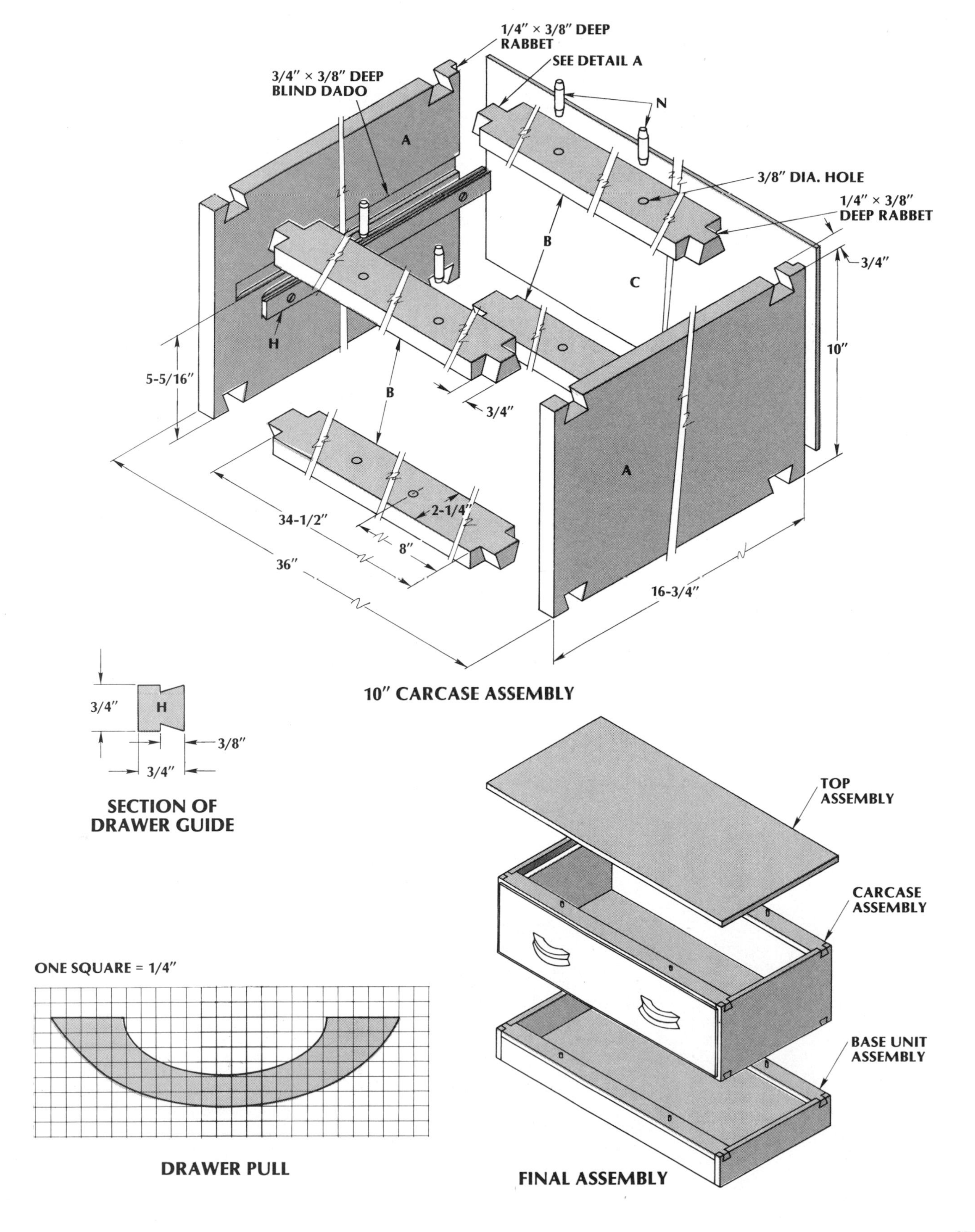
1/4″ × 3/8″ DEEP RABBET
SEE DETAIL A
3/4″ × 3/8″ DEEP BLIND DADO
N
A
3/8″ DIA. HOLE
1/4″ × 3/8″ DEEP RABBET
3/4″
B
C
H
10″
5-5/16″
B
3/4″
A
34-1/2″
2-1/4″
8″
36″
16-3/4″
10″ CARCASE ASSEMBLY
3/4″
H
3/8″
3/4″
SECTION OF DRAWER GUIDE
TOP ASSEMBLY
CARCASE ASSEMBLY
ONE SQUARE = 1/4″
BASE UNIT ASSEMBLY
DRAWER PULL
FINAL ASSEMBLY

CHILD'S DESK & CHAIRS

From *HANDS ON* Mar/Apr 82

Every child deserves a desk of their very own to store their favorite coloring books and crayons, paints and paper, and their own small library of books. Here's a project that uses only one piece of 4 × 8 plywood (we found 1/2" worked well). You get a full 4' desk top and storage shelf plus two chairs just right for that special little person in your life and his or her little friend.

Carefully follow the cutout diagram in marking all the pieces on a sheet of plywood. You can use fir plywood, interior or exterior glue, good one side (A/D) or good two sides (A/B) or special order a sheet of Medium Density Overlay plywood that's specifically made for painting. Make all straight cuts first, then drill holes on the inside of the lines for cutting out the curved pieces. These can be cut on the jigsaw or a hand-held saber saw.

Sharp exposed plywood edges pose a splinter hazard for young hands, so round over these edges with sandpaper or a carbide-tipped 3/8" rounding over router bit.

Dry-assemble all pieces. It helps to drill pilot holes and to use some of those new drywall/particleboard utility screws with a variable speed drill. After positioning all pieces, disassemble and glue. Put it all back together using the screws to clamp the project together.

Fill edge voids with wood putty and apply a primer coat before final painting with a *lead-free* paint. Then bring it out of the shop and watch as the kids create their projects on it!

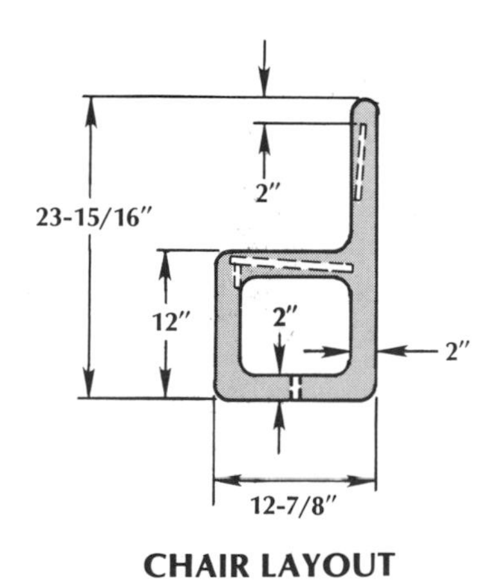

CHAIR LAYOUT

NOTE: 1-1/4" RADIUS TYPICAL EXCEPT WHERE NOTED

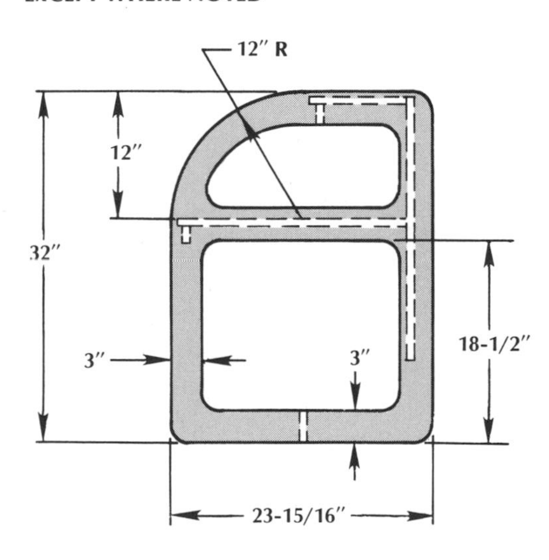

DESK LAYOUT

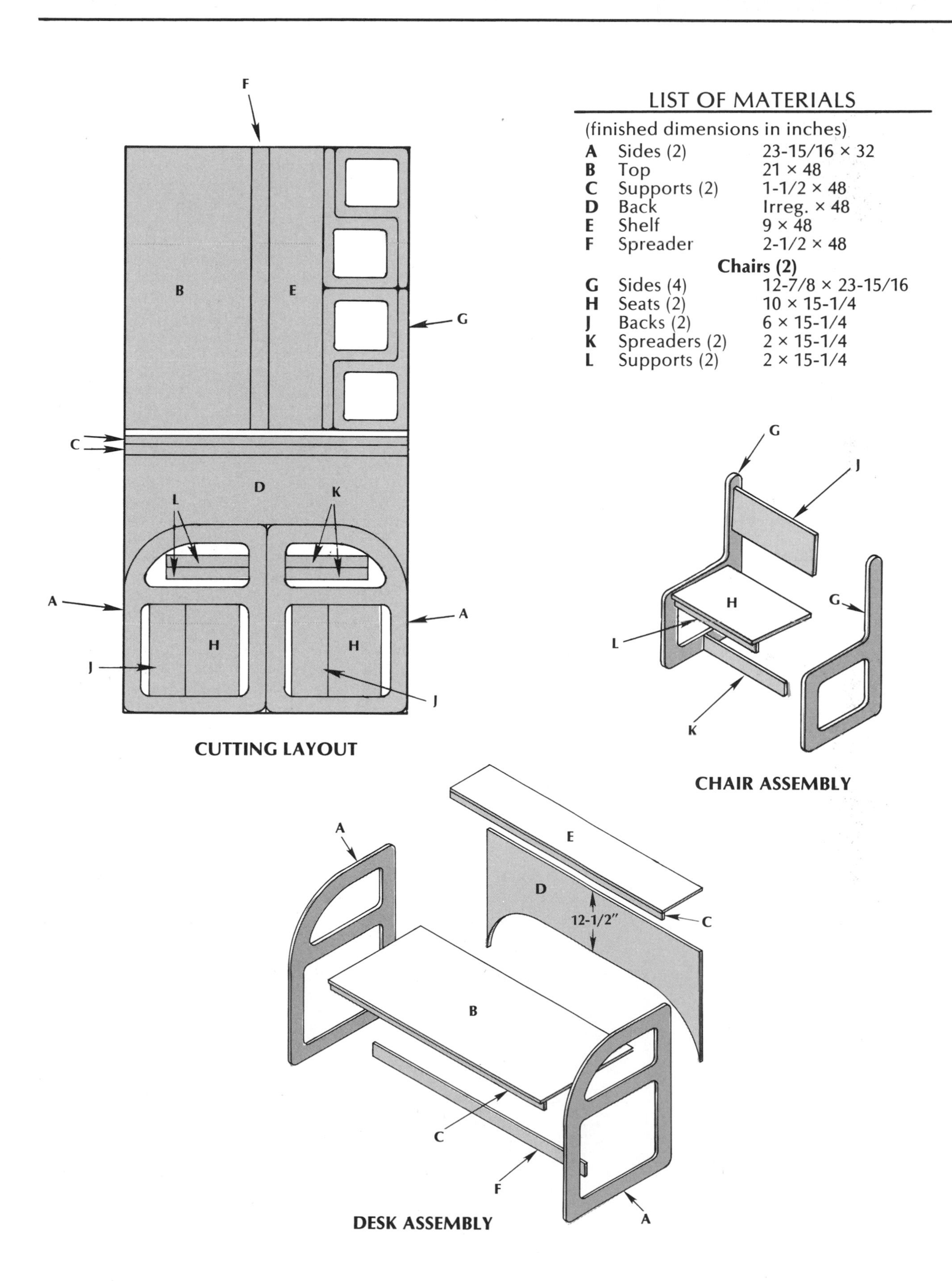

CUTTING LAYOUT

CHAIR ASSEMBLY

DESK ASSEMBLY

LIST OF MATERIALS

(finished dimensions in inches)

A	Sides (2)	23-15/16 × 32
B	Top	21 × 48
C	Supports (2)	1-1/2 × 48
D	Back	Irreg. × 48
E	Shelf	9 × 48
F	Spreader	2-1/2 × 48
	Chairs (2)	
G	Sides (4)	12-7/8 × 23-15/16
H	Seats (2)	10 × 15-1/4
J	Backs (2)	6 × 15-1/4
K	Spreaders (2)	2 × 15-1/4
L	Supports (2)	2 × 15-1/4

HEIRLOOM CRADLE

From *HANDS ON* Apr/May/June 83

One of the greatest joys in woodworking is to see the project you've made used and appreciated. This cradle will not only succeed at this, but will continue to be used and appreciated for generations to come. Because of this, the cradle will be an heirloom—a part of you that will be around well into the 21st century.

Designed with simple classic lines, the construction of this cradle is basic and the joinery rugged. Features include wide feet to prevent tipping, a locking pin on the basket, and wedges that knock out so the whole cradle can break down and store easily.

1. Glue-up stock where necessary according to the List of Materials. Use a hand-held belt sander to smooth the glued-up sections.

2. Transfer the patterns onto all the contoured parts (A,B,C,D,E,F). Mark the location of the holes in the headboard (E) and footboard (F). Do not cut any of the contours yet.

3. Cut the mortises in the feet (A), posts (B), and stretcher (C) with the mortising attachment. If you do not have a mortising attachment, drill several holes and chisel out the waste. We used the drilling method and left the mortises round on the posts so that we could have rounded tenons.

4. Cut the tenons on the bottoms of the posts (B) and ends of the stretcher (C) using a dado attachment. Round the tenons of the stretcher with a rasp.

5. Drill holes. First drill the 1/2" diameter holes in the feet through the post for the pegged mortise and tenon joint with the two parts assembled. Then, drill the 3/4" diameter pivot holes in the posts (B), headboard (E), and footboard (F). Finally, line-up a post with the headboard and drill the locking pin hole through the post into the headboard.

6. Cut the contours on the posts (B), stretcher (C), sides (D), headboard (E), and footboard (F) using the bandsaw. Sand all of these edges using the drum and disc sanders.

7. Assemble the feet to the posts with glue and 1/2" diameter dowels (P). Sand the ends of the dowels flush with the outside surfaces. Tip: Scrub off the excess glue with a wet rag. This works better than chiseling or sanding it off later.

8. Assemble the basket by attaching the sides (D) to the headboard (E) and footboard (F) with glue and #10 × 1-1/2" flathead wood screws. Countersink the screws 3/16" below the surface, and then plug these holes. Use a hand-held belt sander to sand the outside of the cradle smooth and the plugs flush.

The stretcher is joined to the post with classic wedged-through mortise-and-tenon construction.

Cradle pivot pin is a 3/4" diameter hardwood dowel capped with a button.

The post is joined to the foot with a pinned mortise-and-tenon. Pins are hardwood dowels.

Locking pin slips out when you want to rock baby to sleep. The pin is turned from one piece with grain running lengthwise.

9. Cut the cleat strips (G,H) to size, and mount them to the inside of the cradle with #8 × 1-1/4" flathead wood screws.
10. Cut the bottom (Q) to size and bevel the two sides edges. Sand all the edges.
11. Make the spacers (M) by first resawing 3/4" stock to 3/8" thick. Draw 2" circles on the stock, and drill the 3/4" holes. Cut the washers on the bandsaw or jigsaw and sand the edges. Set aside.
12. Make the pivot pins (J) and the pivot lock pin (L). The pivot pins (J) are made of 3" lengths of 3/4" hardwood dowel. The caps to these are turned on the lathe using the screw center. After they are turned, use a jig to hold them while you drill the 3/4" × 1/2" deep holes for the pin. If you are using a good durable hardwood like cherry or maple, you can turn these pins out of one piece of stock.

Turn the locking pin as one piece from a 4" length of 3/4" stock.
13. Make the wedges (N) for the post and stretcher joint. These wedges are cut-to-fit and should be centered and fit snugly with a tap from a mallet.
14. Finish sand all the subassemblies with a fine grit sandpaper. Then apply a nontoxic finish of your choice.

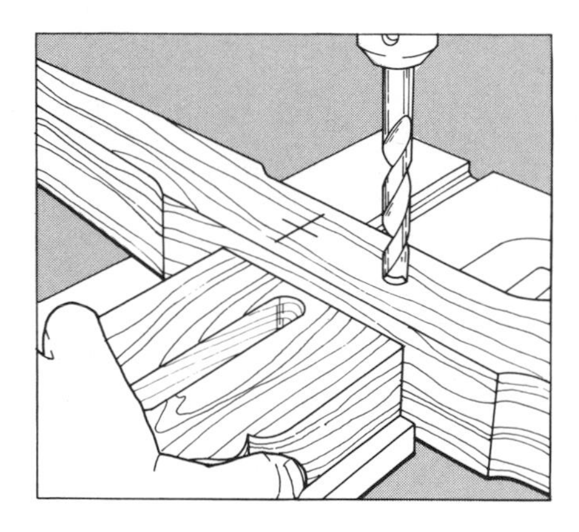

Drilling the 1/2" holes for the pegged joint.

Using a simple jig to hold the caps while drilling.

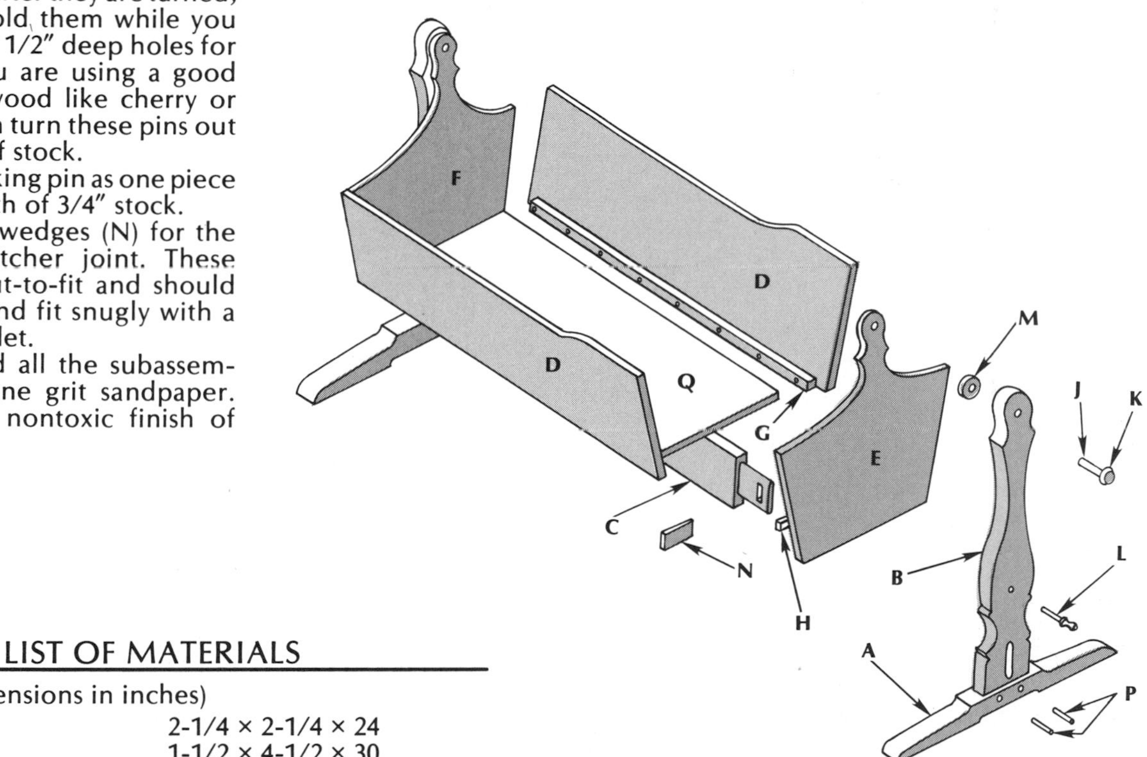

LIST OF MATERIALS

(finished dimensions in inches)

A	Feet (2)	2-1/4 × 2-1/4 × 24
B	Posts (2)	1-1/2 × 4-1/2 × 30
C	Stretcher	1-1/4 × 4-1/2 × 42-3/4
D	Sides (2)	3/4 × 12 × 35
E	Headboard	3/4 × 19-5/8 × 20-1/4
F	Footboard	3/4 × 18-7/8 × 20-1/4
G	Cleat strips (2)	3/4 × 3/4 × 33-1/2
H	Cleat strips (2)	3/4 × 3/4 × 14-3/16
J	Pivot pins (2)	3/4 dia. × 3
K	Pivot pin caps (2)	1-1/2 dia. × 3/4
L	Pivot lock pin	3/4 dia. × 3-3/8
M	Spacers (2)	2 dia. × 3/8
N	Wedges (2)	9/16 × 1-7/8 × 3-3/8
P	Dowels (4)	1/2 dia. × 2-1/4
Q	Bottom	1/4 × 15-11/16 × 33-7/16
	Flathead wood screws	#10 × 1-1/2
	Flathead wood screws	#8 × 1-1/4
	Flathead wood screws	#6 × 1-1/2

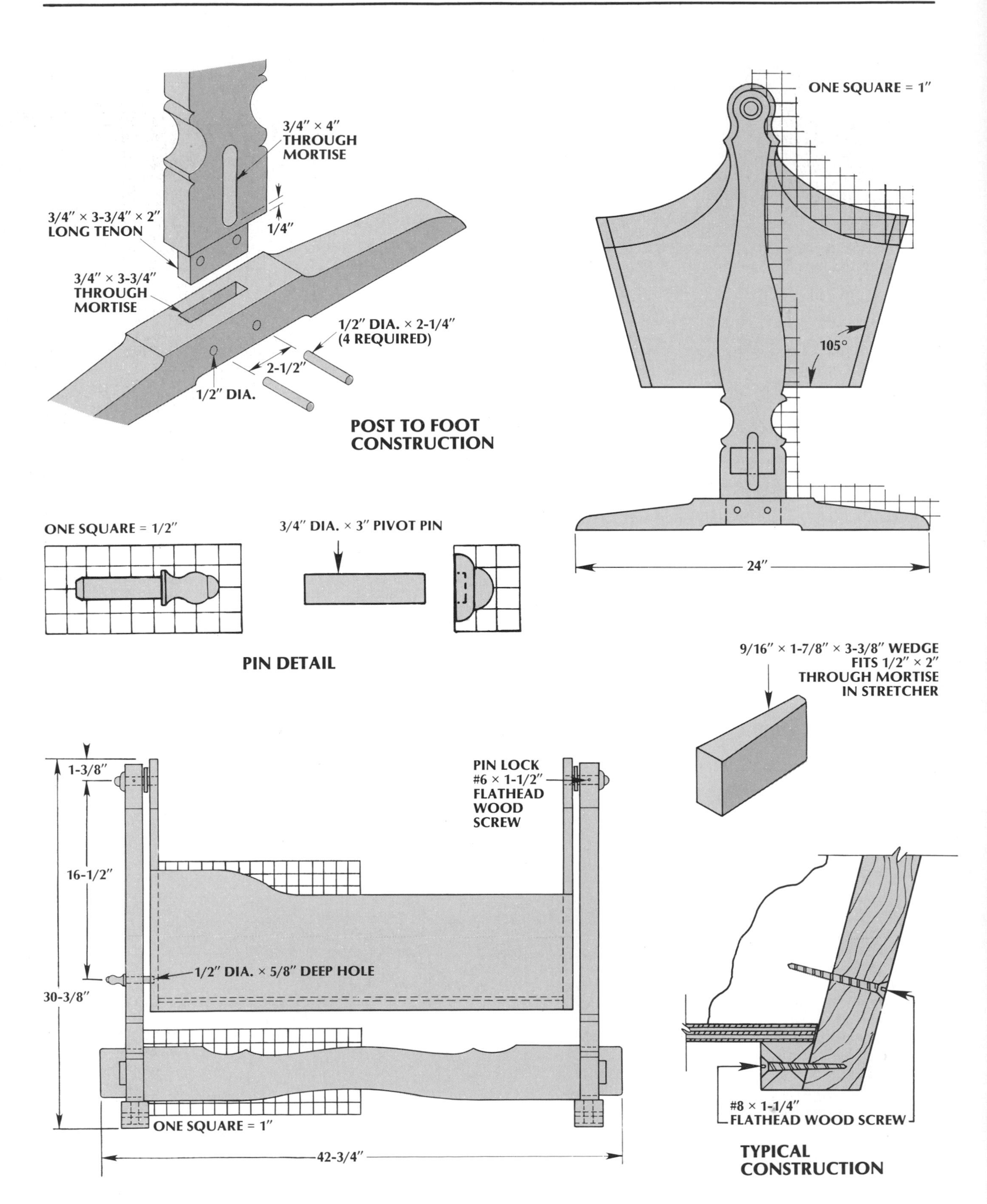
3/4″ × 4″
THROUGH
MORTISE
3/4″ × 3-3/4″ × 2″
LONG TENON
1/4″
3/4″ × 3-3/4″
THROUGH
MORTISE
1/2″ DIA. × 2-1/4″
(4 REQUIRED)
2-1/2″
1/2″ DIA.
POST TO FOOT
CONSTRUCTION
ONE SQUARE = 1″
105°
24″
ONE SQUARE = 1/2″
3/4″ DIA. × 3″ PIVOT PIN
PIN DETAIL
9/16″ × 1-7/8″ × 3-3/8″ WEDGE
FITS 1/2″ × 2″
THROUGH MORTISE
IN STRETCHER
1-3/8″
PIN LOCK
#6 × 1-1/2″
FLATHEAD
WOOD
SCREW
16-1/2″
1/2″ DIA. × 5/8″ DEEP HOLE
30-3/8″
ONE SQUARE = 1″
42-3/4″
#8 × 1-1/4″
FLATHEAD WOOD SCREW
TYPICAL
CONSTRUCTION

From *HANDS ON* Sept/Oct 80

A home sound system is a big investment, so why not get maximum performance from your speakers? A tilted speaker stand can greatly enhance the quality of sound, and it's amazingly easy to construct.

1. You'll need three standard-sized dowels to make the speaker stand— 1-1/4", 3/4", and 3/8". Cut the dowels to length using a bandsaw.

2. Smooth the ends of the dowels with a disc sander.

3. Take eight of the 1-1/4" dowels and drill 3/8" diameter holes 1-1/16" deep in one end of each dowel.

4. Cradle the dowels on the drill press by tilting the table and rip fence to form a V. Clamp a stop block on the fence to accurately position the stretcher holes.

5. Drill 3/4" diameter stretcher holes 5/8" deep in the 1-1/4" dowels. Make sure the top end of the dowel always faces the same direction.

5. Assemble as shown, using wax on the 3/8" dowels and glue on the 3/4" dowels. Stain and finish according to preference.

7. Small pieces of felt can be glued to the stand to prevent it from scratching the speaker.

Note: By adjusting the length of the dowels, you can accommodate larger or smaller speakers. For example, use 3/8", 1/2", and 1" dowels for smaller speakers.

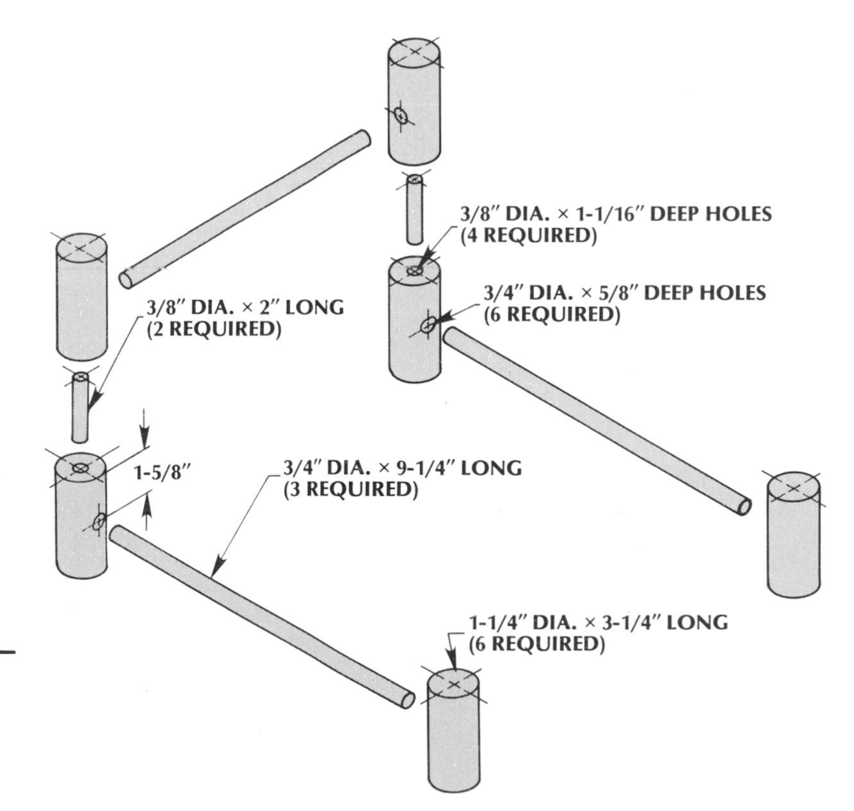

LIST OF MATERIALS

(finished dimensions in inches)

A	Dowels (4)	2 × 3/8 dia.
B	Dowels (6)	9-1/4 × 3/4 dia.
C	Dowels (12)	3-1/4 × 1-1/4 dia.

BOOKCASE

From *HANDS ON* Sept/Oct 85

LIST OF MATERIALS

(finished dimensions in inches)

A	Sides (2)	3/4 × 11-1/4 × 78
B	Top	3/4 × 11-1/4 × 35-1/4
C	Bottom	3/4 × 11-1/4 × 35-1/4
D	Shelves (as many as you need)	3/4 × 11 × 34-1/2
E	Top face frame	3/4 × 3 × 32-1/2
F	Bottom face frame	3/4 × 2-1/2 × 32-1/2
G	Side face frame pieces (2)	3/4 × 1-3/4 × 78
H	Top front molding	3/4 × 2-1/2 × 40
I	Top side moldings (2)	3/4 × 2-1/2 × 14
J	Base front	3/4 × 5 × 37-1/2
K	Base sides (2)	3/4 × 5 × 12
L	Base cleats (7)	3/4 × 3/4 × 4
M	Back	1/4 × 35-1/4 × 74-3/4
N	Dowels (8)	3/8 dia. × 2

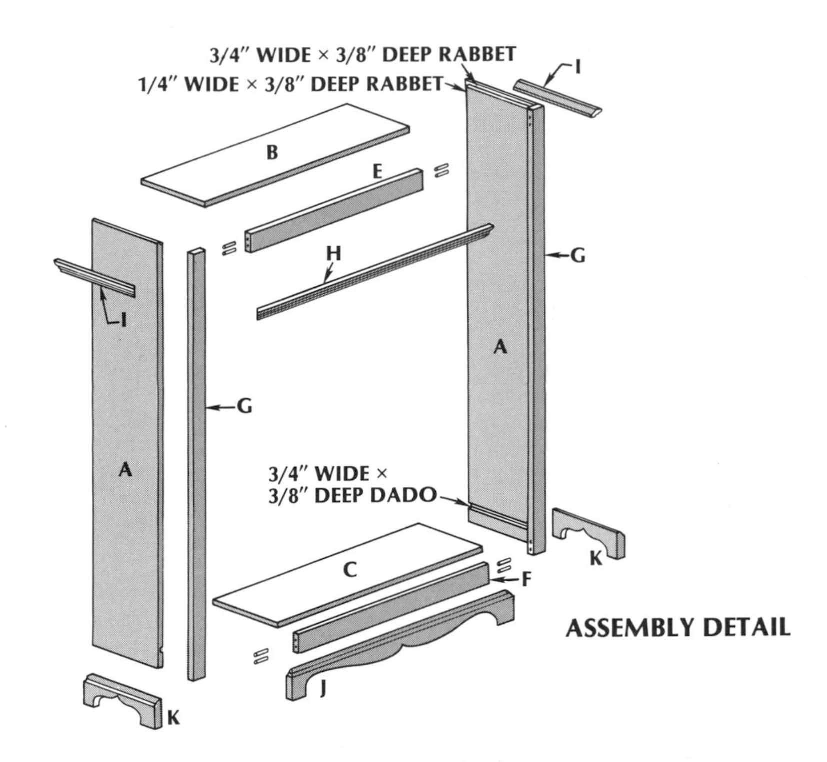

ASSEMBLY DETAIL

A simple bookcase—sides, shelves, and a back, held together with nails—is very easy to make. But with just a little extra effort, a simple bookcase can look like one purchased from a quality furniture store. Here are the plans for an elegant simple bookcase that has adjustable shelves.

1. Cut the two sides, the top, and the bottom to the dimensions given in the List of Materials. Cut 1/4″ deep by 3/8″ wide rabbets in the back edges of all four pieces. Then cut 3/4″ wide by 3/8″ deep dadoes in the sides to accommodate the top and bottom pieces.

2. This bookcase utilizes a hole-and-peg system to support the adjustable shelves. To mark the location of the holes, use a 6′ long stick that is marked at 1-1/2″ intervals. Using the marked stick as a guide, indicate the locations of two rows of holes on the inside of each side piece at the 1-1/2″ intervals; then drill the 1/4″ diameter by 3/8″ deep holes.

3. Assemble the top, bottom, and sides, then measure for the back. Cut the back to size, and glue and nail the bookcase together with 6d finish nails. The back will help keep the bookcase square.

4. Cut out the top, bottom, and side face frame pieces. Drill the dowel holes horizontally.

5. Assemble the face frame with dowels and glue, then attach it to the bookcase with glue and countersunk 6d finish nails.

6. Form the molding as indicated on the drawing. Cut it to length and then attach it to the bookcase

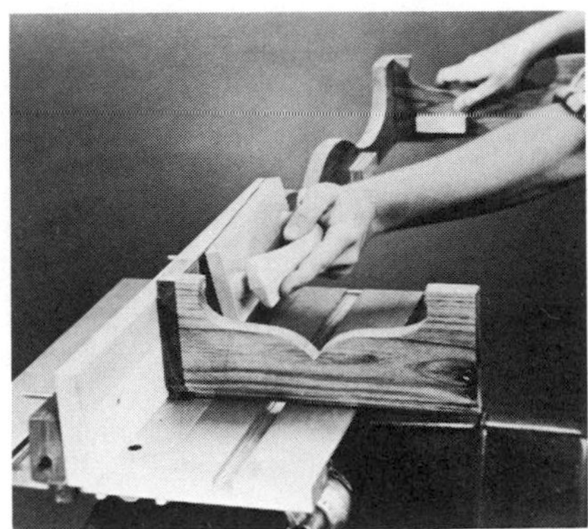

Using the molder to form the contour on the top edge of the assembled base.

with glue and countersunk 6d finish nails.

7. Cut the base pieces to size according to the List of Materials. Transfer the patterns from the drawings to the base front and sides; then use a jigsaw or bandsaw to cut out the base pieces.

8. Sand the contours of the base pieces with a drum sander. Assemble the base pieces, using a molder to form the profile on the top edge.

9. Using glue and #8 × 1-1/4" flathead wood screws, attach the cleats to the inside of the base.

10. Rip and crosscut the shelves to size, then use a molder or shaper with a nosing cutter to shape the front edge of each shelf. Install the shelves.

11. Sand the completed bookcase thoroughly, then finish as desired.

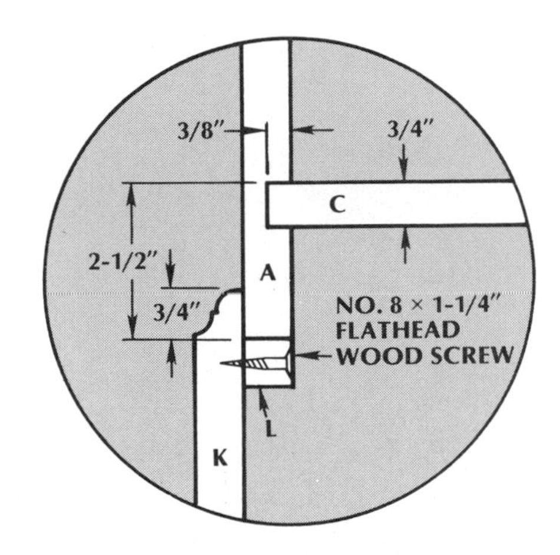

BOTTOM CONSTRUCTION DETAIL

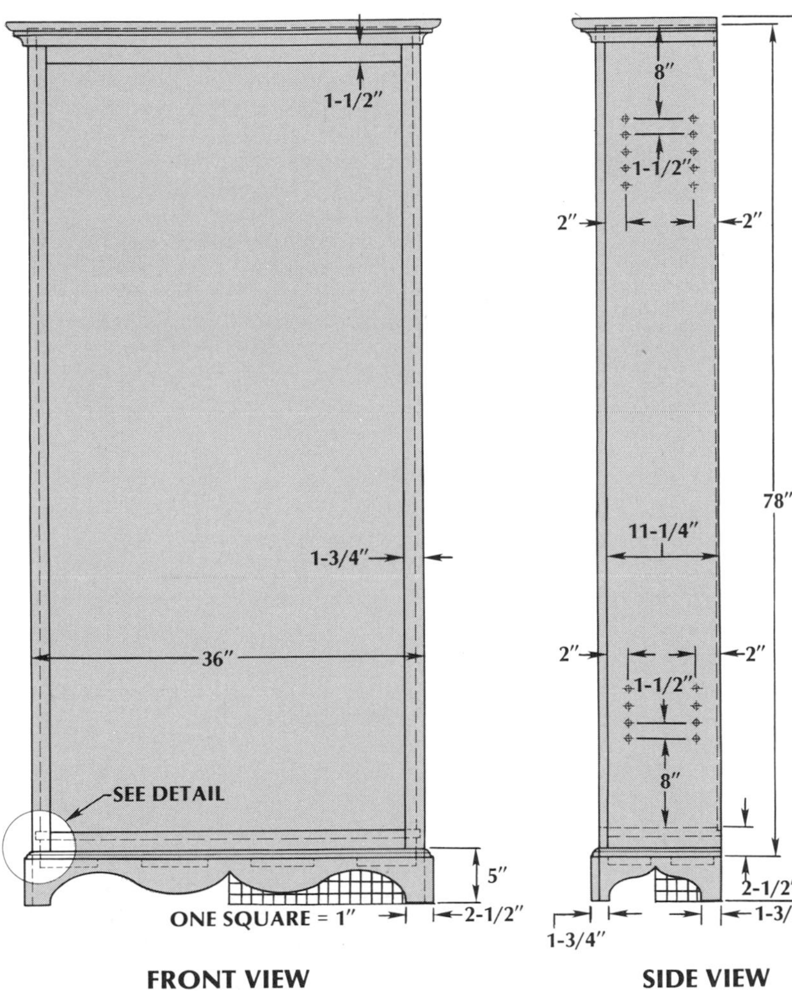

FRONT VIEW

SIDE VIEW

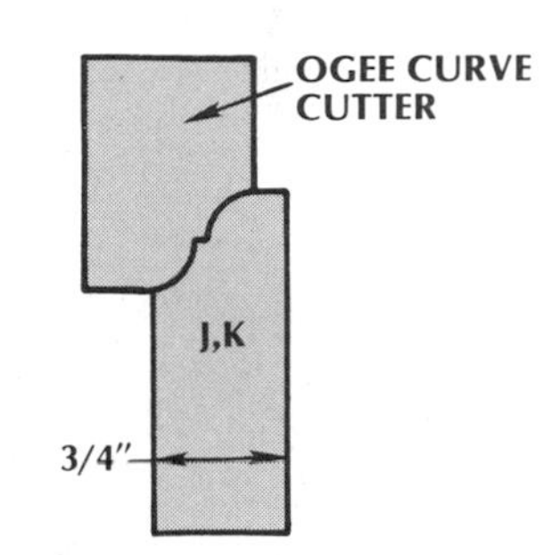

BASE MOLDING DETAIL

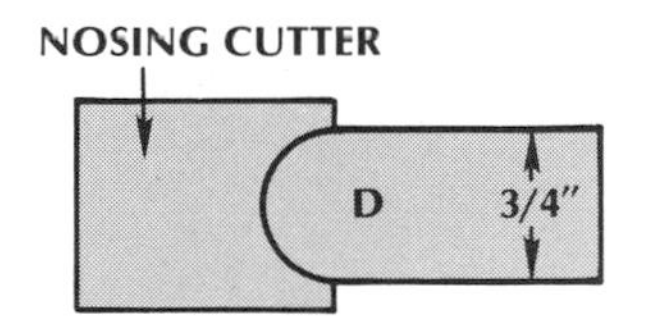

SHELF EDGE DETAIL

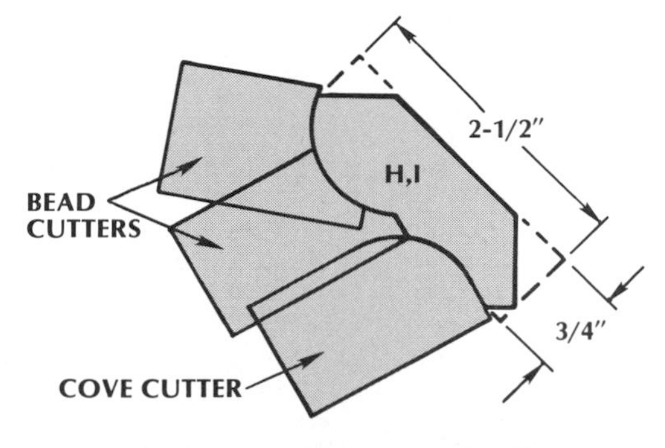

TOP MOLDING DETAIL

POOR MAN'S BUTLER

From *HANDS ON* Nov/Dec 81

Somehow jackets and coats always manage to drape themselves across every available table and chair. If it's getting so you can't see your furniture for the clothes, perhaps you need a 'poor man's butler'.

This particular butler, though traditional in design, is made from contemporary materials. The large panels and shelf are cut from a single piece of 3/4" plywood. Don't try to rip this sheet by yourself—get one or two helpers. We found a carbide-tipped blade worked best; a plywood blade will heat up and begin to wobble in thick stock during a long cut.

Cut the mirror opening in the back panel with a saber saw. We chose to cut a simple oval, 22-1/2" wide × 34-1/2" tall; but you can make the opening any shape or dimension that suits your fancy. The lid can be cut from the seat on a bandsaw—or very carefully on a table saw, finishing up with a handsaw.

The joinery is a snap—most of it consists of simple butt joints and rabbets, all reinforced with glue and countersunk wood screws. The one difficult joint—a stop rabbet in the front stiles—is made by carefully lowering the stock onto the dado blade and rabbeting to a predetermined mark. Make several passes, taking a little more stock off with each pass. Square the ends of the stop rabbet with a chisel.

Drill 1" holes for the pegs in the back stiles, then attach the shelf brackets. Assemble the back stiles to the back panel, build the storge box, and attach the seat and lid.

Screw the front stiles to the storage box, then dowel the arms to both sets of stiles. Add the shelf, trim, and rails. Cover the inside edge of the mirror opening with veneer tape. Turn the pegs and glue them into the back stiles.

If you build from fir plywood, apply a light coat of plywood sealer to help it take a stain evenly. Finish with something that won't be affected by wet raincoats—polyurethane or spar varnish.

Attach the mirror to the back with screws and nylon washers. Finally, collect all the clothes off your other furniture and cover the wooden butler with coats and jackets.

LIST OF MATERIALS

(finished dimensions in inches)

A	Back stiles (2)	1-1/2 × 1-1/2 × 84
B	Front stiles (2)	1-1/2 × 1-1/2 × 23-1/2
C	Arms (2)	1-1/2 × 1-1/2 × 17-1/4
D	Seat Brace	1-1/2 × 1-1/2 × 27
E	Front and back rails (5)	3/4 × 1-1/2 × 27
F	Side rails (2)	3/4 × 1-1/2 × 15
G	Back panel	3/4 × 28-1/2 × 77
H	Front panel	3/4 × 10-1/4 × 28-1/2
J	Side panels (2)	3/4 × 10-1/4 × 16-1/8
K	Seat and Lid	3/4 × 17 × 29-1/2
L	Bottom	3/4 × 15-3/4 × 27
M	Shelf	3/4 × 7-3/4 × 29-1/2
N	Shelf brackets (2)	3/4 × 7-1/4 × 7-1/4
P	Seat and shelf trim	1/4 × 3/4 × 105
Q	Upper pegs (2)	1 dia. × 6-1/2
R	Lower pegs (2)	1 dia. × 5
S	Dowels	3/4 dia. × 1-1/2
T	Mirror opening trim	3/4 × 93
	Veneer tape	
	Mirror	24″ × 36″
	Flathead wood screws (50)	#10 × 1-1/4
	Roundhead wood screws (8)	#12 × 1
	Nylon washers (8)	1/4″
	Hinges (1 pair)	1 × 2

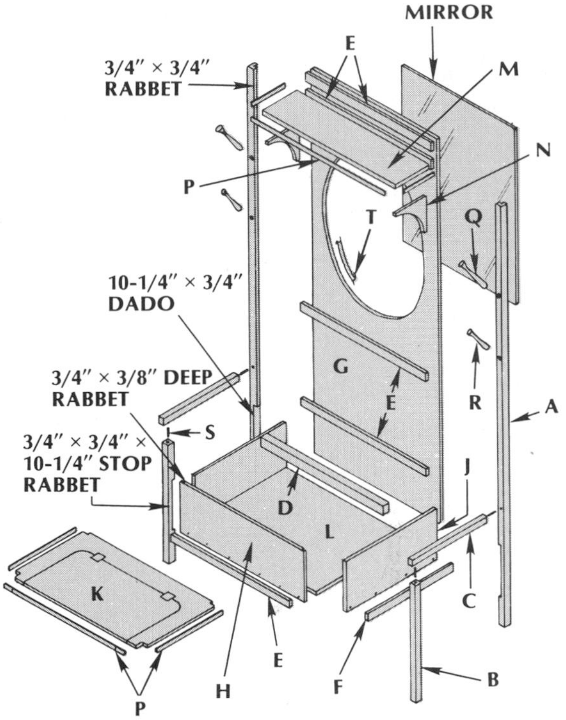

BUTLER ASSEMBLY

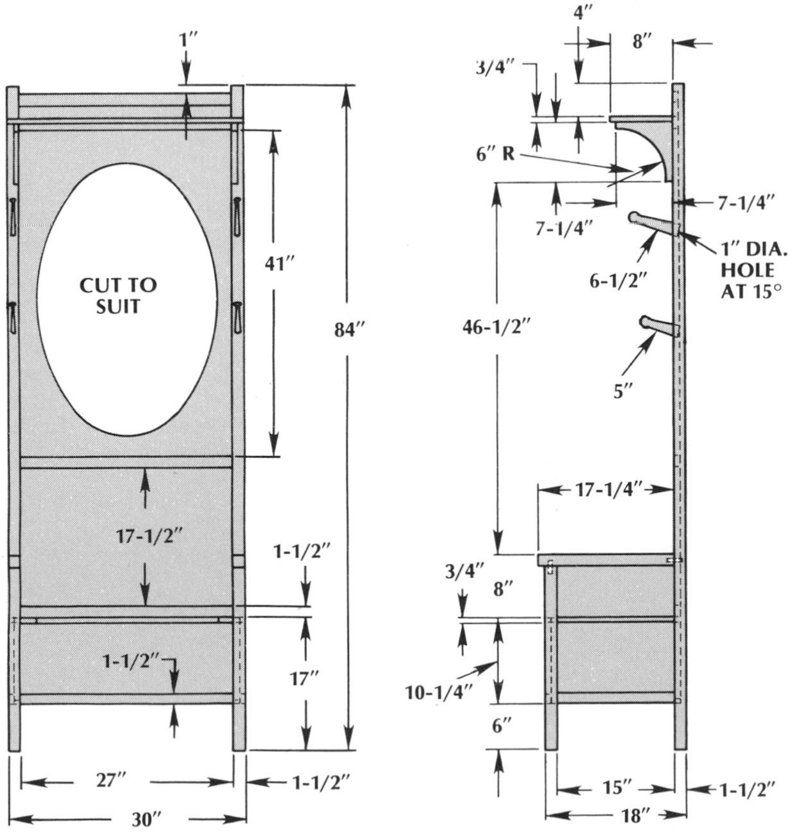

BUTLER LAYOUT

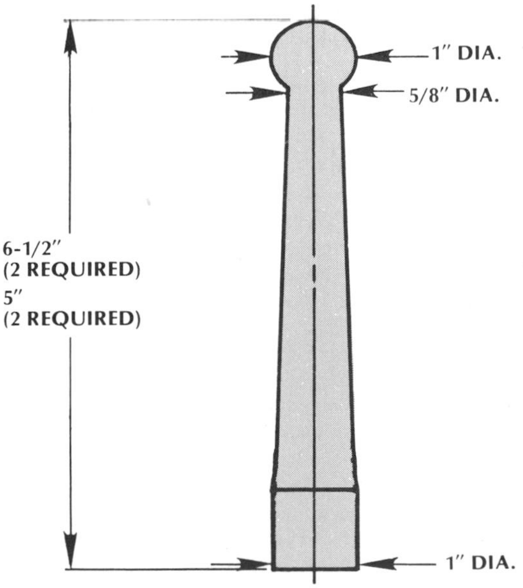

PEG LAYOUT

HALL TREE

From *HANDS ON* Jan/Feb 82

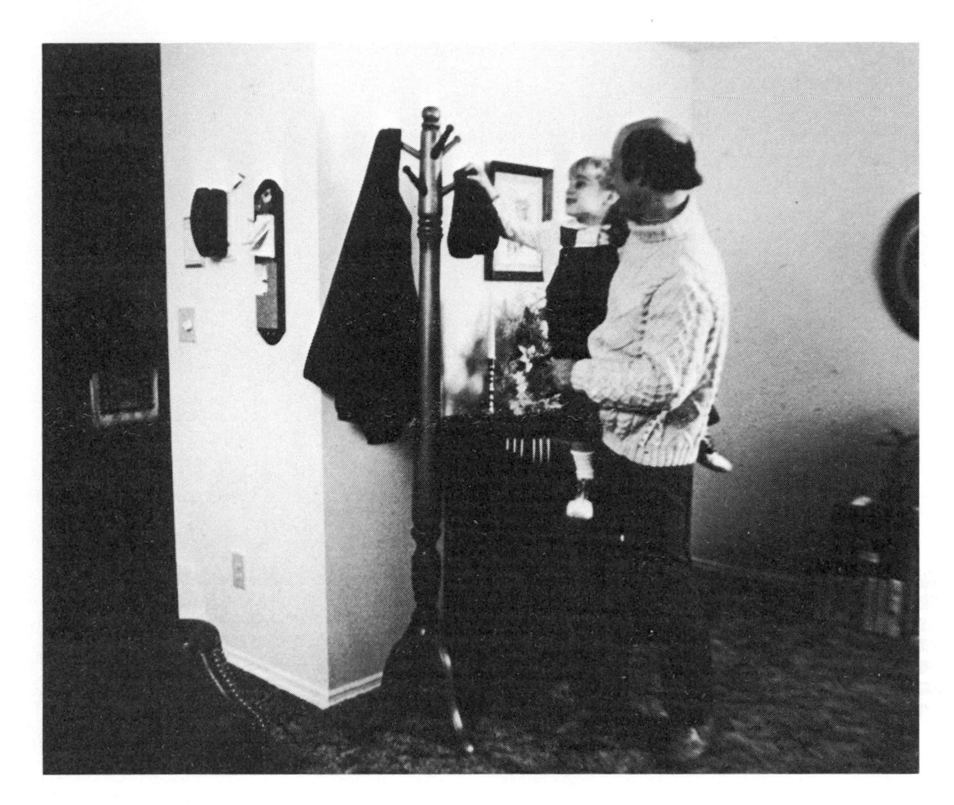

This hall tree, made almost entirely with the lathe, is a simple but classically elegant design suitable for almost any decor.

For this project, you'll need a 4″ × 4″ × 8′ and a 2″ × 4″ × 6′ piece of wood. We used redwood for its rich color and ease of turning. Cut the stock to length according to the plans, allowing about 1/2″ extra stock on each end. Turn the three parts that form the main spindle and finish-sand them while they are still on the lathe.

Next, resaw some of the 4 × 4 stock into 1-1/8″ × 1-1/8″ × 12″ and turn the pegs. These can be turned two at a time from a single piece of stock. Finish-sand these pieces.

Now your turning is complete. The next step is to lay out the legs on the 2 × 4 stock. Cut the angle for the tops of the legs and drill them using horizontal boring. Use a stop block to get even spacing. Finish cutting the legs and sand the contours on a drum or belt sander.

Next, with the drill press, drill the holes for the legs in the bottom section of the hall tree. Measure very accurately or use dowel finders for the proper spacing.

Turning two coat pegs from one piece of stock. Use bandsaw to separate after turning.

The six holes for the pegs in the tapered top are positioned to divide the column in three equal sections. Wrap a piece of paper around the top section and mark the paper for the diameter of the top. Then measure the paper and mark it off into three equal sections. Transfer these marks onto the wood. With the worktable at 30° and a V-block to hold your work, drill the peg holes with a brad-point bit or, better, use a Forstner bit.

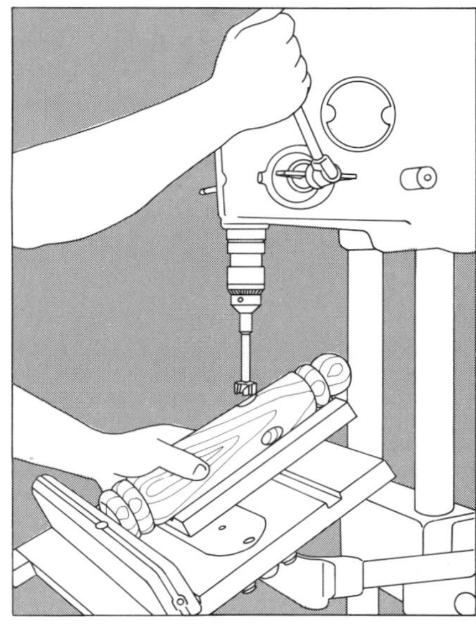

Worktable at 30° with V-block fence forms stop.

For the final assembly, you will need to drill pilot holes into the bottom of the top section, both ends of the middle section and the top of the bottom section. With a 3/16″ bit, drill to a depth of about 1-1/4″. Apply a little soap or paste wax to both ends of the dowel screws and assemble the body of the hall tree with plenty of glue on the end grain.

Glue and dowel the legs into place, then glue the coat and hat pegs in. Apply the finish of your choice. Place it near the door. Then, your final challenge is to get everybody to use it!

LIST OF MATERIALS

(finished dimensions in inches)

A	Top spindle	2-1/2 dia. × 13-3/4
B	Middle spindle	3-1/4 dia. × 33
C	Bottom spindle	3-3/8 dia. × 22
D	Legs	1-1/2 × 3-1/2 × 14
E	Pegs (3)	1 dia. × 6
	Pegs (3)	1 dia. × 5
F	Dowel pegs (8)	3/8 dia. × 2
G	Dowel screws (2)	5/16 dia. × 2-1/2

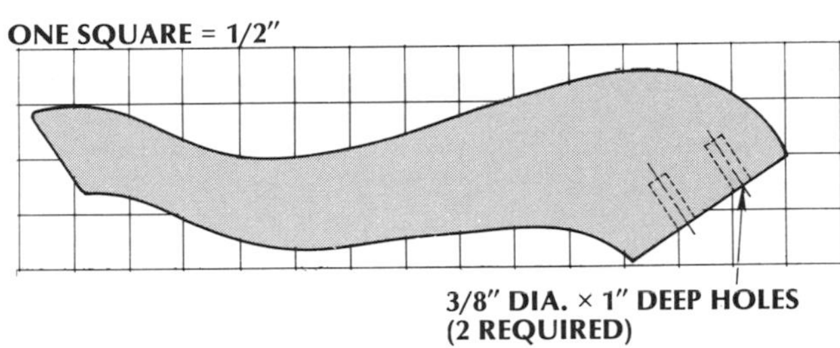

LEG PATTERN

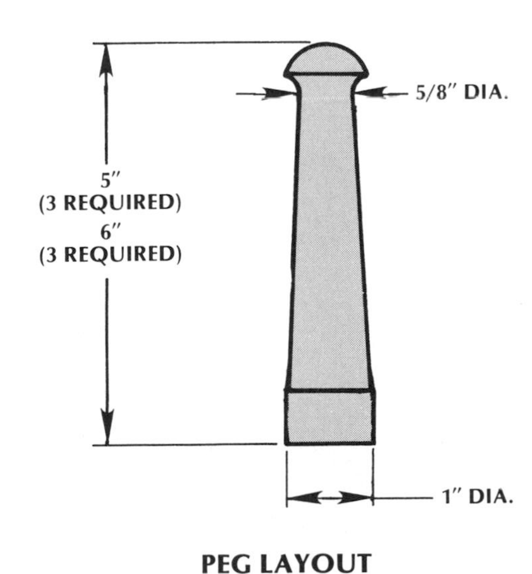

PEG LAYOUT

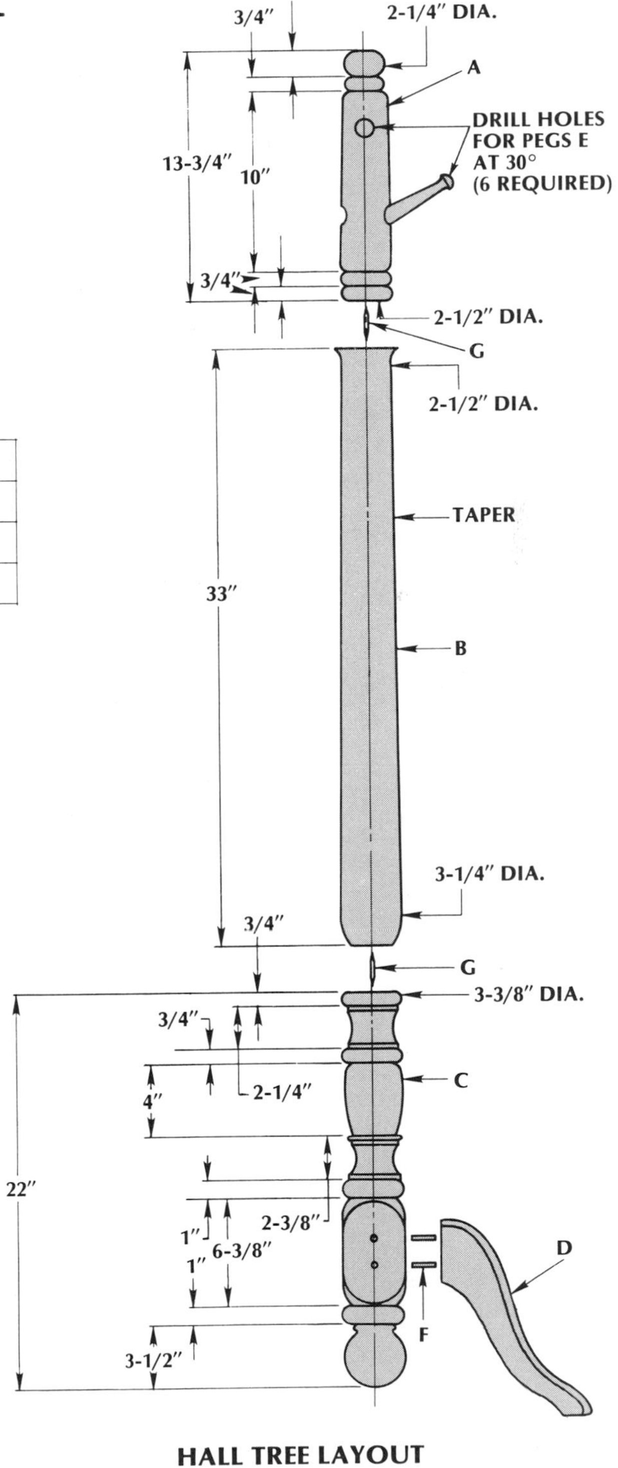

HALL TREE LAYOUT

ELEPHANT BED

From *HANDS ON* May/June 82

Here's a bed that makes use of the vertical space in a small bedroom. Sitting up on high but very stable legs (that's why we call it the "Elephant Bed"), this bed opens up space underneath for a desk and shelves.

This simple structure inspires children to creative activity. Active children, for instance, just might try to climb the shelving! That's why we designed them extra-sturdy.

Also note: *For safety's sake, install a maximum of three shelves with a minimum of 10″ between each shelf. Be sure the top shelf is 10″ below the bottom of the bed.*

The bed frame is built to handle a twin size mattress with about 7″ to spare in width. We recommend using portable tubular guard rails that slip under the mattress to keep children safe from rolling out of the bed. Furniture stores sell a variety of guard rails for this purpose.

To make the bed frame, start by cutting the contour in the tops of the sides and ends on the bandsaw. Sand the contours with a drum sander and mount the cleat strips on the inside of the pieces with screws and glue spaced about 10″ apart. Assemble the bed frame with nails or screws and glue, using simple butt joints. Set the plywood bottom into the frame and fasten.

Assemble the legs. Take the leg assemblies one at a time and clamp them into their relative position on the bed frame. Drill 1/4″ pilot holes for the hex head bolts and then unclamp the legs. Drill the 5/16″ holes for the T-nuts.

Make a desk from the leftover plywood and wood pieces and attach it to the legs.

To make the ladder, it's helpful to mark all waste stock before you start to cut. Cut the hooks to shape on the bandsaw and set aside. Set the miter gauge at 78° and cut the top and bottom ends on the sides. Keep the miter gauge set at 78° and use the dado blades to cut the 3/4″ × 3/8″ deep dadoes for the steps and the lap joint for the hook on one side. Move the miter gauge to 78° in the other direction and cut the dadoes for the other side. Next, tilt the table to 12° and cut the bevel on the front and backs of the steps.

Round off all exposed edges on the bed. Apply a nontoxic finish of your choice.

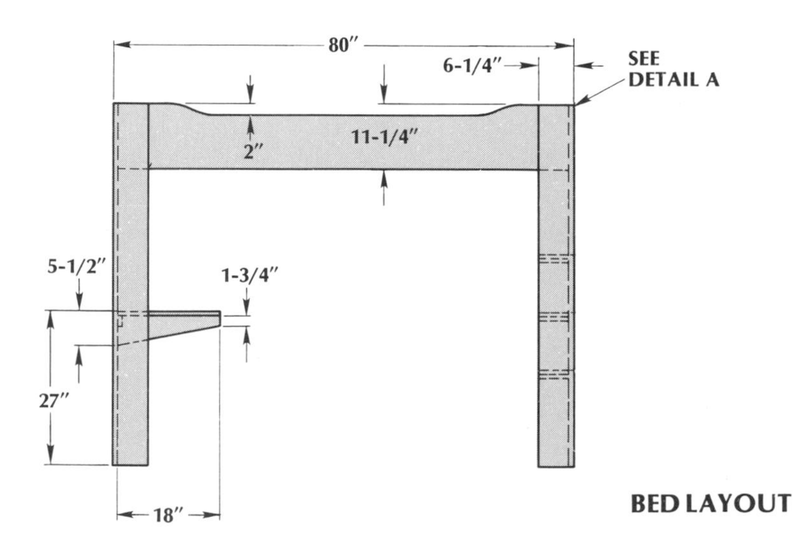

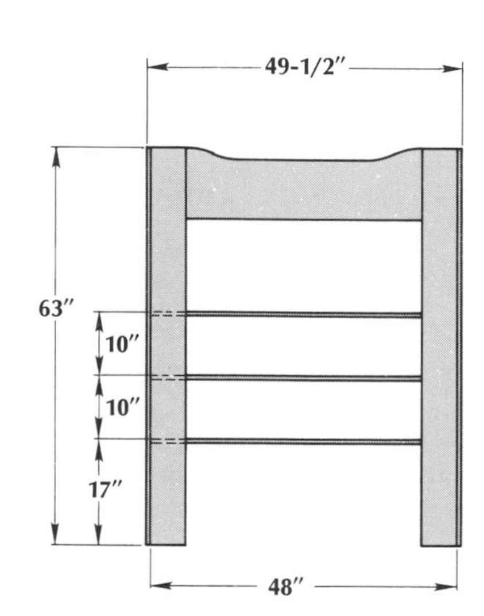

BED LAYOUT

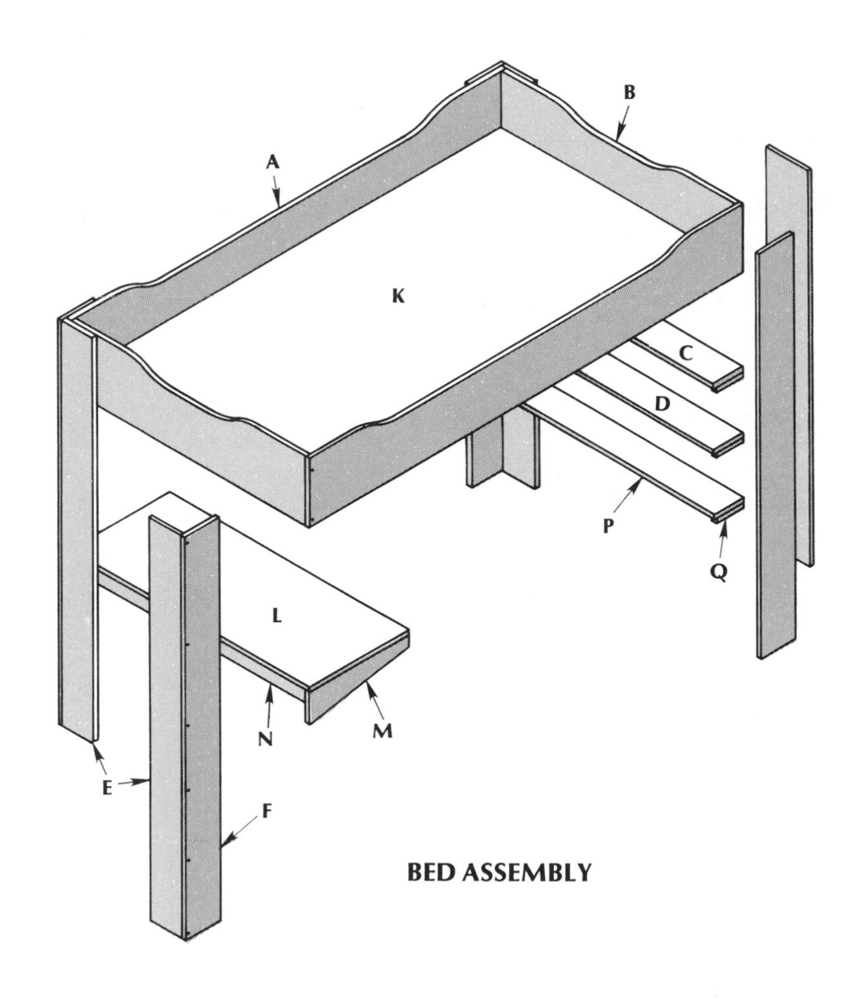

BED ASSEMBLY

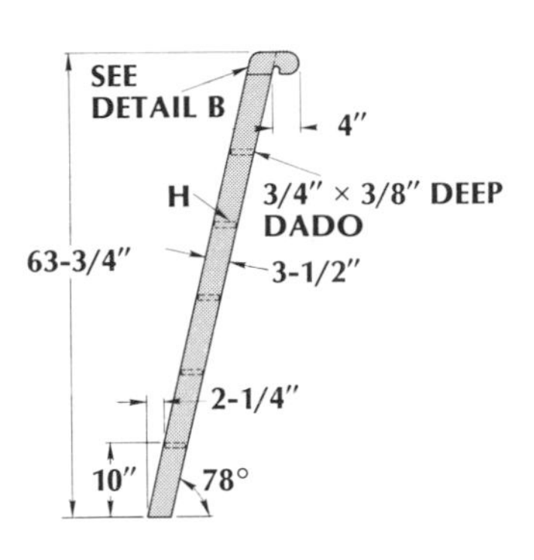

LADDER LAYOUT

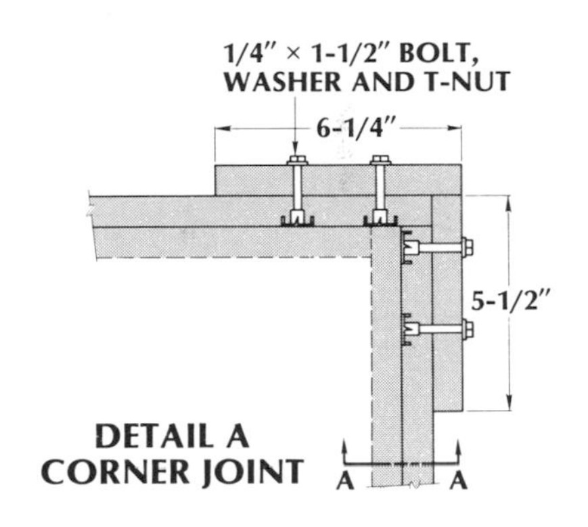

DETAIL A
CORNER JOINT

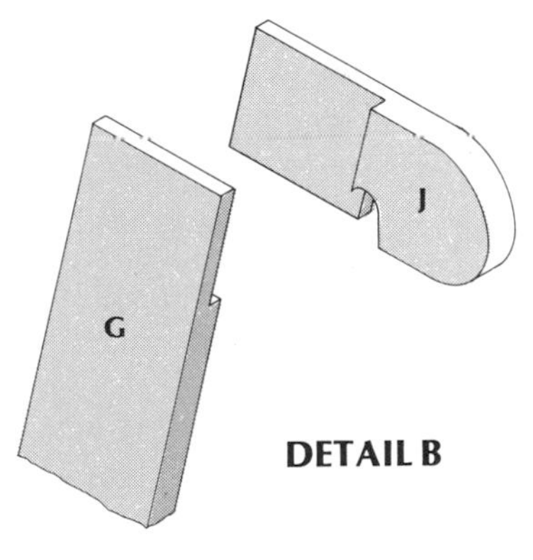

DETAIL B

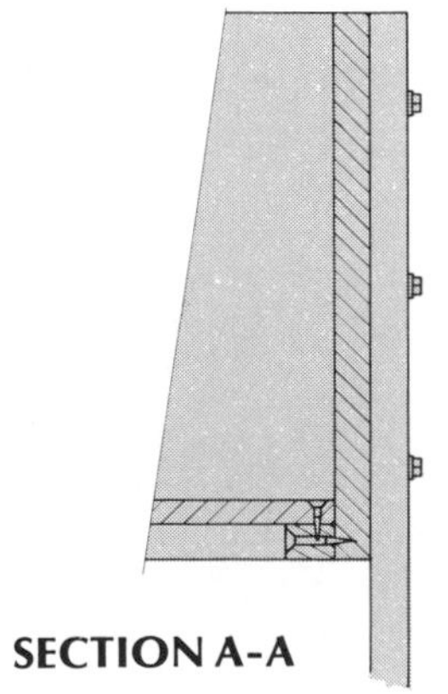
SECTION A-A

LIST OF MATERIALS

(finished dimensions in inches)

A	Frame sides (2)	3/4 × 11-1/4 × 78-1/2
B	Frame ends (2)	3/4 × 11-1/4 × 46-1/2
C	Side cleats (2)	3/4 × 1 × 75-1/2
D	End cleats (2)	3/4 × 1 × 46-1/2
E	Leg sides (4)	3/4 × 5-1/2 × 63
F	Leg sides (4)	3/4 × 6-1/4 × 63
G	Ladder sides (2)	3/4 × 3-1/2 × 66-1/4
H	Steps (5)	3/4 × 3-1/2 × 14
J	Ladder hooks (2)	3/4 × 3-1/2 × 7-1/4
K	Bottom	1/2 × 46-1/2 × 77
L	Desk Top	1/2 × 18 × 48
M	Desk supports (2)	3/4 × 5-1/2 × 18
N	Desk braces (2)	3/4 × 2 × 46-1/2
P	Shelves (3)	3/4 × 5-1/2 × 48
Q	Shelf cleats (6)	3/4 × 1 × 5
	Hex head machine bolts (46)	1/4 × 1-1/2
	Flat washers (46)	1/4
	T-nuts (46)	1/4
	Flathead wood screws (approx. 100)	#10 × 1-1/2

LUGGAGE STAND

From *HANDS ON* Sept/Oct 84

Here's a project that'll please your overnight guests—an attractive, folding luggage stand that's not only practical but shows off your woodworking skills in an unusual way. However, two stands are better than one. Once you have your woodworking tools set up for the various required operations, it takes only a little more time and effort to make a second stand.

1. Prepare the stock. For the best results, use clear straight hardwood. Rip all stock to width then crosscut to length. Leave an extra 2" on the spindle (A) for waste stock.

2. Turn the spindle (A). Keeping the distance between the shoulders at 18", turn the spindle according to the plans or create your own design. Final-sand the spindle while it's still on the lathe. Next, trim off the waste stock after removing the spindle from the lathe.

3. Make the rails (B). Use the disc sander to round both ends of each rail. Next, use a rasp or a router with 1/4" quarter-round bit and round over the sharp edges of the rails. Sand the rails.

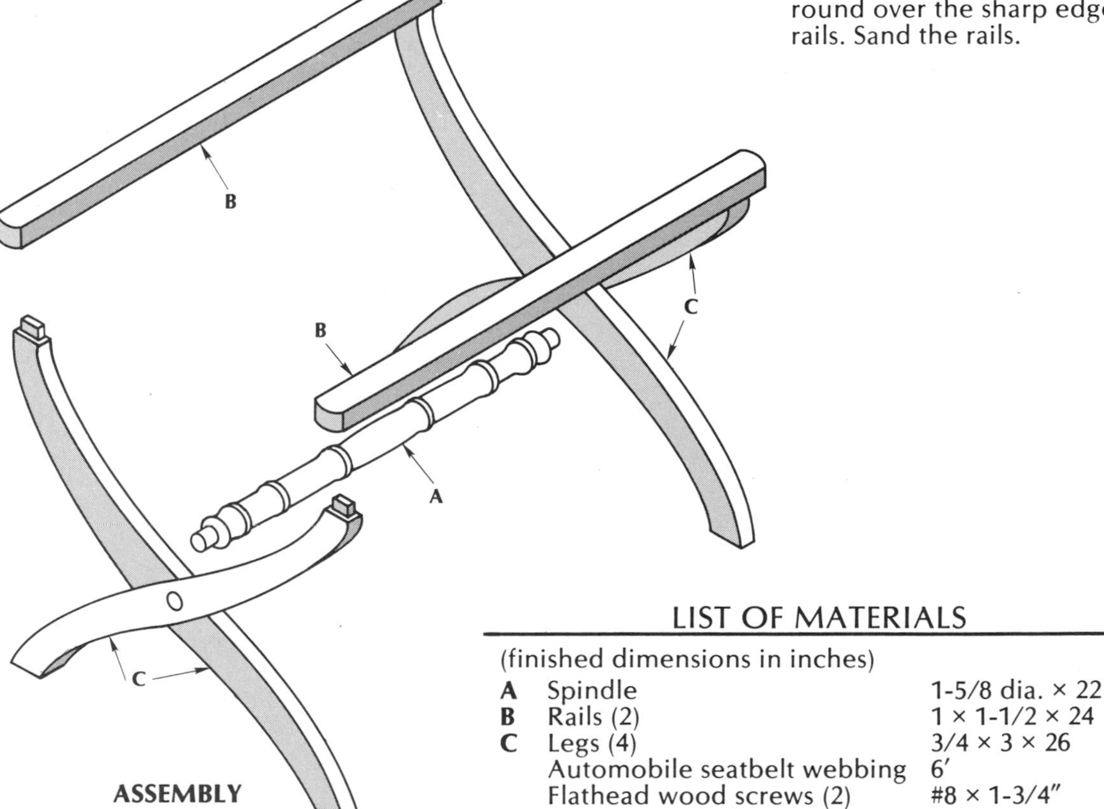

LIST OF MATERIALS

(finished dimensions in inches)

A	Spindle	1-5/8 dia. × 22
B	Rails (2)	1 × 1-1/2 × 24
C	Legs (4)	3/4 × 3 × 26
	Automobile seatbelt webbing	6′
	Flathead wood screws (2)	#8 × 1-3/4″
	Carpet or upholstery tacks (18)	#8
	Flat washers (2)	1″ I.D.

Mortise the rails. Note the different locations of the mortises for each rail. To allow for excess glue, make the mortises 1/16" deeper than the length of the tenon.

4. Make the legs (C). Use a cardboard template to transfer the pattern to the stock. Using a bandsaw, cut out the legs and use the disc and drum sanders to sand the edges.

Mark each leg for its location on the stand and cut the tenons to fit the mortises.

Stack the legs and tape them together. Pad drill the 15/16" hole in the center. Prevent splintering by backing up the stock with scrap.

Next, use a decorative shaper cutter or router bit to shape the edge.

5. Apply a finish to all parts except the mortises and tenons.

6. Assemble the stand. By building a simple jig, the assembly of the stand will be much easier. Attach two scrap 2 × 4s 15" apart on a 2' square piece of plywood. Dry-fit the rails, spindle, and legs. Apply glue and place the stand in the jig. Use #8 × 1-3/4" flathead wood screws to secure the spindle to the outside legs.

7. Install the webbing. Cut the webbing into 2' lengths. Fold back 5/8" on each end of each strip and use three #8 carpet or upholstery tacks to attach the webbing to the rails.

RAIL DETAIL

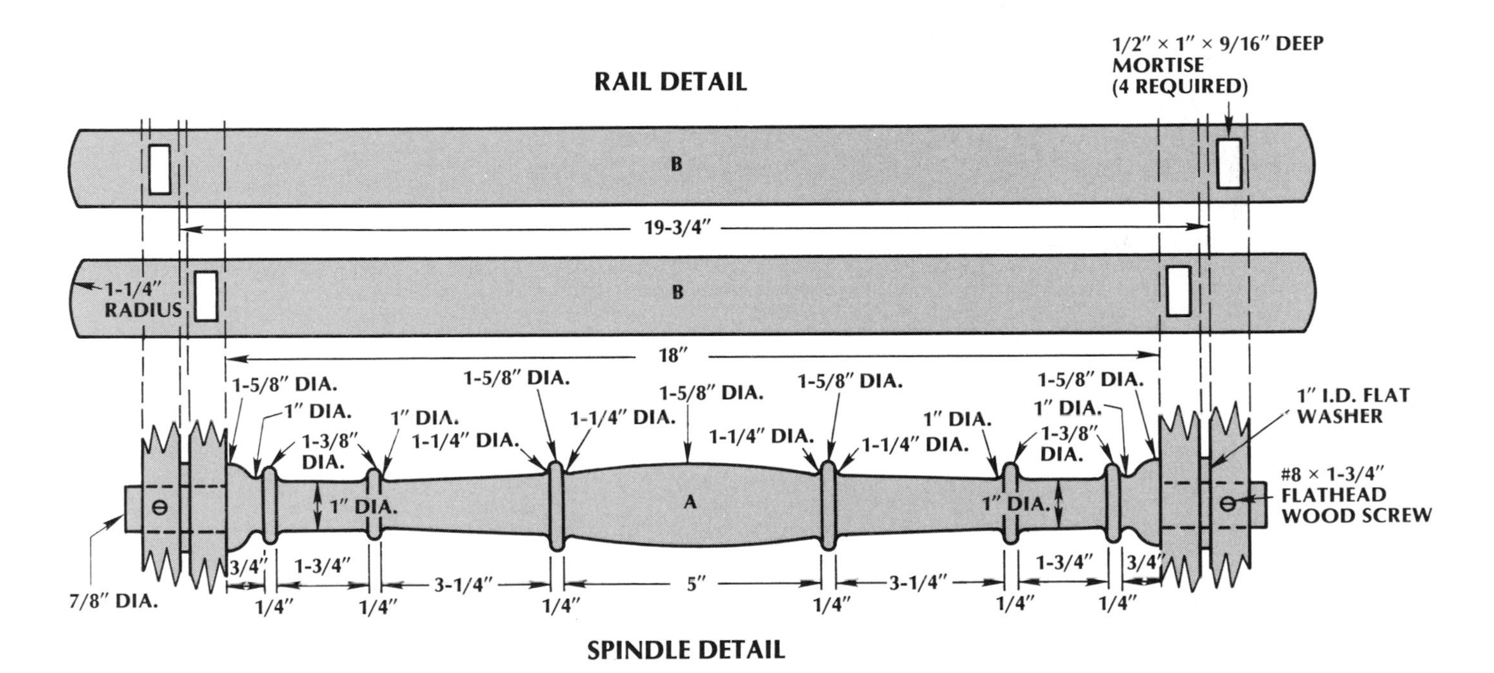

SPINDLE DETAIL

ONE SQUARE = 1"

1/2" × 1" × 1/2" LONG TENON

C

15/16" DIA.

LEG DETAIL

NESTING TABLES

From *HANDS ON* May/June 82

Here's an attractive project that takes less time than it might appear. Many of the setups can be "borrowed" from one nesting table to the next.

You can make these tables from the hardwood of your choice. Stock for the legs should be straight-grained and clear wood due to the tapers you'll form in them.

Glue the wood for the three tabletops, then cut all rails to size according to the List of Materials. Make sure all ends are square.

Cut all the legs to size, but leave them untapered for now.

Locate and drill holes for dowels in the rails. Use the miter gauge and a stop block held with a C-clamp for duplicating hole locations in each set of the three or four rails. Use dowel centerfinders for locating the mating holes in each leg.

Drill the stabilizing dowel holes in the tops of the front legs of the medium and large tables.

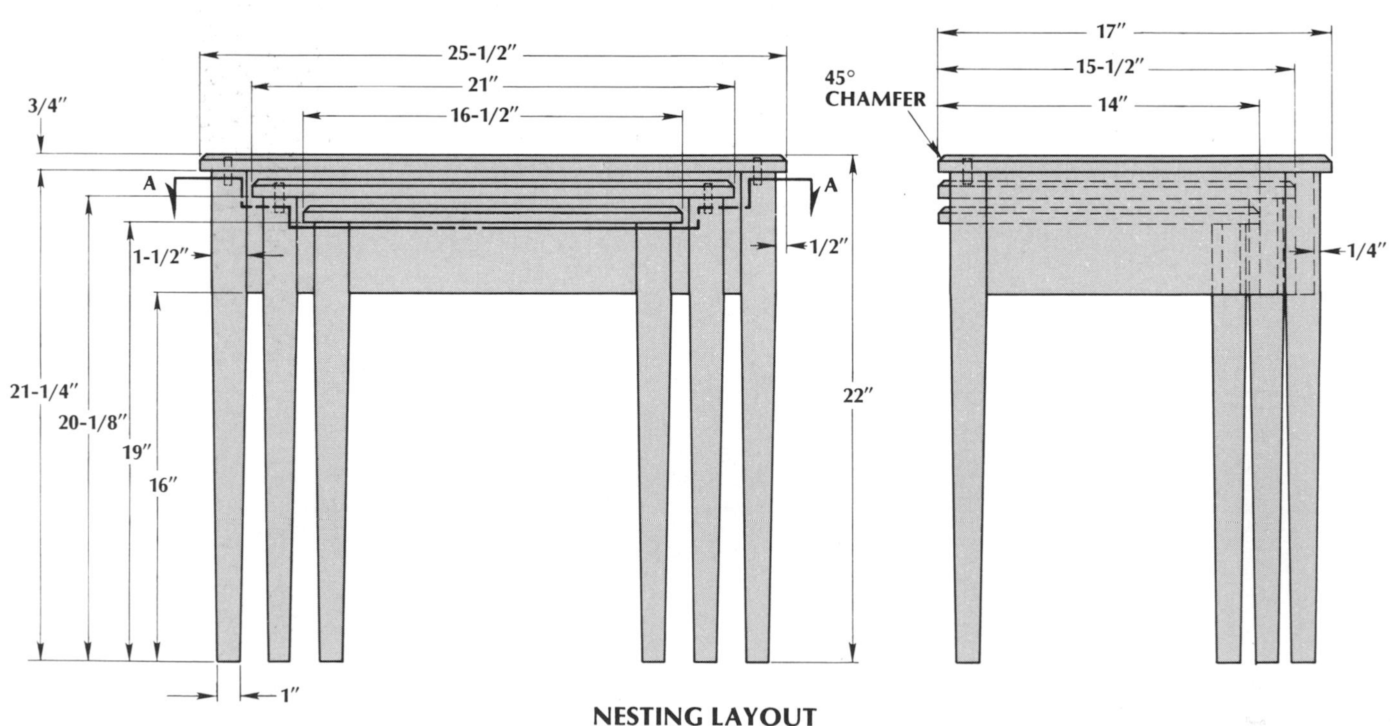

NESTING LAYOUT

Now set the jointer depth to 7/64". Use a stop block at the starting position and make two passes on all four sides of the legs. The taper is the same length on all 12 legs. Then reset the depth of the jointer to 1/32", remove the stop block, and make one final pass over the jointer to clean up the tapered portion.

Use a planer blade to cut the groove on the inside of all ten rails. This groove will accept the retainer clips that will hold the tabletops to the base assemblies.

Cut the tops to size, then set the jointer fence to 45° and cut the chamfer on all the table edges.

Assemble all three bases and finish-sand them. Locate and drill the stabilizing dowel holes in the medium and large tabletops. Apply the finish of your choice. Then attach the tops with the retainer clips and dowels.

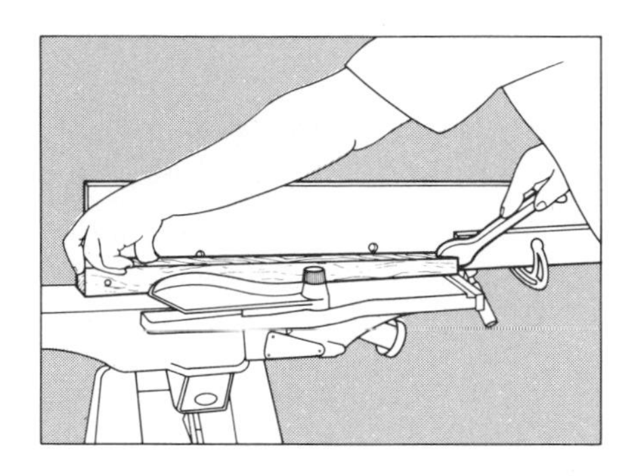

Tapering process for all legs. Note use of stop block and safety push stick.

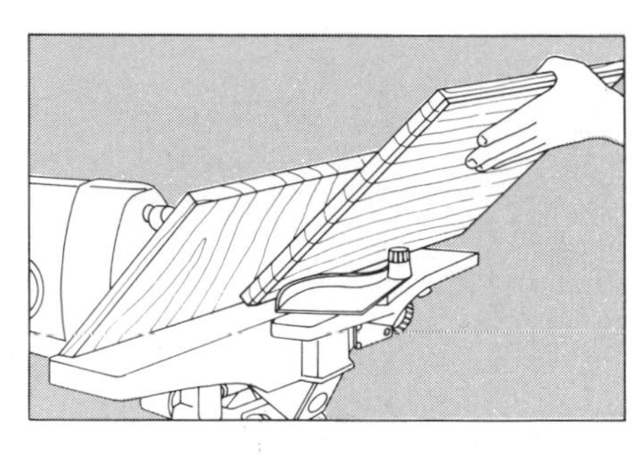

Forming chamfer on tabletops. Wood extension fence increases accuracy and safety.

LIST OF MATERIALS

(finished dimensions in inches)

	Large Table	
A	Rails (2)	3/4 × 5-1/4 × 13
B	Rail	3/4 × 5-1/4 × 21-1/2
C	Top	3/4 × 17 × 25-1/2
D	Legs (4)	1-1/2 × 1-1/2 × 21-1/4
	Medium Table	
A	Rails (2)	3/4 × 4-1/8 × 11-1/2
B	Rail	3/4 × 4-1/8 × 17
C	Top	3/4 × 15-1/2 × 21
D	Legs (4)	1-1/2 × 1-1/2 × 20-1/8
	Small Table	
A	Rails (2)	3/4 × 3 × 10
B	Rails (2)	3/4 × 3 × 12-1/2
C	Top	3/4 × 14 × 16-1/2
D	Legs (4)	1-1/2 × 1-1/2 × 19
	Miscellaneous	
	Dowels (44)	5/16" dia. × 1-1/2"
	Mirror retainer clips (20)	
	Roundhead wood screws (20)	#6 × 1/2"

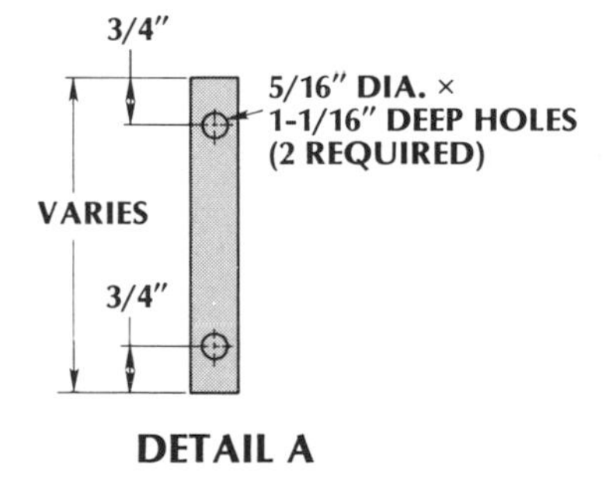

DETAIL A

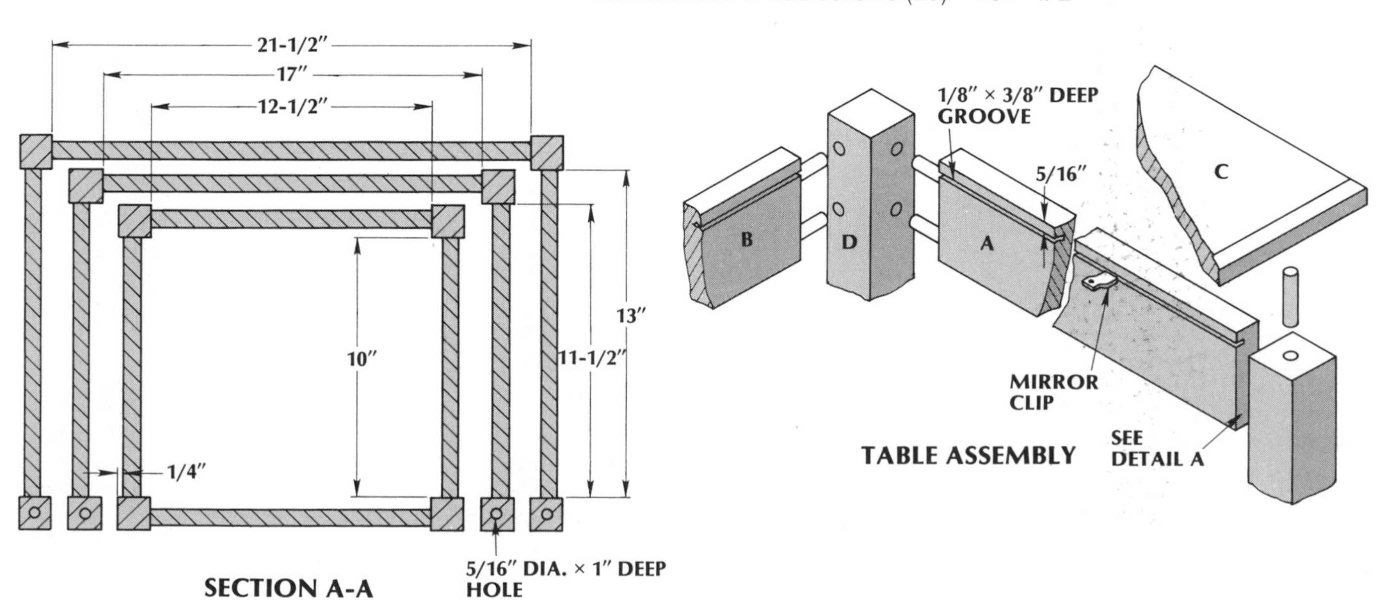

CHAIR-TABLE

From *HANDS ON* July/Aug 83

The origin of the chair-table design dates back to 16th century England. The chair-table is an excellent example of multipurpose furniture—a chair that provides draft-free seating by the fireside, storage below the seat, and a table when the back is lowered. The idea of the chair-table was popular among furniture-makers on both sides of the Atlantic well into the 19th century. Today, we still have the need for functional furniture, and you can build this versatile chair-table by following these simple steps.

1. Cut out all parts according to the List of Materials. See Step 2 for special instructions on cutting out the top (J). The pins (R,S) can all be turned from a single piece of 1-1/2 × 1-1/2 × 13″ stock (see Step 7).

2. Make the top (J) by first drawing a 42″ diameter circle on your shop floor. Arrange your boards on the circle to maximize the use of your stock. Cut to length and joint the edges. Glue and clamp together the boards for the top. Cut out the top. An option is to use 3/4″ plywood for the top with veneer edge banding to cover the plywood edge. Sand the edge.

3. Drill the dowel holes in parts (A,B,C,D,G). First drill the ends of the sides (C), end (D) and rails (G). Next, locate the dowel positions on the legs (A), and drill these holes. Dry-assemble the sides, ends, rails, and legs. Locate the dowel holes in the tops of the legs for the arms (B). Locate the matching dowel holes for the arms, and then disassemble the chair. Drill the remaining dowel holes.

Round the back end of the arms (B). Locate and drill the 5/8″ holes for the pivot pins (R) in the arms (B), and drill the hole for the locking pin (S) in the front of one arm. Mark the location of the pin holes in the battens (K), and drill. *Note:* One batten has two holes, one for the pivot pin (R) and one for the locking pin (S). Set the battens aside.

4. Assemble the chair. First glue and clamp each of the legs (A) to the sides (C). After these have set up, glue these assemblies to the end (D) and rails (G). Check for squareness as you go. Glue the arms (B) into place.

Attach the drawer runners (F) to the drawer guides (E) with #8 × 1-1/4″ flathead wood screws. Attach these assemblies to the inside of the chair assembly.

Cut out the notches for the legs in the seat (H) and attach the seat with #8 × 1-1/4″ flathead wood screws. Countersink the screws 1/4″ and use dowel plugs to fill the holes.

5. Make the drawer by first checking the size of the drawer opening on the assembled seat. Cut the drawer front (L) and back (N) to allow for 1/8″ total clearance on the width. Cut the front, back, and sides to allow for 1/16″ clearance on the height.

Cut the 1/4″ groove for the bottom with dado blades or with a routing attachment.

Make the 3/4″ wide × 3/8″ deep dado in the sides for the back with the dado attachment. Then, form the locking drawer joint using the dado attachment. Assemble the drawer by gluing and clamping the front, sides, and back together. Check for squareness. Slide in the bottom and secure with 2d wire nails.

6. Contour and drill the battens (K) according to the drawings. Use the bandsaw to cut the angles. Drill screw pockets and pilot holes for the #10 × 1-1/2″ roundhead wood screws. Use an oversized pilot hole to allow for expansion of the top.

Center the chair assembly upside down on the bottom of the tabletop to locate the position of the battens. The battens must run at right angles to the grain of the top boards to provide strength and prevent warping. Mount the battens to the top with the screws. Cap the screw pocket holes with dowel buttons.

7. Turn the pins (R,S) from the 1-1/2″ square stock. Turn all three pins at one time. Note that the locking pin is shorter since it is not a through pin. Next, turn the knob for the drawer. Use the screw center to mount the stock on the lathe.

8. Finishing touches: Final-sand the project and apply the finish of your choice to all surfaces. Cut out felt washers to go between the arms and the battens in order to protect the wood.

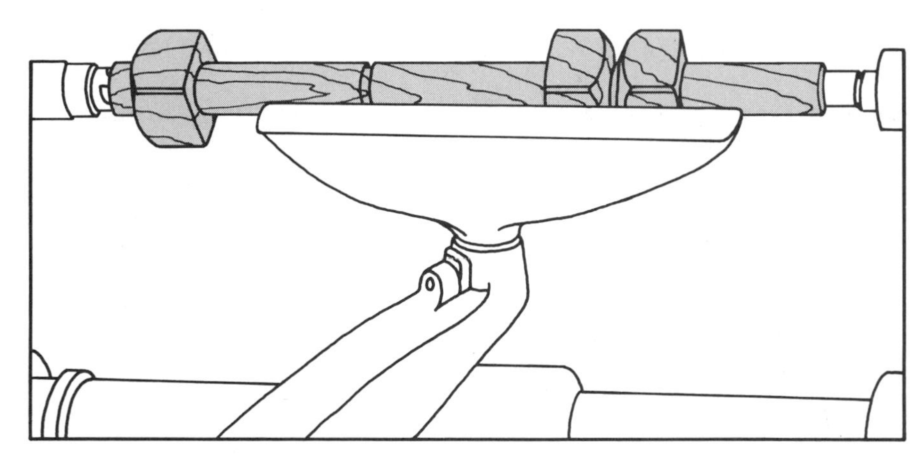

Turning the three pins at one time on the lathe out of a single piece of stock.

ONE SQUARE = 1/4″

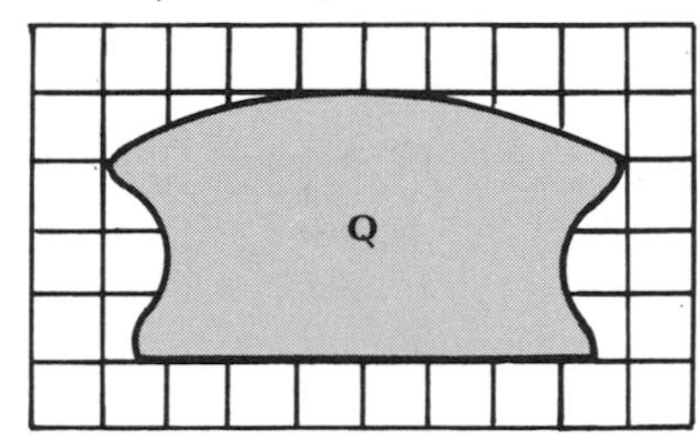

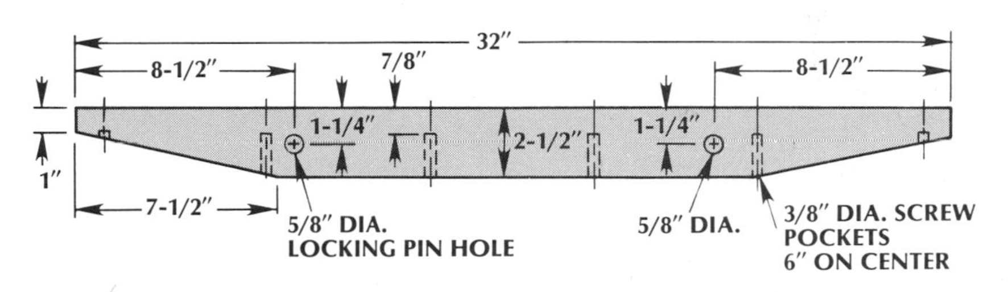

K BATTEN LAYOUT

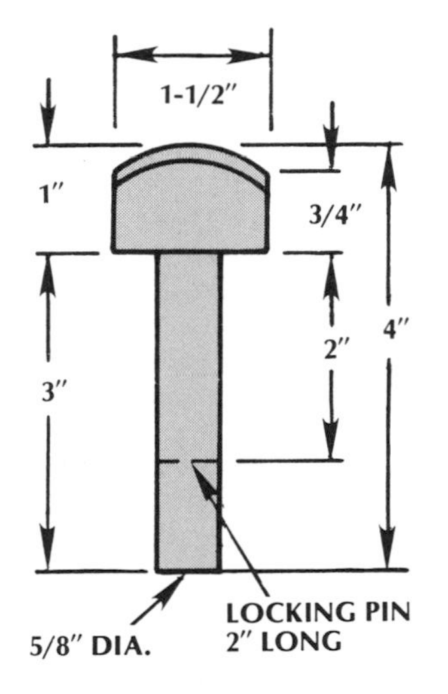

PIN LAYOUT

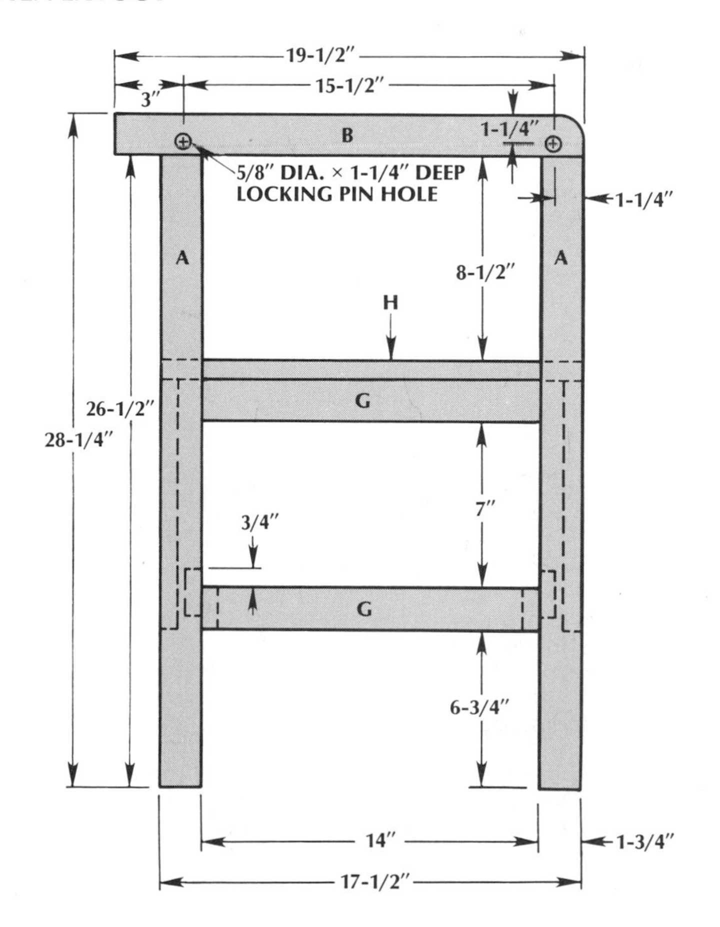

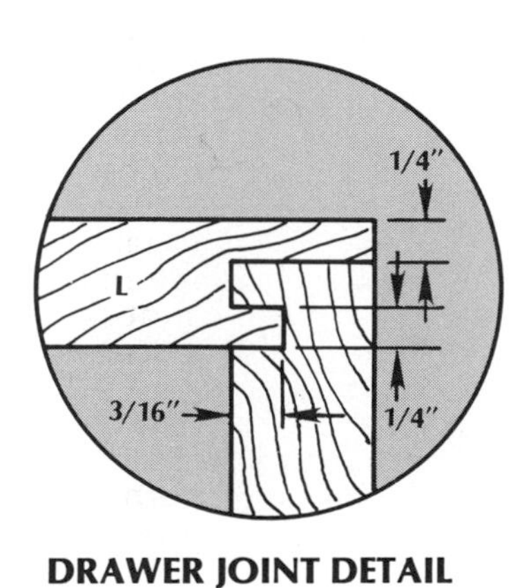

DRAWER JOINT DETAIL

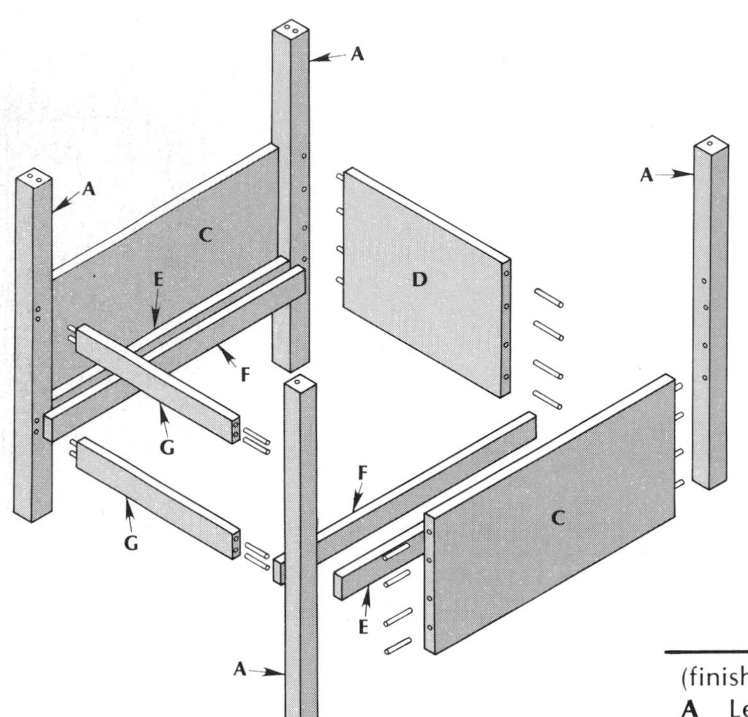

BASE ASSEMBLY

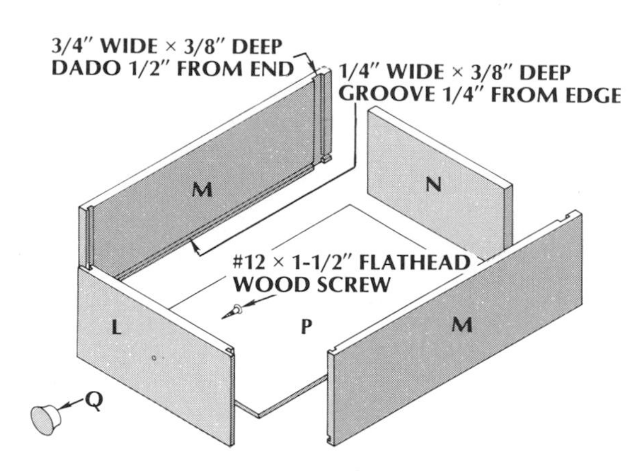

DRAWER ASSEMBLY

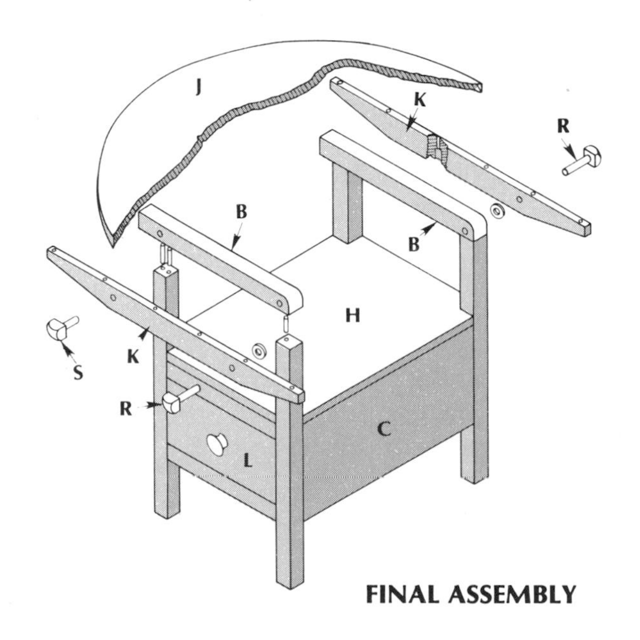

FINAL ASSEMBLY

LIST OF MATERIALS

(finished dimensions in inches)

A	Legs (4)	1-3/4 × 1-3/4 × 26-1/2
B	Arms (2)	1-3/4 × 1-3/4 × 19-1/2
C	Sides (2)	3/4 × 10-1/2 × 21-1/2
D	End	3/4 × 1-1/2 × 14
E	Drawer guides (2)	3/4 × 1-3/4 × 21-1/2
F	Drawer runners (2)	3/4 × 1-3/4 × 23-1/2
G	Rails (2)	3/4 × 1-3/4 × 14
H	Seat	3/4 × 17-1/2 × 25
J	Top	3/4 × 42 dia.
K	Battens (2)	3/4 × 2-1/2 × 32
L	Drawer front	3/4 × 7 × 14
M	Drawer sides (2)	3/4 × 7 × 24
N	Drawer back	3/4 × 6-1/2 × 13-1/4
P	Drawer bottom	1/4 × 13-1/4 × 23-1/8
Q	Drawer knob	2 dia. × 1
R	Pivot pins (2)	1-1/2 × 1-1/2 × 4
S	Locking pin	1-1/2 × 1-1/2 × 3
T	Dowel pins	3/8 dia. × 2
U	Dowel buttons (12)	3/8
	Felt washers (2)	5/8 I.D. × 1-1/2 O.D.
	Flathead wood screw	#12 × 1-1/2
	Roundhead wood screws	#10 × 1-1/2
	Flathead wood screws	#8 × 1-1/4
	2d Wire nails	

PICNIC TABLE

From *HANDS ON* June/July/Aug 84

Picnics in the backyard are as American as fireworks on the Fourth of July. And what better base for a picnic than your own home made picnic table.

1. Select the stock. Redwood is the best wood to use for this table. It's attractive, easy to work, and naturally weather resistant. Pressure-treated lumber or cedar is also acceptable.

2. Crosscut parts (A,B,C,F) to length (see the cutout diagram). Set the miter gauge at 90° and use an extension table to support the stock. Use a miter gauge extension for added support and control. Rip a 5′ long 2 × 10 in half, then crosscut parts (D,E) to length.

3. Bevel the ends of parts (E,G). Set the miter gauge at 90°.

4. Cut the miters on parts (B,C,F). Adjust the miter gauge to 30°.

5. Assemble parts (B,C,F) with 5/16″ × 3-1/2″ carriage bolts. Use two bolts per joint. Use #12 × 2-1/2″ flathead wood screws to attach the top and seats (A) to the frame assemblies. The seat and top supports (E,G) are also attached with #12 × 2-1/2″ wood screws.

6. Cut the braces (D) to fit. With the stock on edge, tilt the miter gauge 25° and bevel one end of each brace. Hold the brace in place and mark the lower end for length. Set the miter gauge at 67°, and then cut the bevel.

7. Finish the table to your liking, but consider weathering when making your choice.

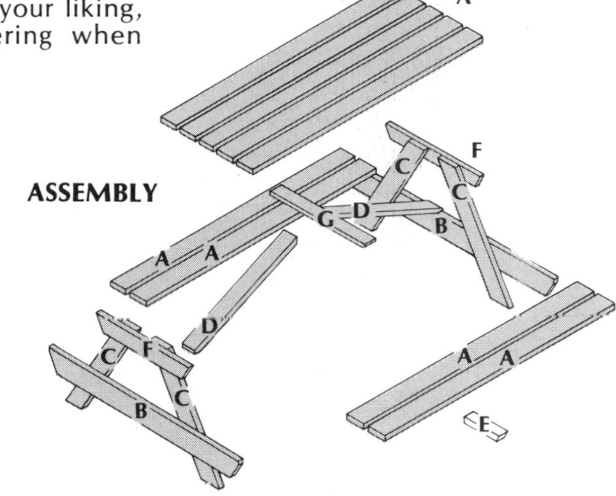

ASSEMBLY

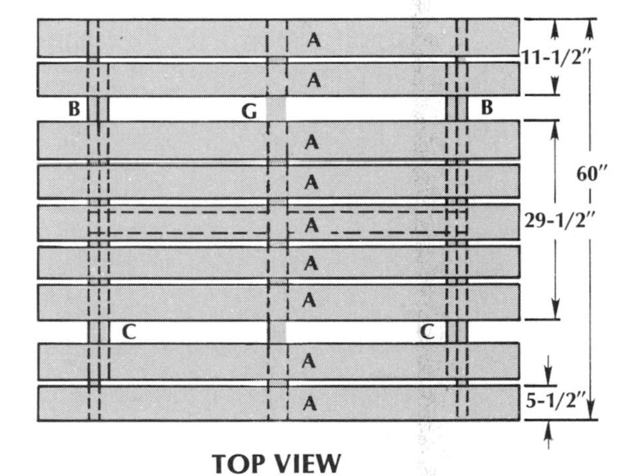

TOP VIEW

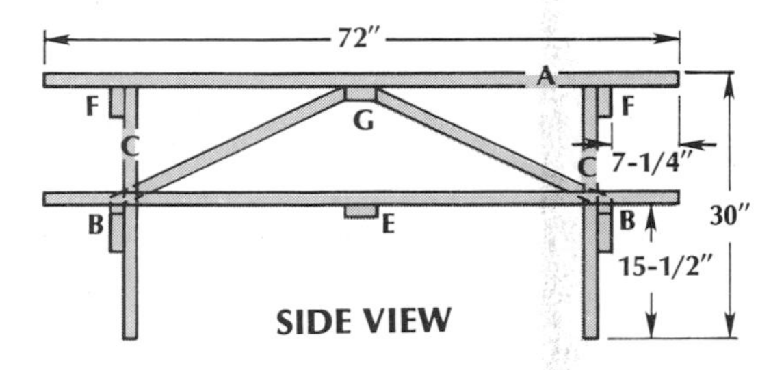

SIDE VIEW

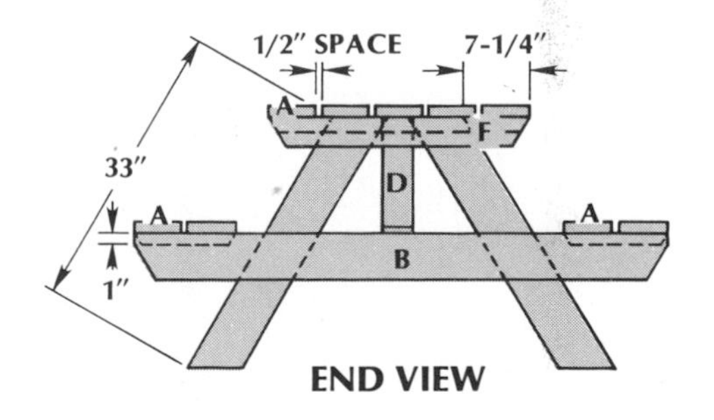

END VIEW

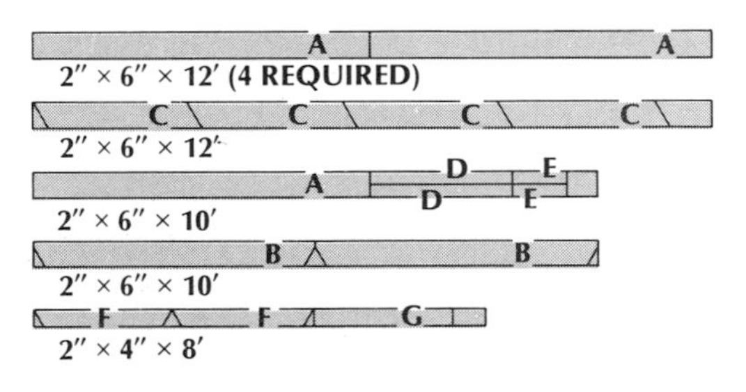

CUTOUT DIAGRAM

LIST OF MATERIALS

(nominal standard lumberyard dimensions in inches)

A	Top and seats (9 pieces)	2 × 6 × 72
B	Seat supports (2)	2 × 6 × 60
C	Legs (4)	2 × 6 × 36
D	Braces (2)	2 × 3 × 30
E	Center seat supports (2)	2 × 3 × 11-1/2
F	Tabletop supports (2)	2 × 4 × 29-1/2
G	Center top support	2 × 4 × 29-1/2
	Flathead wood screws (60)	#12 × 2-1/2
	Carriage bolts (16)	5/16 dia. × 3-1/2

GARDEN BENCH

From *HANDS ON* June/July/Aug 85

If you've priced sturdy, well-designed, outdoor furniture, chances are you know you're ahead of the game if you can build it yourself. This plan gives you the opportunity to construct a sturdy, easy-to-build garden bench at a fraction of retail prices—and enjoy it for years to come.

Mortise-and-tenon joinery is used extensively on this project and makes for a bench that's long-lasting and durable. Here are the plans for a 6′ bench, but don't let our dimensions keep you from building the bench any size you want—this bench plan is easy to adapt to any length.

1. Cut all the stock to size according to the List of Materials. For our bench, we used economical pressure-treated pine, but redwood, oak, cedar, teak, or other weather-resistant wood will also work. Outdoor woods usually require no upkeep and age beautifully over the years.

2. Transfer the pattern of the back legs (B) to 4 × 6 stock and the patterns of the back rail (F) and armrests (E) to 2 × 6 material. Do not cut the contours yet.

3. With a square, accurately mark the locations of the mortises and tenons on all parts.

4. Cut all the mortises in the front and back legs (A,B). Because of the length and bulk of the parts for this bench, be sure to properly support your stock when cutting the mortises.

5. Now cut the tenons on parts (C,D,E,F,G,J) to fit the mortises. Again, because of the length and bulk involved, be sure to support your stock.

Cut the 3/4″ wide × 1/2″ deep grooves in the upper and lower back rails (F,G).

6. Using a bandsaw, cut out the contours on the upper back rail (F), legs (B), seat supports (C), armrests (E), and brackets (L). Use a drum sander to smooth out the saw marks.

7. Check the armrests (E) for fit with the back legs—the armrests should fit so they'll be parallel to the ground. Use the disc sander to bevel the back end to get a flush fit. Next, drill the armrests and back legs for 1/2″ diameter × 3″ long dowel pins.

8. Assemble the sides one at a time. Use plastic resin glue and clamps. (Water resistant plastic resin glue is available at home centers and hardware stores.)

9. Attach the splat spacers (I) to the upper and lower back rails with glue; then assemble the back with clamps. Use glue to assemble the back assembly and the seat stretcher (J) to the sides. Using glue and 6d galvanized finish nails, attach the brackets (L).

10. Use 8d galvanized finish nails to attach the seat boards (K). The front board is cut to fit between the two front legs.

11. Reinforce all the joinery with two 10d galvanized finish nails per joint.

12. Round off all the edges with a rasp or coarse sandpaper, and then sand the bench thoroughly to remove any roughness or splinters.

Outdoor woods need no additional finishing beyond sanding. But, if you want to apply a finish, use finishes that are made especially for outdoor use. Oil-based primer is necessary before painting, and spar varnish or an exterior polyurethane are suitable natural finishes.

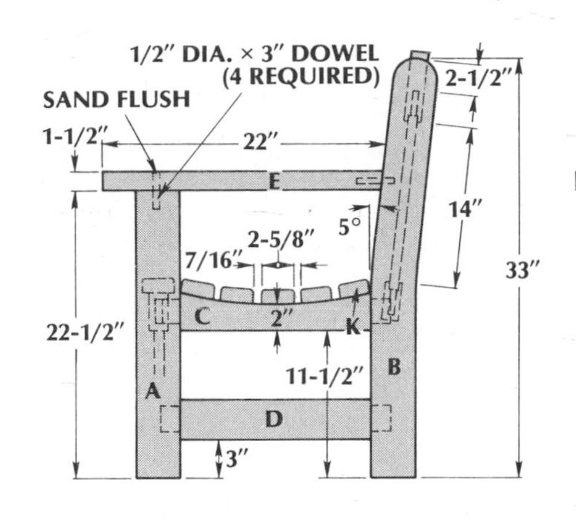

SIDE VIEW

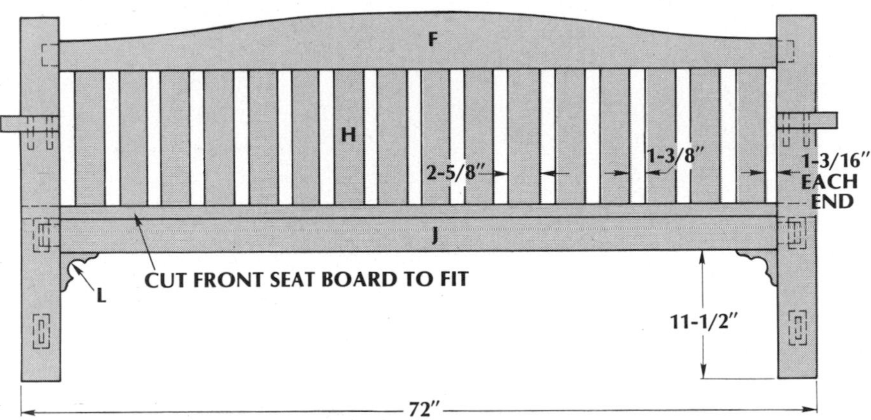

FRONT VIEW

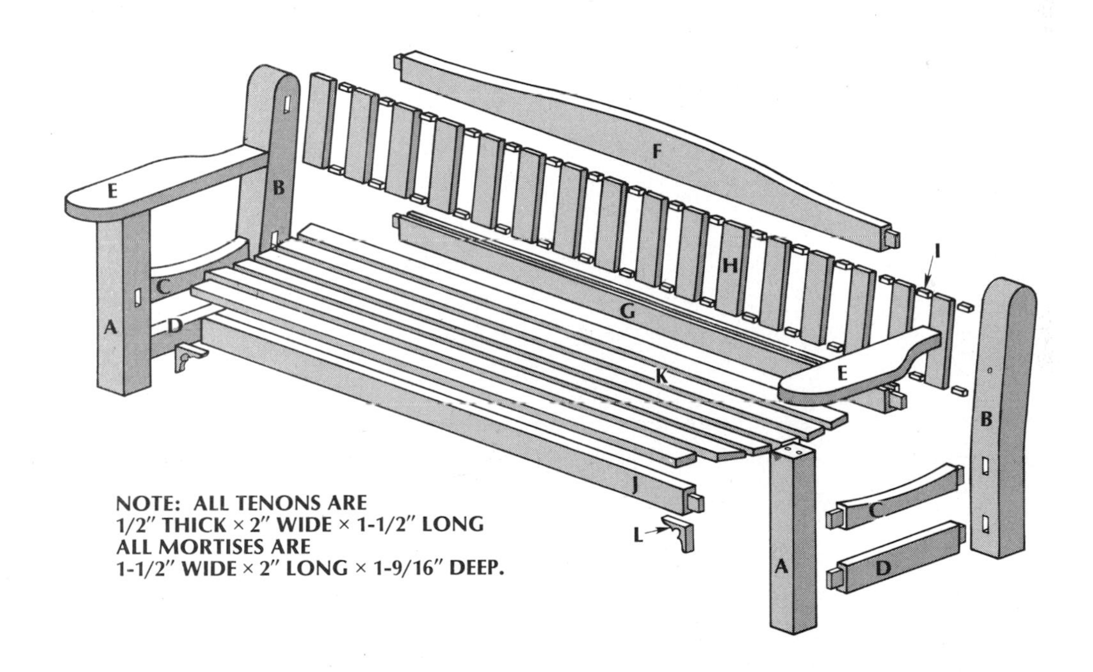

NOTE: ALL TENONS ARE
1/2" THICK × 2" WIDE × 1-1/2" LONG
ALL MORTISES ARE
1-1/2" WIDE × 2" LONG × 1-9/16" DEEP.

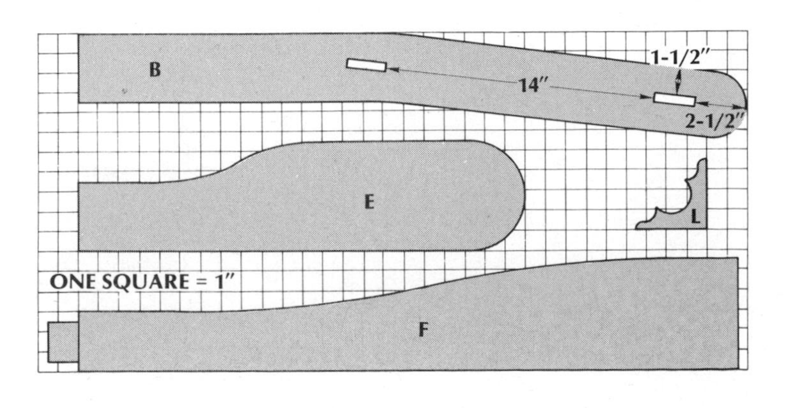

LIST OF MATERIALS

(finished dimensions in inches)

A	Front legs (2)	3-1/2 × 3-1/2 × 22-1/2
B	Back legs (2)	3-1/2 × 5-1/2 × 33
C	Seat supports (2)	1-1/2 × 3 × 18
D	Leg rails (2)	1-1/2 × 3 × 18
E	Armrests (2)	1-1/2 × 5-1/2 × 22
F	Upper back rail	1-1/2 × 5-1/2 × 68
G	Lower back rail	1-1/2 × 3 × 68
H	Splats (16)	3/4 × 2-5/8 × 14
I	Splat spacers (34)	1/2 × 3/4 × 1-3/8
J	Seat stretcher	1-1/2 × 3 × 68
K	Seat boards (6)	1-1/8 × 2-5/8 × 72
L	Brackets (2)	3/4 × 3-1/2 × 3-1/2
	Dowel pins (8)	1/2 dia. × 3

Accessories

Entertainment, kitchen, and accent pieces are among the twenty projects found in this section. These items can add decorative touches as well as serve practical purposes. What makes these projects, as well as those contained in the other two sections, even more valuable is the fact that you can build them yourself.

PENCIL/STAMP HOLDER

From *HANDS ON* Mar/Apr/May 85

Need a project to give as a gift? This pencil/stamp holder is the perfect answer. By using a bandsaw, these hardwood holders are easy to make. They don't involve precision measurements or joinery, and are fun to give.

The following procedure illustrates the necessary steps in making the holders. These steps, however, are the same for any bandsaw box. After practicing the technique, feel free to change the dimensions and design shown in the drawings, and experiment and create your own project.

Here's how to make the holders:

1. Prepare a piece of stock measuring 3″ × 3-1/2″ × 15″—enough for three holders. If you don't have 3″ stock, laminate thinner stock (using one kind, or laminating a variety of contrasting woods) to achieve the required thickness. **Warning:** All stock must be at least 15″ long to allow safe milling later in the project.

2. After squaring the stock, crosscut it into three equal pieces.

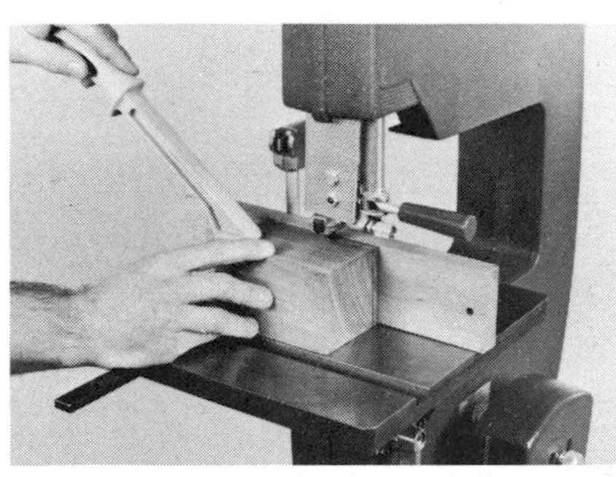

3. Next, using a bandsaw with a 1/2″ blade, cut 1/4″ thick sides from each block (see detail A). Keep the pieces together so that the boxes can be reassembled with the wood in the original position.

4. Switch to a 3/16″ blade and cut out the drawer block (see detail B). Take the drawer block and cut 1/4″ sides from it by resawing (see detail C).

5. Use a 3/16″ blade to cut out the inside contour of the drawer (see detail D).

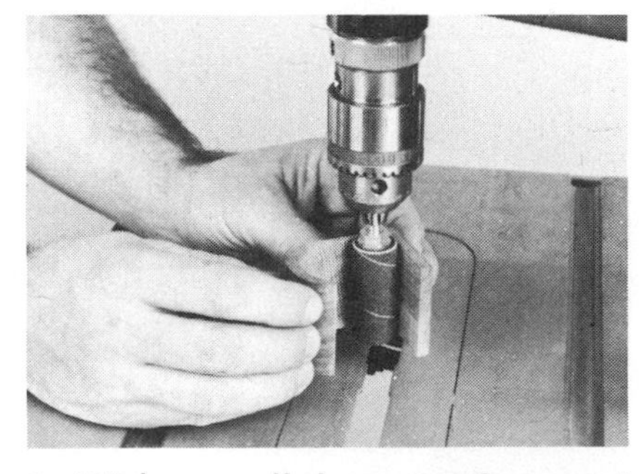

6. With a small drum sander, sand the inside of the drawer. Then, using a disc or belt sander, smooth the sides of the drawer body and the surfaces of the drawer sides. Glue and clamp the drawer together.

7. Measure the width of the reassembled drawer and sand the main body to allow 1/16" extra space. Sand the sides smooth, then glue and clamp the main body together.

8. Drill the three holes for the pencils in the top of the main body (see drawings) and drill the knob mounting hole in the drawer.

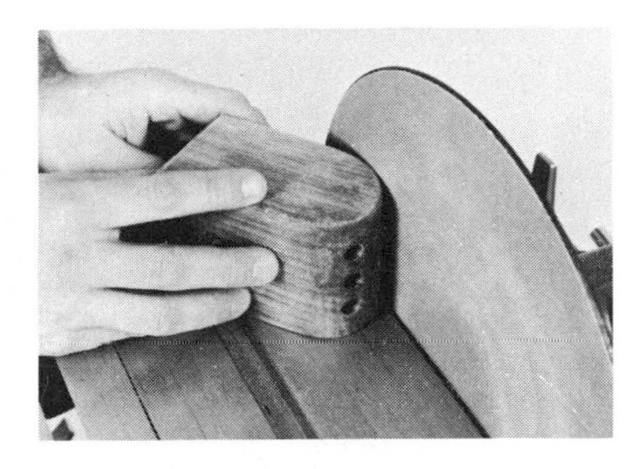

9. Use a 3/16" blade to cut the top contour (see detail E). Sand the holder and apply the finish of your choice.

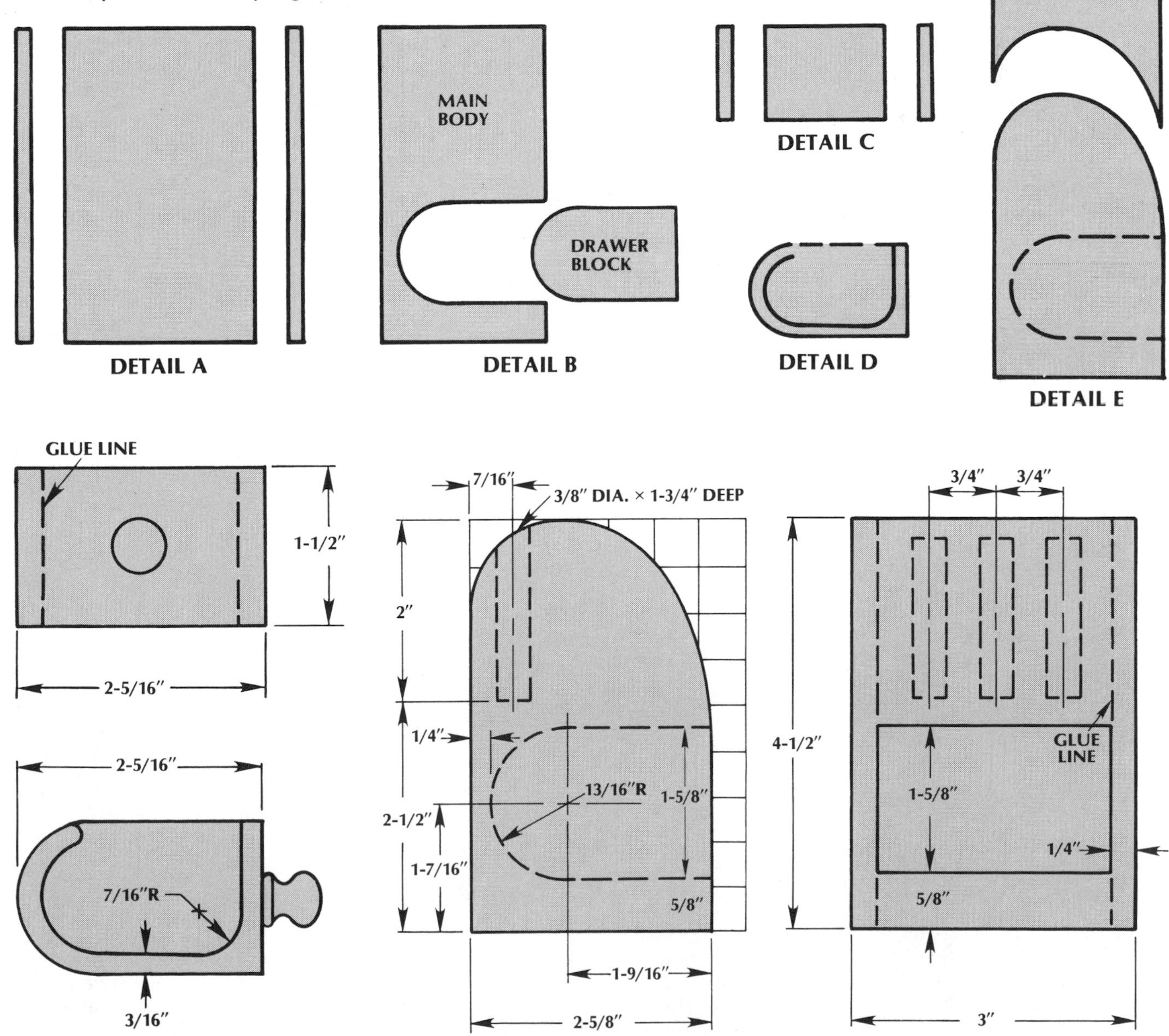

ROLLING PIN

From *HANDS ON* Jan/Feb 82

Compliments of Rude Osolnik

This project is not only very useful, but it's interesting to produce. Cutting laminated hardwood and turning stock diagonally adds tremendous visual appeal and interest. When this utensil is not in use, a holder can be made for displaying it on the kitchen wall.

1. Select the stock. Suggested woods for this project are close-grained hardwoods such as walnut or maple. But you can even use Baltic birch plywood to add a creative flair.

2. Glue up the stock into a 2-1/2" × 8" × 18-1/2" block. Use a waterproof glue such as resorcinol so the rolling pin can be cleaned up in soap and water after it's used. Allow the clamped block to dry for at least 24 hours.

3. Make 2-1/2" wide slices of the stock at a 10° to 15° angle. The angled cuts reveal more end grain of the wood layers.

4. Square the ends of the diagonally cut laminated stock using a bandsaw or table saw.

5. Mount the stock between centers. Use the gouge to rough it to round, using the calipers to assure uniform diameter. Be careful that the exposed plies don't catch the lathe tool and tear.

6. Mark for the handles and cut using calipers to get the diameter of the middle portion of the knobs. Cut the knob nearest the tailstock first, each knob should be as wide as it is thick.

7. Sand the project while it is still on the lathe. Apply a nontoxic salad bowl finish or mineral oil.

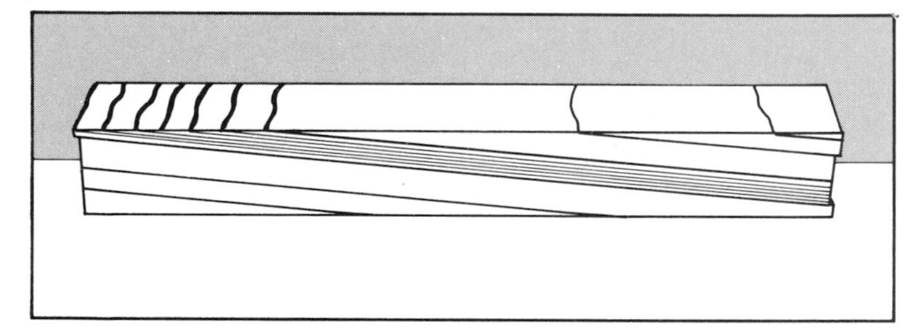

Glued-up stock for laminated rolling pin. Note that stock is cut at an angle on the bandsaw to reveal the laminated plywood and solid wood layers.

ONE SQUARE = 1"

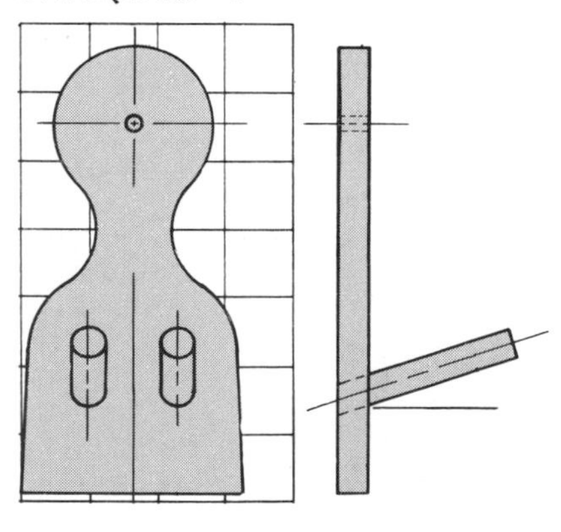

HOLDER

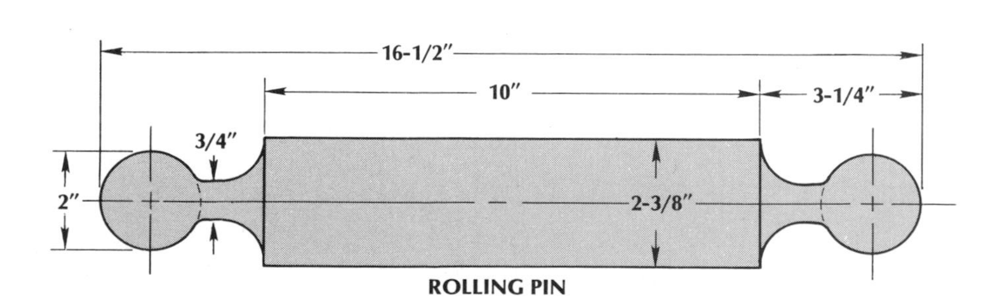

ROLLING PIN

KNIFE BLOCK HOLDER

From *HANDS ON* Nov/Dec 84

This knife block holder can add a touch of professional charm to your kitchen countertop. It is decorative as well as functional and it's a relatively easy project to put together.

1. Prepare seven 3/4" × 5-1/4" × 10" pieces of stock.
2. Glue up five pieces to form a 3-3/4" × 5-1/4" × 10" block.
3. Follow the plans to form the slots for the knives and knife sharpener.
4. Glue the remaining pieces of stock to the block.
5. Belt sand or disc sand the entire block smooth, then round the edges.
6. Apply the finish of your choice.
7. Attach rubber feet to the base.

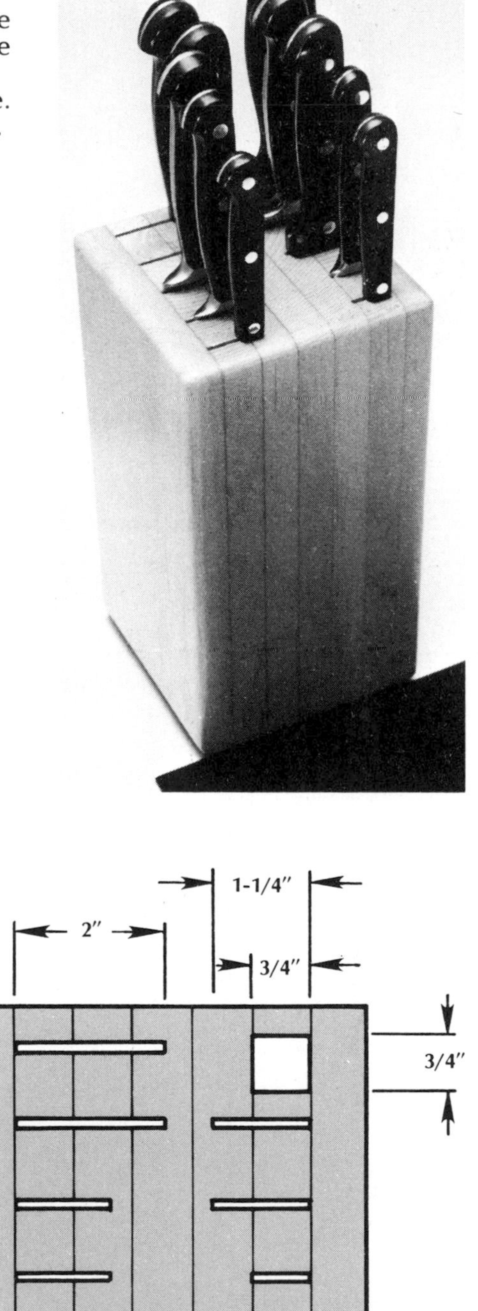

10"
5-1/4"
RUBBER FEET (4 REQUIRED)

1-1/4"
2"
3/4"
3/4"
1"
1-1/4"
3/4"

NOTE: ALL KNIFE SLOTS ARE 1/8" WIDE.

SNACK TRAY

From *HANDS ON* Sept/Oct 80

Here is an idea for snack trays that can take as many unique forms as the variety of snacks you can create to serve in them.

Cut out a template of a tray with as many compartments as you want. On a router arm, make a routing fixture by attaching this template to the underside of a laminated sink cutout and pin routing recesses in the plastic laminate.

Cut blanks from hardwood stock. (This stock should be 1" to 1-1/2" thick and can be laminated from different colors of hardwood.) Attach the blanks to the fixture with nails or screws. Pin rout the recesses using a 3/4" core box bit and 3/4" table pin. Use a 3/8" straight bit and 3/8" pin to clean up the edges of the recesses. Remove the blank from the fixture and cut the outside contour of the tray on a bandsaw.

Round the top edges with a 1/4" round-over bit, and sand with flutter sheets. Finish with salad bowl finish.

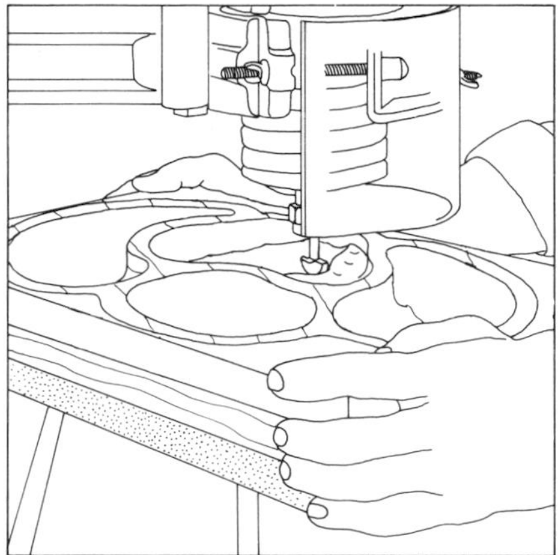

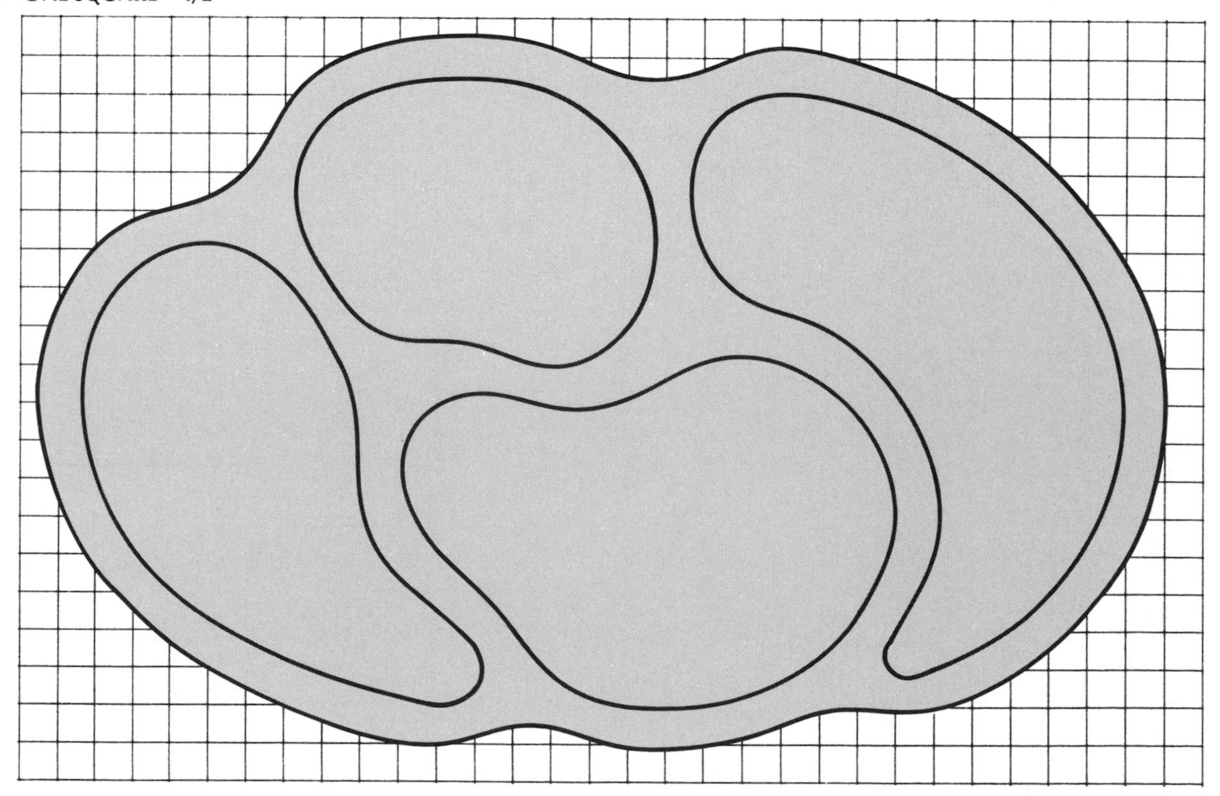

MAGAZINE RACK

From *HANDS ON* Nov/Dec 84

This handy magazine rack not only makes a nice accent piece, but it also serves an important function in keeping your magazines neat and handy. It makes a perfect gift for a friend or for yourself.

1. Prepare a 3/4″ × 9-1/2″ × 22″ piece of stock.
2. Use a jigsaw to cut the base (B) from the top (A).
3. With the shaper, round the inside edge of the top.
4. Cut the outside contour of the top and shape the edge. Shape the outside edge of the bottom.
5. Drill the 3/8″ diameter × 1/4″ deep holes in the top.
6. Tilt the saw table 10° and drill the 3/8″ diameter × 1/2″ deep holes in the bottom.
7. Cut the dowels to length and lightly sand.
8. Assemble the rack by first gluing the dowels into the top then glue them into the bottom.
9. Sand the project and apply the finish of your choice.

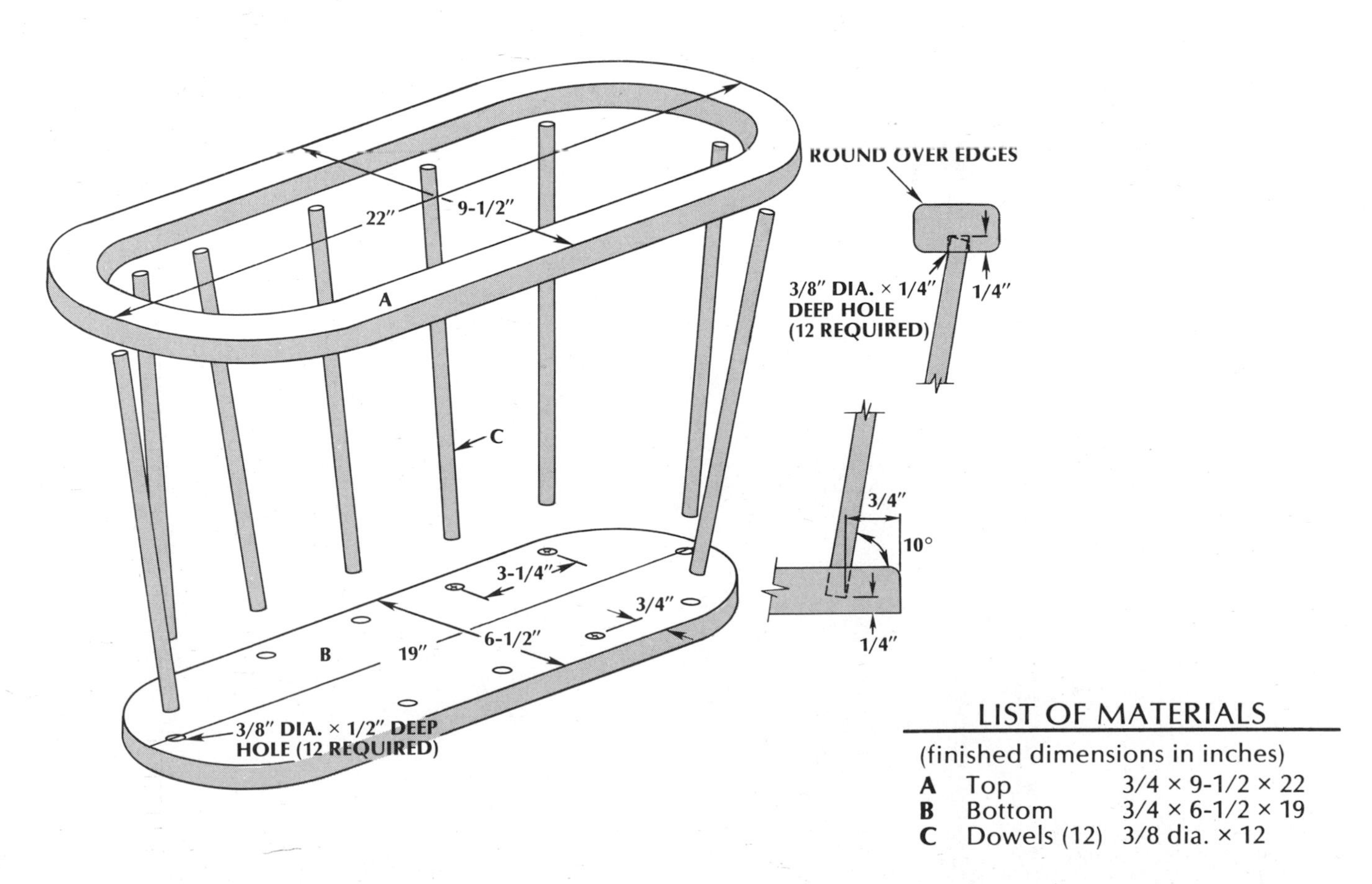

LIST OF MATERIALS

(finished dimensions in inches)

A	Top	3/4 × 9-1/2 × 22
B	Bottom	3/4 × 6-1/2 × 19
C	Dowels (12)	3/8 dia. × 12

MIRROR FRAME

From *HANDS ON* Nov/Dec 84

A framed mirror adds depth and warmth to a room. This project will give you a beautiful addition to any room.

1. Glue up and square a 3/4″ × 15″ × 21″ piece of stock.
2. Cut out the 11″ × 17″ oval center.
3. Shape the inside and outside edge contours using a shaper or router.
4. Form a 5/16″ wide × 5/16″ deep rabbet on the back of the oval.
5. Sand the frame.
6. Apply the finish of your choice.
7. Paint the inside of the rabbet black so the mirror will not reflect the wood.
8. For mounting the frame to the wall, attach a picture hanger or use a router with a T-slot bit. Install the mirror.

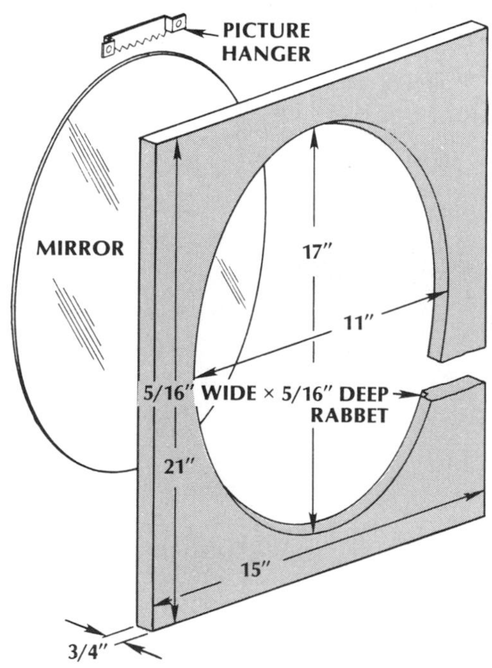

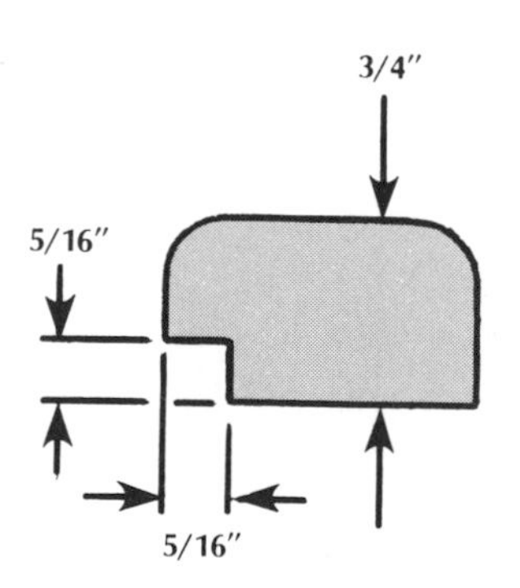

FRAME CROSS SECTION

BUTTERFLY BOXES

From *HANDS ON* May/June 80

The sides of these ingenious boxes can be made from hollow tree limbs. Take a walk through a forest (with permission from the owner) and select a dead, dry branch 6" to 10" in diameter. Cut off a 5" to 8" length, peel off the bark, and sand the hollow with a sanding drum. If you don't want to use a dead branch, you can also cut up an old porch post or turn a hollow cylinder.

Cut out a bottom and assemble it to the base of your box. Then glue up stock for the lid, at least 1-1/2" thick. You may want to use some scraps you have laying around and laminate contrasting woods. These laminations create an intriguing effect when the lid is sculpted.

Cut out a circle for your lid. Then make an S-shaped cut through the center of the circle. Shape the tops of the two lid halves, using the various sander/sculpture techniques. Let your imagination go and make any contours you wish. Smooth out the contours on the 'soft' side of the sander. However, confine most of your sanding to the tops of these pieces, and don't do anything more than remove the mill marks from the sides. When you're done sculpting, the pieces should still fit together exactly and the lid should fit the top of the box.

Hinge the two lid pieces to the box with metal pins. Be sure to use metal, not wooden dowels—wood will not operate smoothly in humid weather. When you've finished, the lid should close tightly, giving no clue to how it's hinged; then swing apart like two wings.

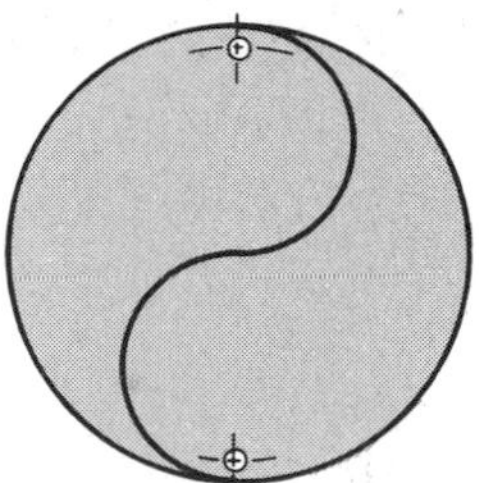

Cut lid apart as shown and drill for hinge pins.

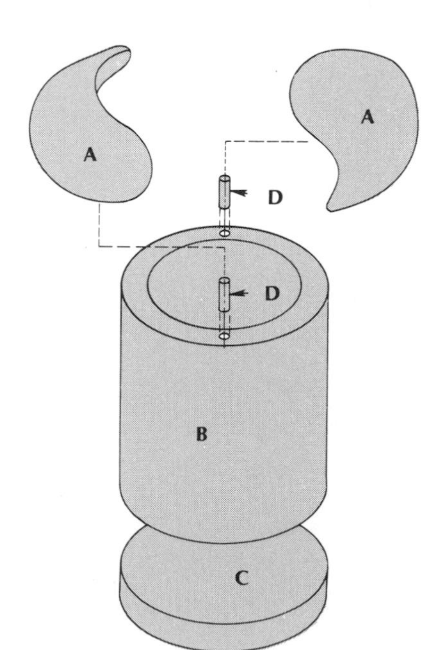

Final shaping of the lid on the 'soft' surface of a belt sander.

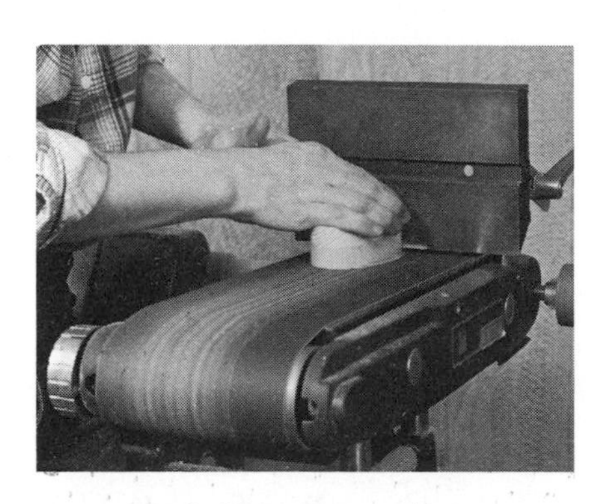

Assemble lid halves, Hinge pins, box, and bottom as shown.

PICTURE FRAMES

From *HANDS ON* Sept/Oct 84

Everyone knows how a beautiful frame enhances a painting or photograph. The challenge is getting the right frame, and one of the best ways to do that is by producing your own frame stock.

Here are four designs for picture frames that you can make by using the table saw and the molder attachment. Use these designs as a starting point, then experiment with the settings—table tilt, rip fence, depth-of-cut, etc. You can even change the look of a frame by using different woods, cutting compound miters, combining finishes, and so on.

Safety Tip: Use stock that's 6' to 8' long, then cut to length after all machining is complete. Use fence extensions, feather boards, push sticks and push blocks.

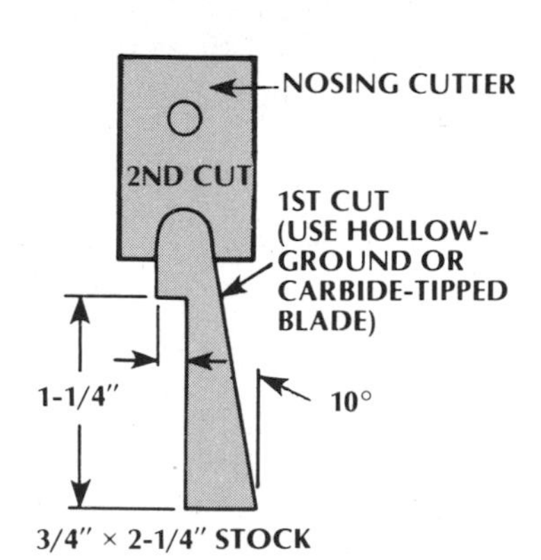

Cut rabbet last. Use dado blades and auxiliary fence. When cutting the miters, use spacer in rabbet so frame will rest flat on miter gauge face.

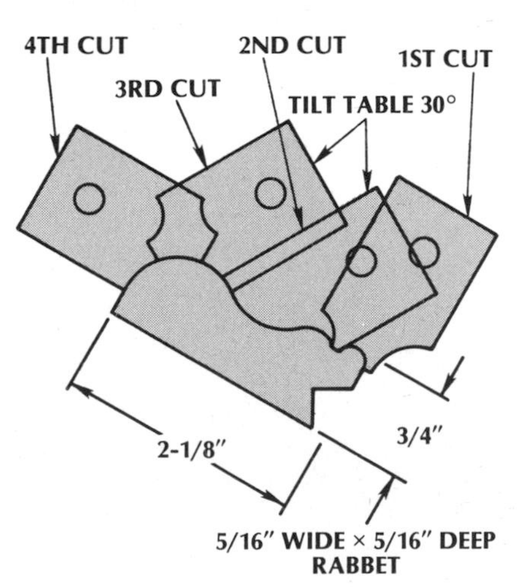

Tilt table 30° and cut rabbet in back. To cut miters, tilt table 21° and set miter gauge at 49°.

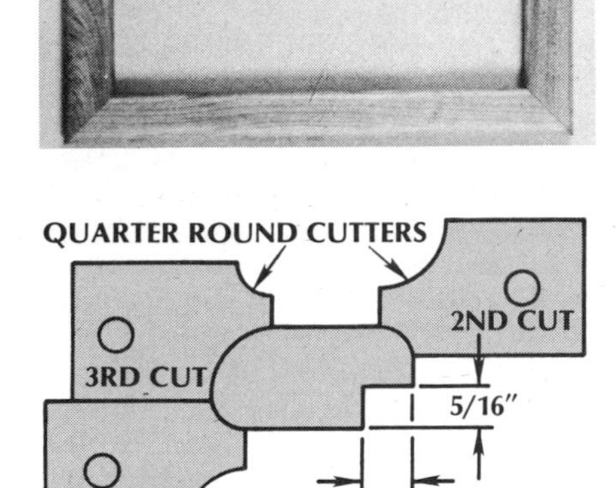

Cut rabbet in back last. Final sand frame after assembly.

2-1/4"
1-3/4"
3/4"
3/8"
5/16" WIDE × 5/16" DEEP RABBET

Use proper coving method. Tilt table 30° and cut rabbet in back. To cut miters, tilt table 21°, set miter gauge at 49°.

From *HANDS ON* Sept/Oct 83

One way to add a touch of class to your dinner table is with this handy casserole holder. Not only does this holder look great, but it is also very functional.

To make one for your table, use 3/4" hardwood stock for the ends and handles and 1/2" dowel rods for the rack. The ends are 3" high and should be 2" longer than the width of the baking dish. The handles measure 4" shorter than the ends and are 1" wide. On the inside of the ends, drill 1/2" diameter × 1/2" deep holes for six dowel rods (see photo for approximate location). On the outside of the end pieces, drill 1/2" dowel rod holes for the handles. Round off all edges on the ends and handles using the shaper. Cut the dowel rods to the length required and assemble the project with glue and clamps.

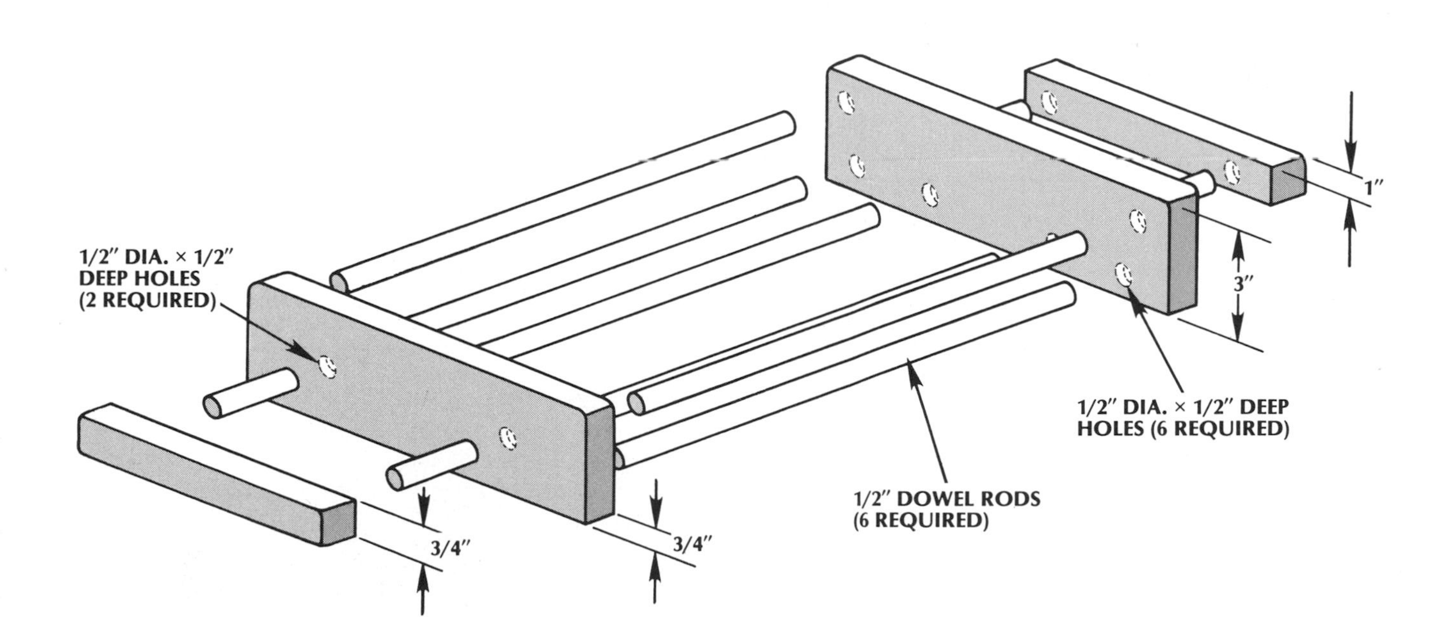

CANDLE BOX

From *HANDS ON* Nov/Dec 84

This candle box not only makes a decorative storage item for your home, but it also makes an excellent gift idea for someone special.

1. Prepare 1/2" stock.
2. Cut all the stock to size according to the List of Materials.
3. Cut out the contours on parts (A,B,C).
4. Assemble parts (A,B,C,D) using glue and 2d finishing nails.
5. Cut the 1/4" wide × 1/4" deep grooves in the three drawer sides (E).
6. Drill the knob mounting hole in the drawer front (F).
7. Glue and nail drawer parts (E,F,G) together.
8. Countersink all the nails and fill the nail holes with wood putty.
9. Use the belt sander to sand the box sides smooth.
10. Attach the base (H) using glue and nails.
11. Apply the finish of your choice.
12. Attach the knob.

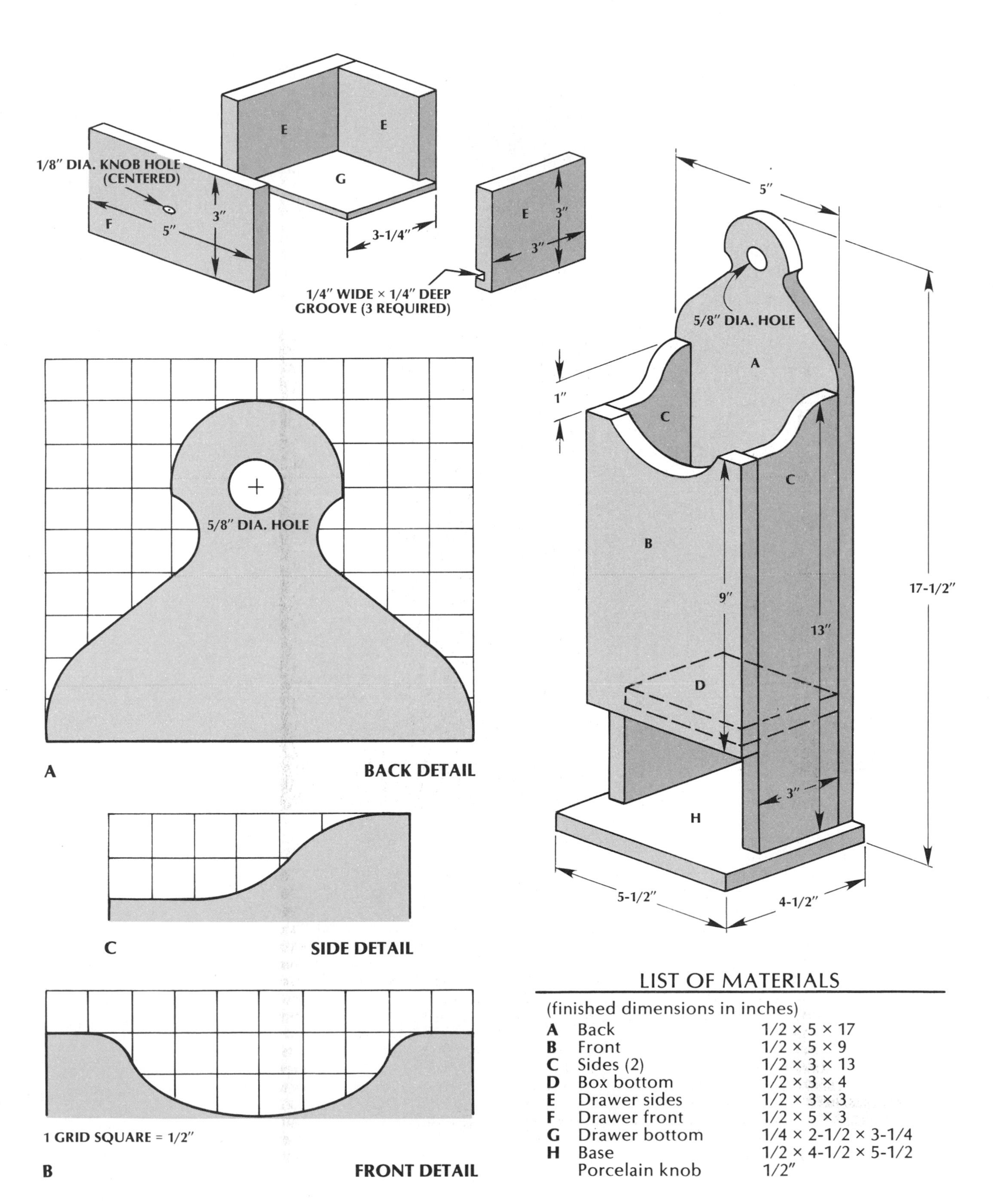

LIST OF MATERIALS

(finished dimensions in inches)

A	Back	1/2 × 5 × 17
B	Front	1/2 × 5 × 9
C	Sides (2)	1/2 × 3 × 13
D	Box bottom	1/2 × 3 × 4
E	Drawer sides	1/2 × 3 × 3
F	Drawer front	1/2 × 5 × 3
G	Drawer bottom	1/4 × 2-1/2 × 3-1/4
H	Base	1/2 × 4-1/2 × 5-1/2
	Porcelain knob	1/2″

WALL DESK

From *HANDS ON* May/June 82

One of the most used "appliances" in the kitchen is the phone. Mounting it on the wall saves space, but leaves no place for the phone book or messages. This wall desk, however, will provide you with such place.

For our wall desk we used maple, but any soft or hardwood will do. You'll need to resaw or plane wood down to the 1/2" thickness required for the shelf, bottom, and drawer parts.

Glue up the wood necessary for the project. Make the two sides (A) from one piece; cut the piece to width, set the miter gauge to 65°, and cut across the middle to make the two sides (A) with a minimum of waste.

Cut 1/2" wide × 3/8" deep dadoes in sides (A) that will accept the bottom and shelf. Cut the same size groove and rabbet in the back (E) for the bottom and shelf.

Cut 1/2" wide × 1/4" deep dadoes in the bottom (G) and shelf (H) for the drawer partition (J).

Cut a 3/4" wide × 3/8" deep stop rabbet in sides (A) for the back.

Now, cut and sand the bottom profiles of sides (A).

Tilt the table 25° and using the extension table and rip fence to guide the work, cut the angled top edge on the back (E). With the table at the same angle, cut the top strip (C) and front (F).

Assemble and glue the partition (J) to the shelf (H) and bottom (G). Then glue and clamp sides (A) to the shelf and the bottom. Then glue and assemble the back (E) and front (F) and top strip (C). Install the hinges on the top and top strip.

Cut and assemble the stock for the drawer, final sand the entire project and apply the finish of your choice.

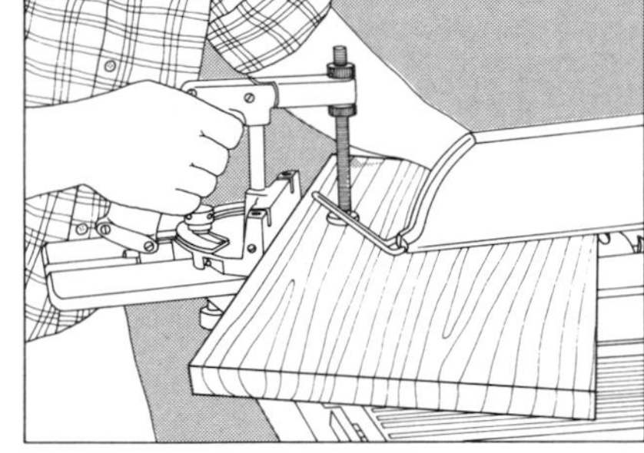

Cutting sides (A). Note use of table extension.

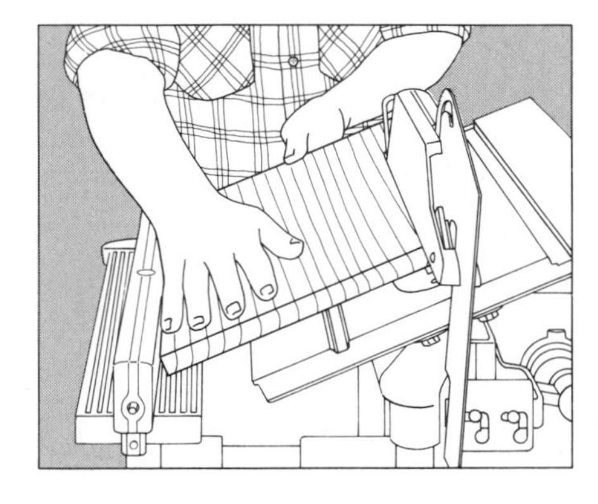

Cutting angled top edge of back (E).

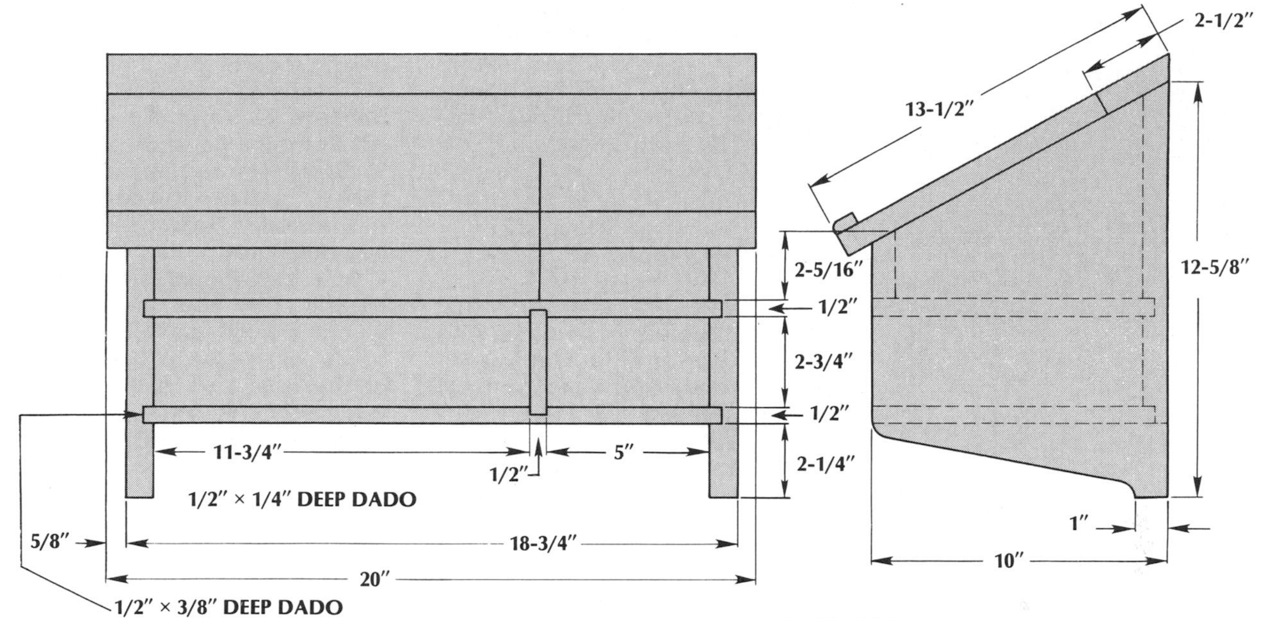

DESK LAYOUT

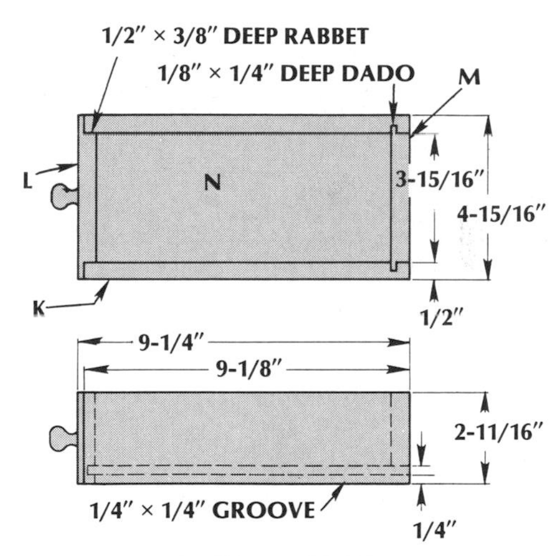

DRAWER LAYOUT

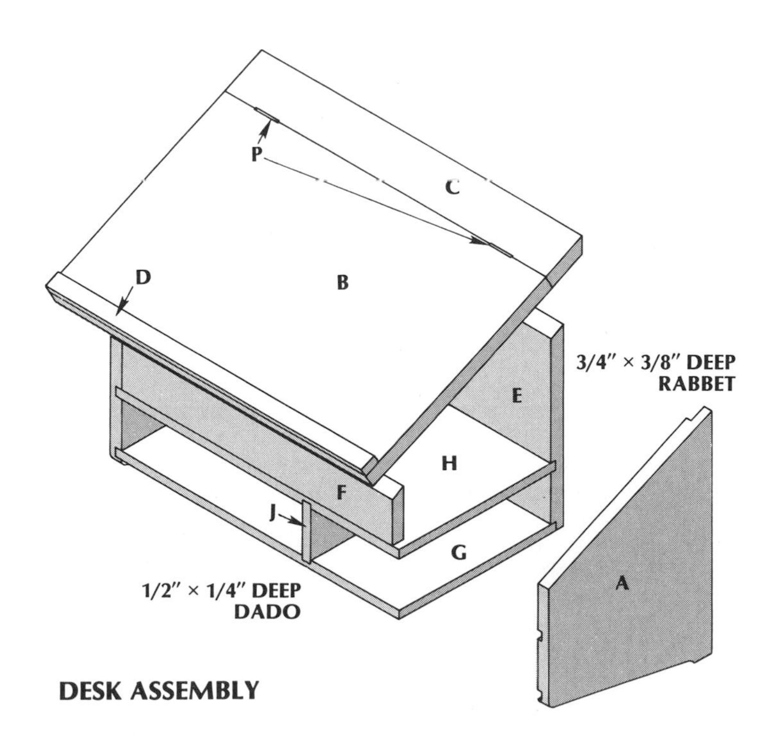

DESK ASSEMBLY

LIST OF MATERIALS

(finished dimensions in inches)

A	Sides (2)	3/4 × 10 × 20-3/4
B	Top	3/4 × 11 × 20
C	Top strip	3/4 × 2-1/2 × 20
D	Ledge	3/8 × 3/4 × 20
E	Back	3/4 × 10-3/8 × 18
F	Front	3/4 × 2-5/16 × 17-1/4
G	Bottom	1/2 × 9-5/8 × 18
H	Shelf	1/2 × 9-5/8 × 18
J	Partition	1/2 × 3-1/4 × 9-1/4
K	Drawer sides (2)	1/2 × 2-11/16 × 9-1/8
L	Drawer front	1/2 × 2-11/16 × 4-15/16
M	Drawer back	1/2 × 2-3/16 × 4-7/16
N	Drawer bottom	1/4 × 4-7/16 × 9
P	Butt hinges (2)	1" × 2"

BIRD HOUSES

From *HANDS ON* Mar/Apr/May 85

Getting the birds to flock to your home is easy when you provide them with elegant low-cost housing. Here are two houses you can build—one for wrens and one for blue jays. You can make these birdhouses for your yard, and while you're at it, make extras to give as gifts. Easy-to-build, these projects will be a hit with your friends (fine-feathered and otherwise).

WREN HOUSE

Wrens are small songbirds that provide sweet sounding music. And wrens are easy to attract because of their willingness to adapt to both rural and city life.

Constructing this wren house is simple and basic. By starting with an 8′ board, you can build four of these houses. Here's how:

1. Cut the ends (A) from a 2′ long 1 × 6. Next, use a bandsaw to resaw the remaining stock in half. Plane the resawn boards to 5/16″ thick, then cut parts (B,C,D) to size.

2. Tilt the saw table 45° and bevel the roof (B), sides (C), and bottom (D) as indicated in the drawings.

3. Drill the entrance hole no larger than 1″ in order to keep out undesirable birds. Next, drill a 1/4″ hole for the perch.

4. Use galvanized nails to assemble the ends, roof, and sides.

5. Use a 3/32″ bit to drill the pilot holes for the screw eyes in the top of the roof and install them. Tap the perch (E) into place (the fit should be snug), and slide the bottom (D) into position.

6. Apply the finish of your choice (see box). After the finish dries, hang the house from your favorite tree.

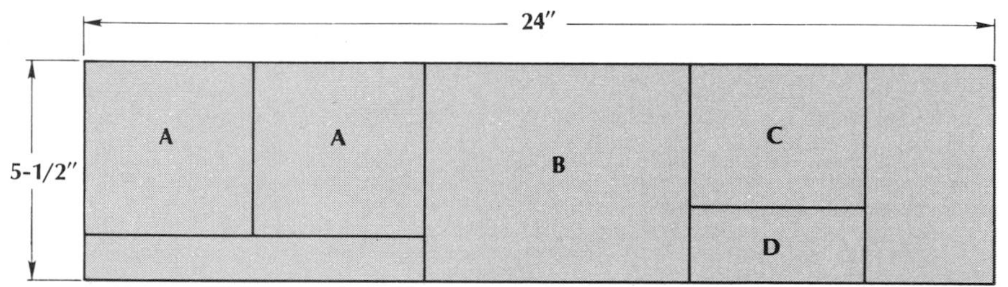

CUTTING DIAGRAM FOR WREN HOUSE

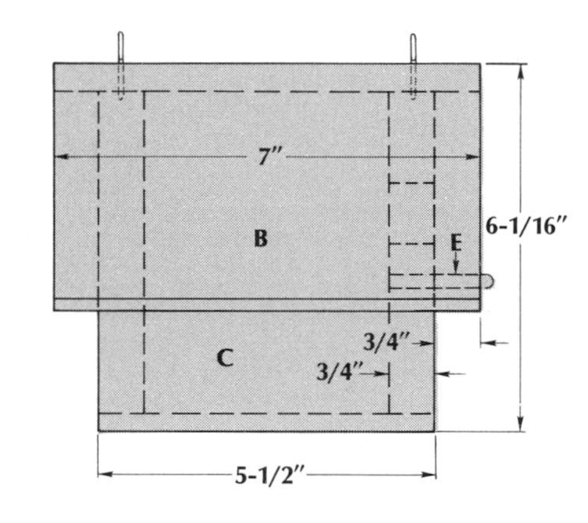

SIDE VIEW

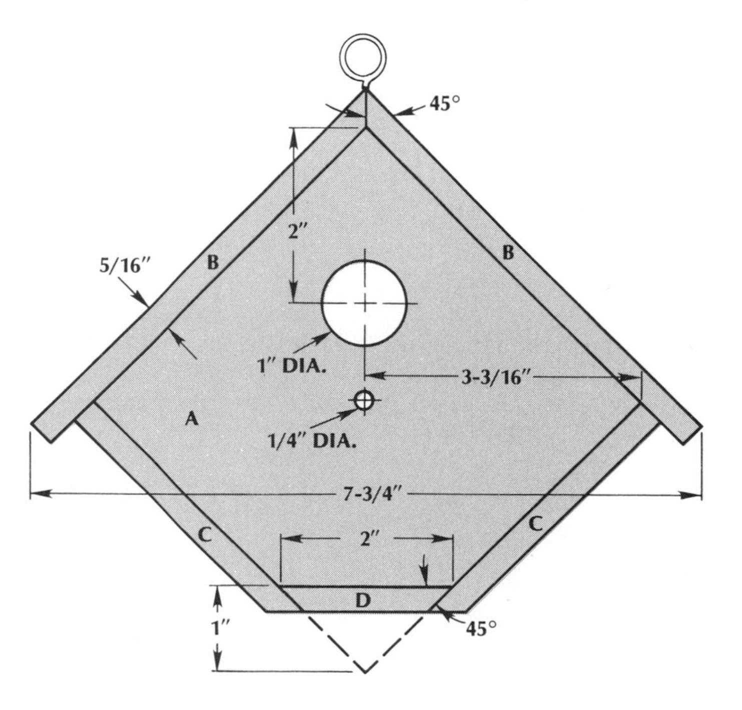

FRONT VIEW

LIST OF MATERIALS

(finished dimensions in inches)

A	Ends (2)	3/4 × 4-1/2 × 4-1/2
B	Roof (2)	5/16 × 5-1/2 × 7
C	Sides (2)	5/16 × 3-1/2 × 5-1/2
D	Bottom	5/16 × 2 × 5-1/2
E	Perch	1/4 dia. × 1-1/2
	Screw eyes (2)	3/8″

BLUE JAY HOUSE

Blue jays, often loud and always protective of their turf, are a beautiful bird to have around. This house provides ample space for blue jays to raise a family. Here's how to make the house:

1. Cut parts (A-D) to length and width from a 3′ section of 1 × 6 redwood. Use a bandsaw to resaw part (E) in half to make two 5/16″ thick boards, then cut these to length.

2. Tilt the saw table 20° and bevel the tops of the front (A), back (B), and the ends of the roof (D).

3. Return the table to "0." Set the miter gauge at 70° and miter the tops of the sides (E).

4. Drill a 1-1/2″ hole in the front (A). Next, drill a 1/4″ hole for the perch (F) and a 1/4″ diameter mounting hole in the back (B).

5. Use 4d galvanized nails to assemble the house. Mount the roof (D) with hinges; tap the perch (F) into place; and apply the finish of your choice. Hang the house on a nail or hook about 6′ to 10′ above the ground.

BIRDHOUSE BUILDING TIPS

Here are a few things you need to know when building birdhouses.

- Use wood that's suitable for the outdoors. Redwood, cedar, and exterior plywood are all good materials. Avoid using pressure-treated lumber—the long-term effects to wildlife are unknown.
- Use only rust-resistant hardware. For nails or screws, use galvanized, stainless, or brass for best results.
- Construct birdhouses so they can be cleaned out at least once a year to control lice. Hinged tops or sliding bottoms are just two constructions that allow for easy cleaning.

- Finish birdhouses with exterior stains or paints. When painting, though, choose light colors in order to prevent heat absorption on hot summer days.

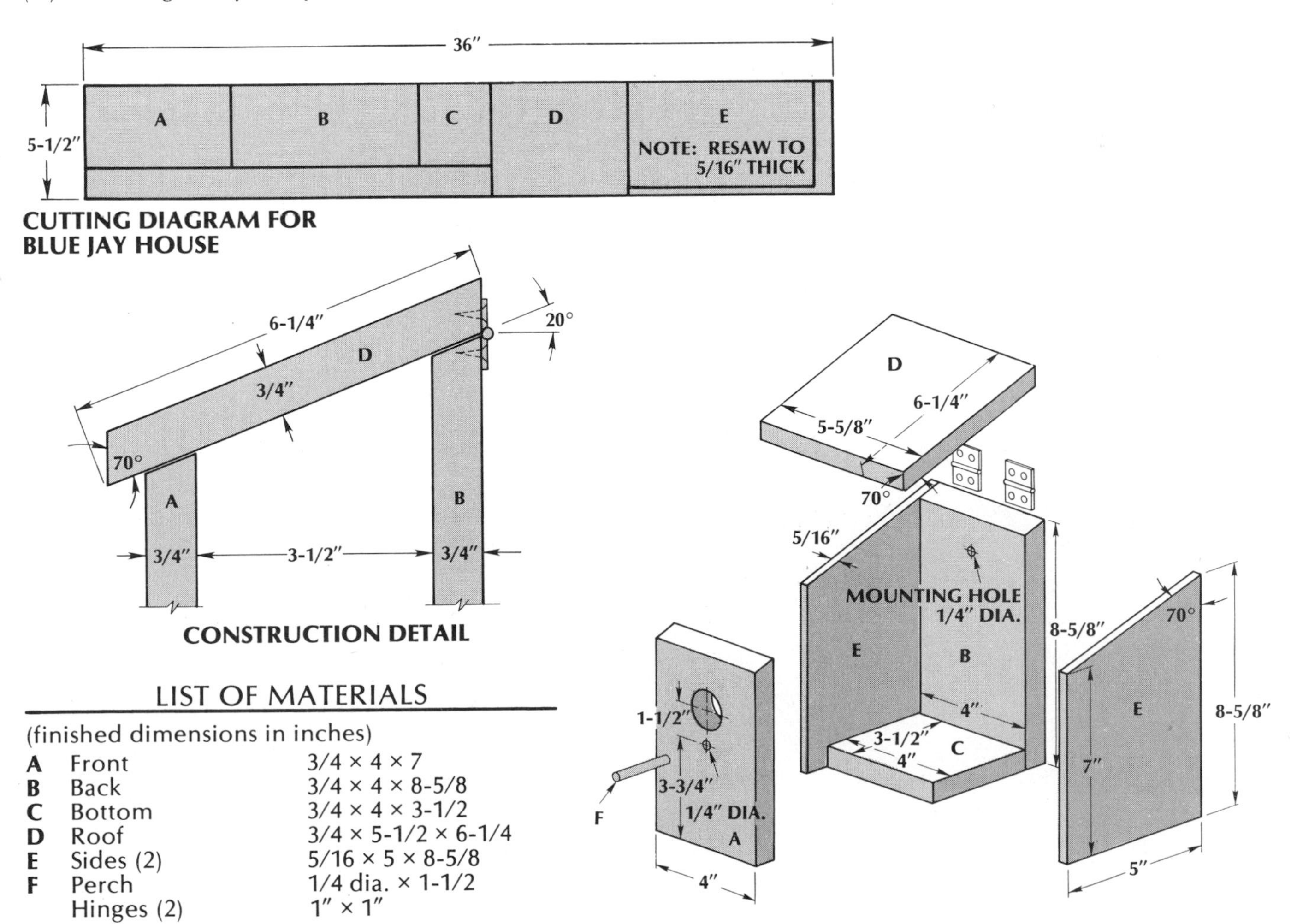

LIST OF MATERIALS

(finished dimensions in inches)

A	Front	3/4 × 4 × 7
B	Back	3/4 × 4 × 8-5/8
C	Bottom	3/4 × 4 × 3-1/2
D	Roof	3/4 × 5-1/2 × 6-1/4
E	Sides (2)	5/16 × 5 × 8-5/8
F	Perch	1/4 dia. × 1-1/2
	Hinges (2)	1″ × 1″

JIGSAW PUZZLES

Jigsaw puzzles are popular with children of all ages. The six designs included here are simple to make and are guaranteed to provide hours of safe fun for the kids.

1. Using a belt or hand sander, sand both surfaces of the stock. The stock should be at least 1-1/2" thick plywood or hardwood.

2. Using the plans and carbon paper, trace the full-scale pattern of the puzzle onto the stock.

3. With a jigsaw, cut out the pattern on the bold line. (The dotted lines are intended for detail painting.)

4. Sand the edges of the puzzle pieces, being careful not to distort the interlocking pattern.

5. Beginning with the large areas, paint the design with non-toxic paint or food coloring. A fine-point permanent marker is good for making the finer details.

6. Finish the puzzle with a good polyurethane varnish.

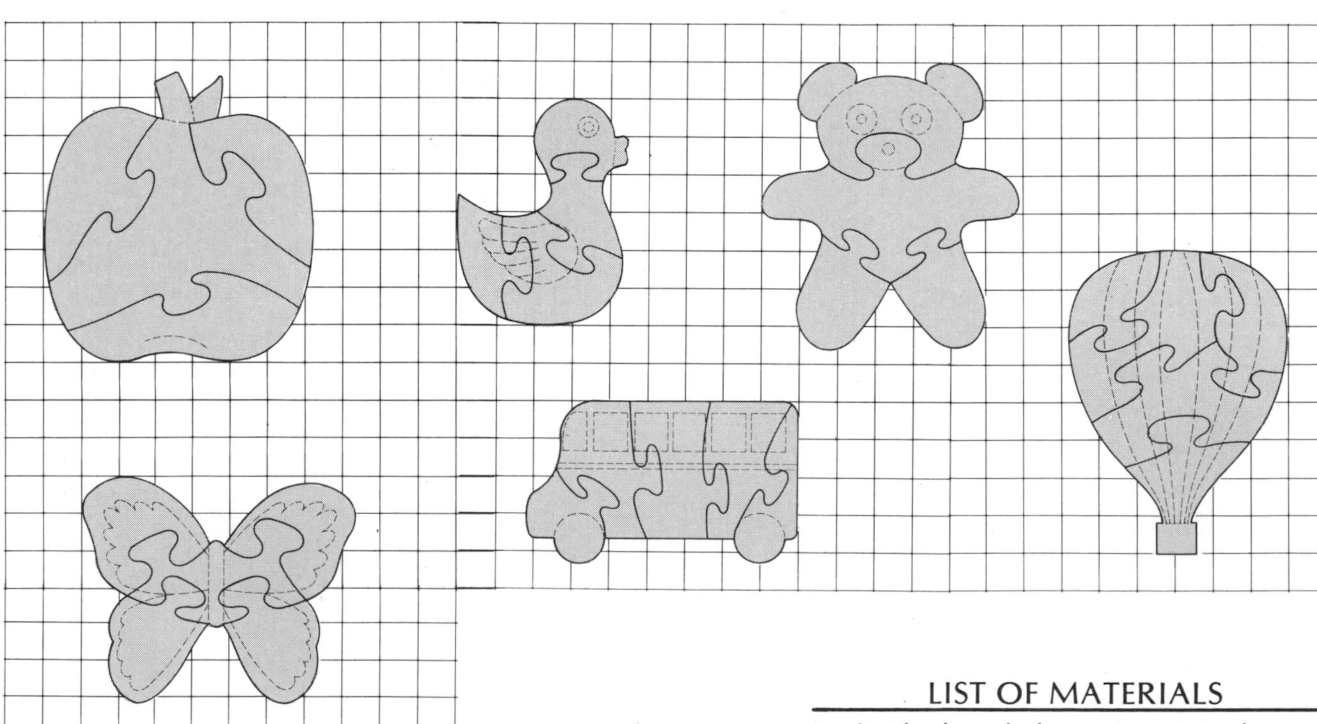

ONE SQUARE = 1"

LIST OF MATERIALS

(unfinished stock dimensions in inches)

A	Duck	1-1/2 × 4-1/2 × 6
B	Bear	1-1/2 × 7 × 8-1/2
C	Apple	1-1/2 × 8 × 8
D	Balloon	1-1/2 × 6 × 8
E	Butterfly	1-1/2 × 7-1/2 × 6
F	Bus	1-1/2 × 7-1/2 × 4-1/2

ADJUSTABLE BOOK RACK

From *HANDS ON* Nov/Dec 84

It's convenient to have your books close at hand for easy reference. This book rack will not only keep your books reachable and organized, but it will also adjust to accommodate your choice of books.

1. Cut all the stock to size according to the List of Materials.
2. Drill the 1/2" diameter × 1/2" deep holes in the ends (A,B).
3. Tilt the table 5° and drill the 9/16" through-holes in the adjustable end (C).
4. Round over the edges using a shaper or router.
5. Sand all the parts. Do not sand the ends of the dowels (D).
6. Assemble with glue and clamp securely. Be careful not to get any glue on part (C).
7. Apply the finish of your choice.

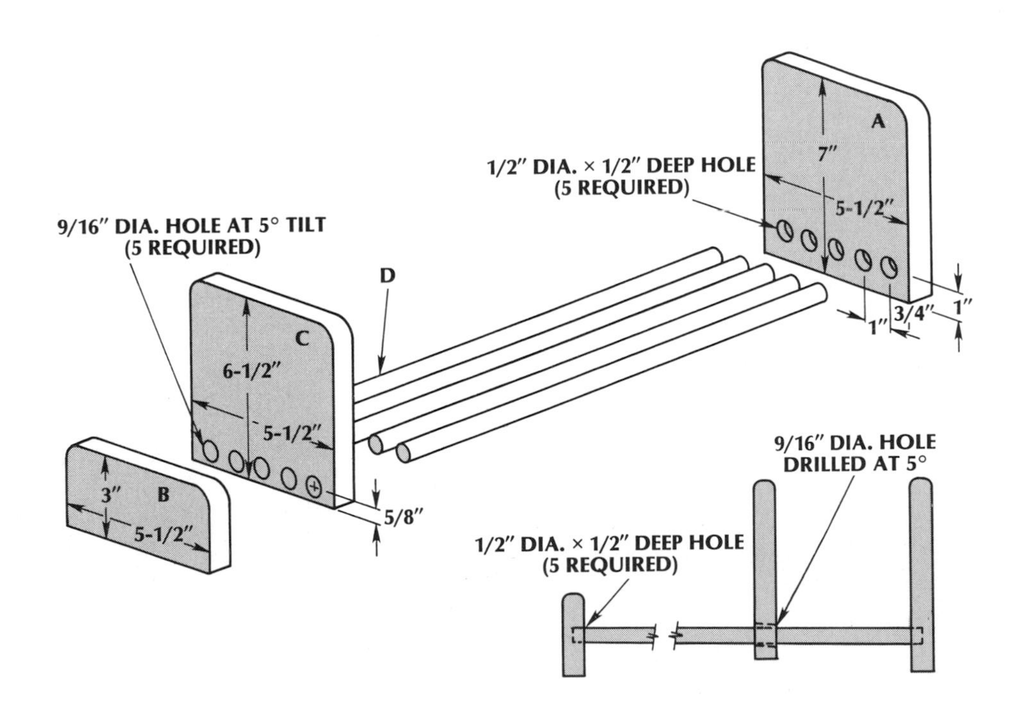

LIST OF MATERIALS

(finished dimensions in inches)

A	Large end	3/4 × 5-1/2 × 7
B	Small end	3/4 × 5-1/2 × 3
C	Adjustable end	3/4 × 5-1/2 × 6-1/2
D	Dowels (5)	1/2 dia. × 18

GARDEN TOOL BOX

From *HANDS ON* June/July/Aug 84

Here's a really handy carrier for your garden tools that's a cinch to put together. The design for this classic toolbox is based on the tool carriers used years ago by carpenters, and that design can easily serve the gardener of today. Roomy enough for a host of small hand tools, gloves, and seed packets, this carrier is so easy to make that you may want to build several. They're equally useful for the plumber, electrician, or mechanic in your home.

1. Select your stock. Pressure-treated or a suitable outdoor wood such as redwood or cedar is best, but any scrap wood will do. The handle is standard 1-1/4″ closet pole stock—or you can use part of an old broomstick.

2. Prepare the stock. Rip the bottom (A), ends (B), and sides (C) to width using the table saw, then crosscut all pieces to length. Cut the contours on the ends (B) with a bandsaw or jigsaw, and sand with the disc sander.

3. Drill the holes for the handle (D). Use a 1-1/4″ Forstner bit to drill these 3/8″ deep holes. Next, drill pilot holes for the assembly screws.

4. Assemble the toolbox with #9 × 1-1/2″ flathead wood screws. Attach the ends (B) to the bottom (A) and insert the handle (D). Attach the sides (C). Round off all sharp edges with a rasp or sandpaper.

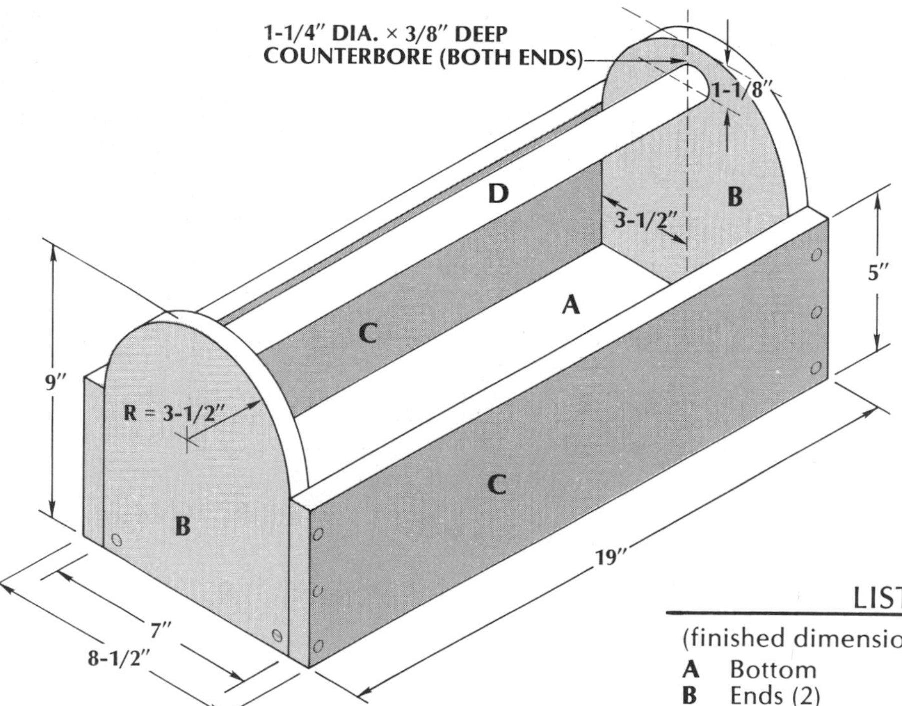

LIST OF MATERIALS

(finished dimensions in inches)

A	Bottom	1/4 × 7 × 17-1/2
B	Ends (2)	3/4 × 7 × 9
C	Sides (2)	3/4 × 5 × 19
D	Handle	1-1/4 dia. × 18-1/4
	Flathead wood screws (22)	#9 × 1-1/2

From *HANDS ON* Jan/Feb 85

To make dominos, carefully resaw and plane a 1-1/4" wide core of either padauk or ash to a thickness of 3/16". Then, build up the domino stock by adding a layer of holly veneer and then a layer of ebony to each side of the core. Once the glue has dried, crosscut the dominos to approximate length and disc sand to final dimensions.

The centerline of each domino is created by using a jigsaw or bandsaw kerf. The dots are revealed by drilling through the outer ebony veneer with a 1/8" twist bit. After the dots are exposed, the disc sander is again used to carefully round all eight edges and four corners of each of the 28 dominos.

The dots on the dominos are revealed by drilling through the top layer of ebony.

SHAKER PEGBOARD

From *HANDS ON* Apr/May/June 83 and Nov/Dec 84

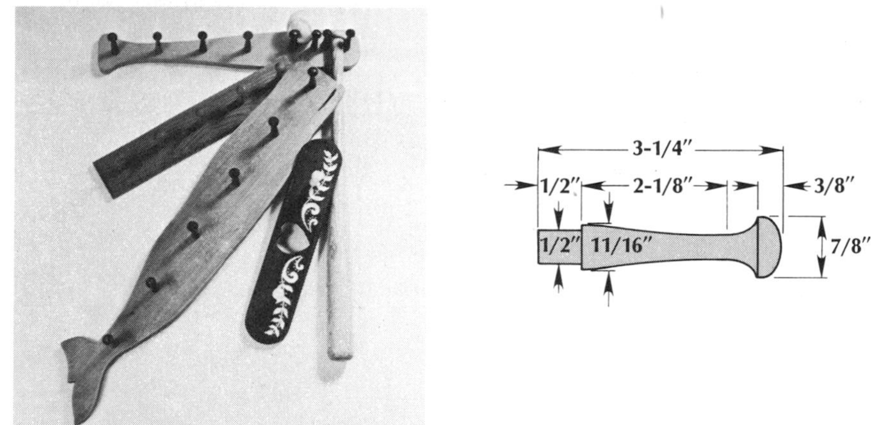

The Shakers had a unique way of storing unused items—they put them on the wall. A pegged board attached to the wall, about 6′ up, provided a perfect place for coats, hats, candle sconces, and even chairs. A Shaker pegged board was about the size of a 1 × 4 with either a plain or a beaded edge. Wooden pegs were set into this board every 2″ to 8″, and the board was attached to the wall.

Even though many of our needs are different from those of the Shakers, there is still the common need for order. And what better place to hang a coat or hat than on a handy peg? Modern production methods have outmoded the old method of turning these pegs one at a time, making such items readily available and inexpensive.

Made out of hardwood, these pegs can fit any room decor in your house. Mount them in a variety of ways: use straight stock and shape the edge; cut out freeform shapes on the bandsaw or jigsaw; or repeat a design on the router arm.

1. Prepare a 3/4″ × 3-1/2″ × 36″ piece of stock.

2. Drill 1/2″ diameter × 1/2″ deep holes for the pegs.

3. Turn the pegs on the lathe, or purchase ready-made pegs.

4. With the profile of your choice, shape the edge of the board.

5. Sand the board.

6. Glue in the pegs and allow glue to dry thoroughly before applying a finish.

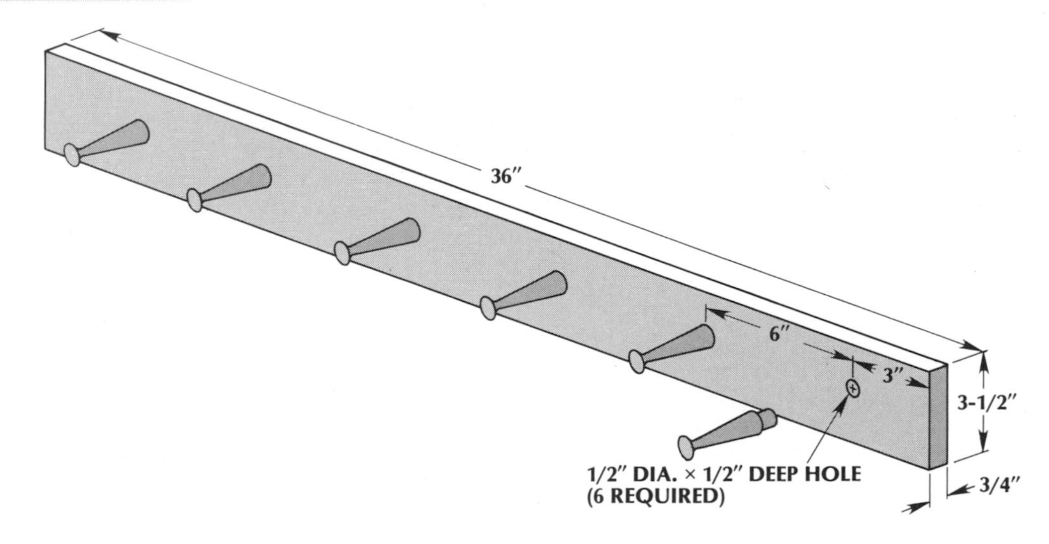

TOWEL HOLDER

From *HANDS ON* Nov/Dec 84

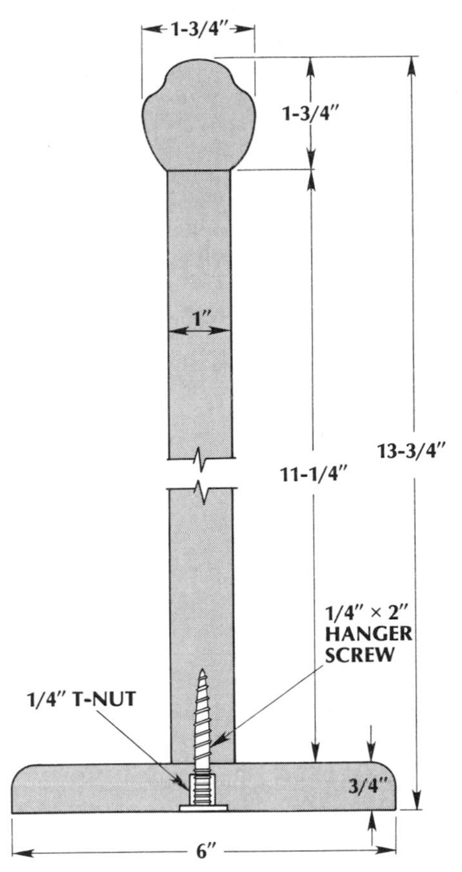

This project proves that a kitchen item can be functional as well as attractive. This towel holder will add a decorative touch to your countertop as well as have the next paper towel at your fingertips.

1. Prepare a 2" × 2" × 14" piece of stock for the towel bar. If you glue up the stock, use yellow woodworker's glue and allow the stock to remain clamped for 24 hours.

2. Turn the towel bar according to the plans. (The knob design at the top of the bar is optional.)

3. Remove the toolrest and sand the towel bar before removing it from the lathe.

4. Remove the finished bar from the lathe and cut off the waste stock.

5. Use the bandsaw or jigsaw to cut out the round base. Remove the saw marks with the disc sander then shape the edge. (Optional: Turn the base on the lathe.)

6. Drill and counterbore the bottom of the base for a 1/4" T-nut.

7. Drill a pilot hole in the end of the towel bar for the anchor screw.

8. Assemble the holder and apply the finish of your choice.

COUNTRY CHARM

From *HANDS ON* March/Apr/May 85

These charming folk art animals are easy to make and great as decorating pieces. To make a collection in your own shop, simply transfer the animal patterns to 3/4" stock and cut out with a bandsaw or jigsaw. Paint the pieces with Early American colors or burn in decorations and finish with a stain. Bases are 3" squares of 3/4" stock and the stems are 3/8" dowel.

From *HANDS ON* Nov/Dec 84

One of the most useful items in a kitchen is a cutting board. By following these easy instructions, you can save your countertop from many unnecessary cuts and slices.

1. Glue up nominal 2" (1-1/2" actual) stock for the large cutting board and 3/4" stock for the smaller cheese board.
2. Surface or sand the stock smooth.
3. Make cardboard templates of the designs then transfer the designs to the stock.
4. Use a bandsaw or jigsaw to cut out the boards.
5. Use the disc and drum sanders to sand the edges of the boards, and hand sand the tight spots.
6. Apply a dark stain to the edges for the 'crust,' then apply a nontoxic finish.

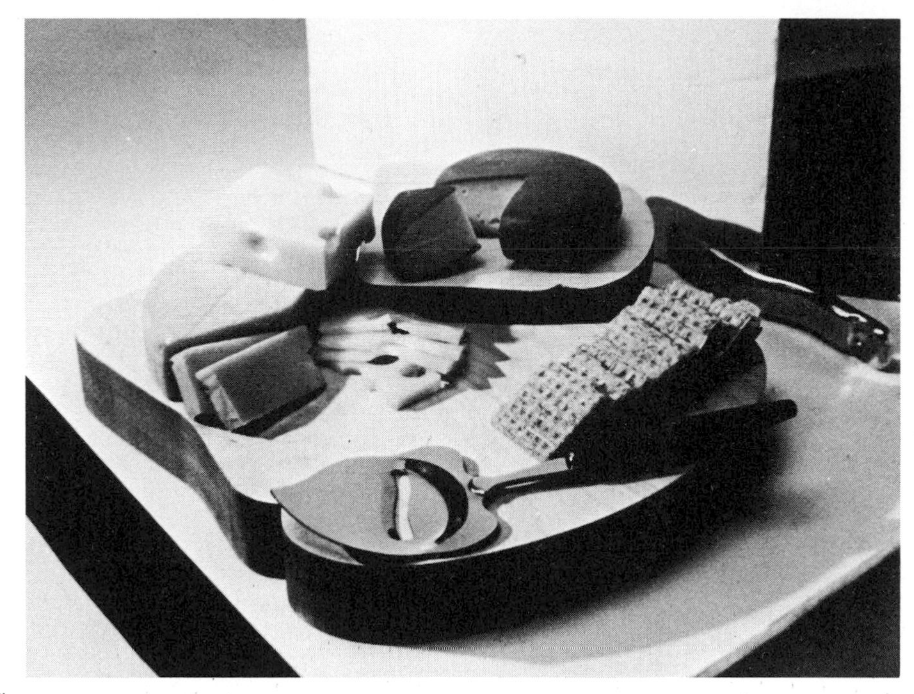

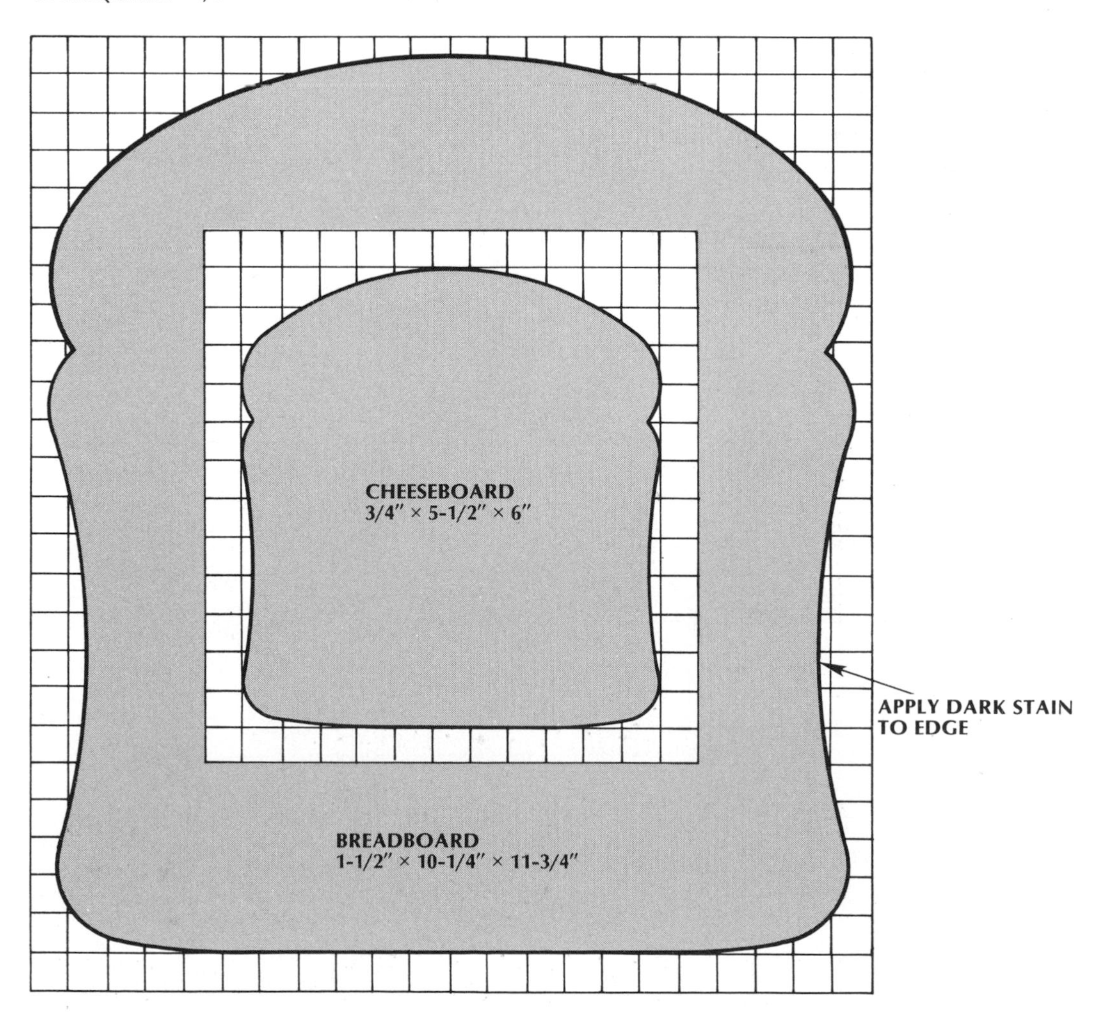

TOOL BOX

From *HANDS ON* June/July/Aug 85

Finding the space to organize all the miscellaneous items in your shop can be a problem. A "lazy susan" storage cabinet could be the solution for you. Using standard storage drawers and less than three square feet of bench space, you can make this handy four-sided storage unit to organize all your small items—even your sandpaper.

Here's how:

1. Start the project by cutting all the parts in the List of Materials to size. Use 1/2" plywood for the main cabinet parts and 1/8" hardboard for the sandpaper shelves.

2. Using a carbide-tipped blade, cut the 1/8" wide × 1/4" deep dadoes for the drawers and trays as indicated on the drawings. Note that the center partition (F) has stopped dadoes with different spacing on each side.

3. Miter the base frame pieces (K) and glue and nail them together. With glue and nails, attach the base (J) to the assembled frame.

4. Assemble the lazy susan by first attaching the parts (E,F,G) together with woodworker's glue and 6d nails. Attach the top (H) and bottom (I) with glue and nails, then attach the sides (A,B,C,D). Attach a ball bearing swivel unit to the base and storage unit.

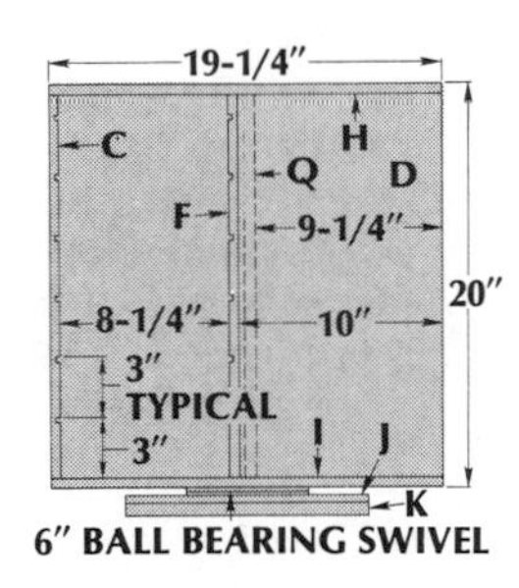

VIEW D

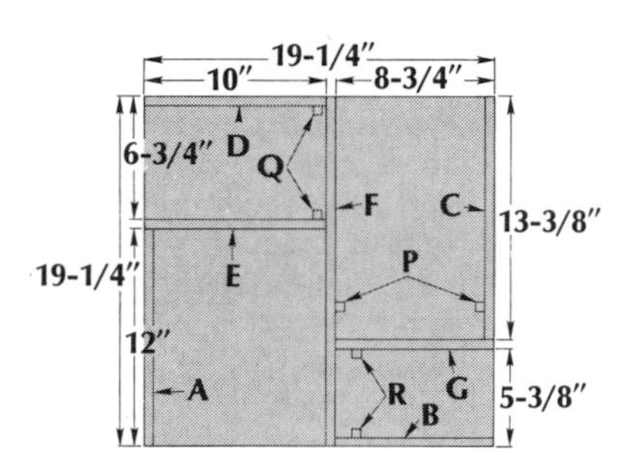

TOP VIEW

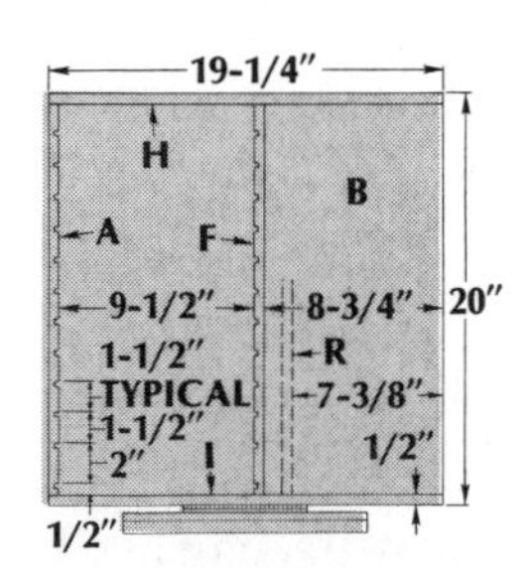

VIEW A

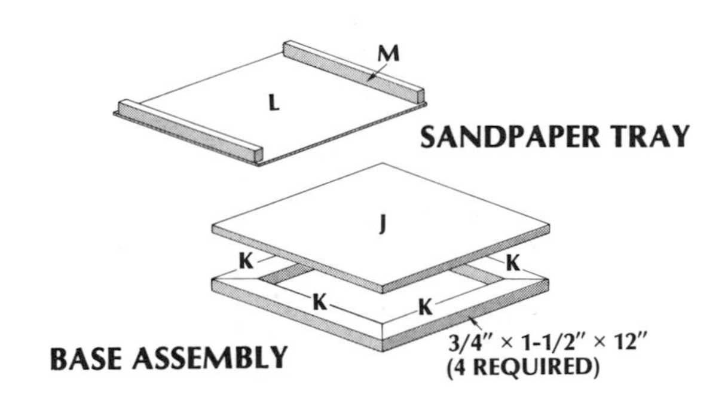

BASE ASSEMBLY

VIEW B

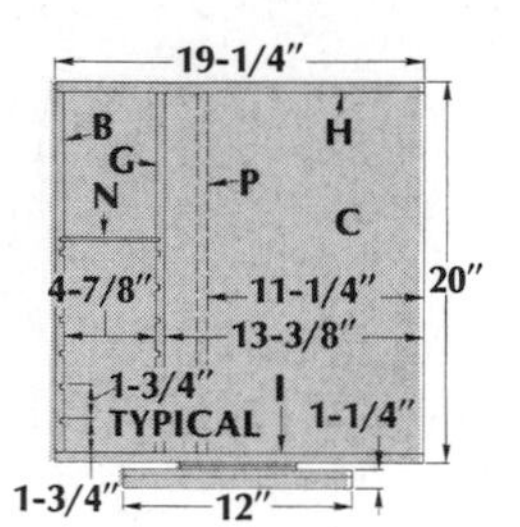

VIEW C

LIST OF MATERIALS

(finished dimensions in inches)

A	Sandpaper side	1/2 × 12 × 19
B	Small drawer side	1/2 × 8-3/4 × 19
C	Large drawer side	1/2 × 13-3/8 × 19
D	Medium drawer side	1/2 × 10 × 19
E	Medium drawer partition	1/2 × 10 × 19
F	Main partition	1/2 × 19-1/4 × 19
G	Small drawer partition	1/2 × 8-3/4 × 19
H	Top	1/2 × 19-1/4 × 19-1/4
I	Bottom	1/2 × 19-1/4 × 19-1/4
J	Base	1/2 × 12 × 12
K	Base frame (4)	3/4 × 1-1/2 × 12
L	Sandpaper trays (12)	1/8 × 10 × 12
M	Sandpaper tray ends (24)	1/2 × 3/4 × 9-1/2
N	Small drawer dust panel	1/8 × 5-3/8 × 8-3/4
O	Medium drawer dust panel	1/8 × 6-3/4 × 10
P	Large drawer stops (2)	1/2 × 1/2 × 19
Q	Medium drawer stops (2)	1/2 × 1/2 × 19
R	Small drawer stops (2)	1/2 × 1/2 × 11
	Ball bearing swivel	6

TABLETOP STORAGE CHEST

From *HANDS ON* Jan/Feb 85

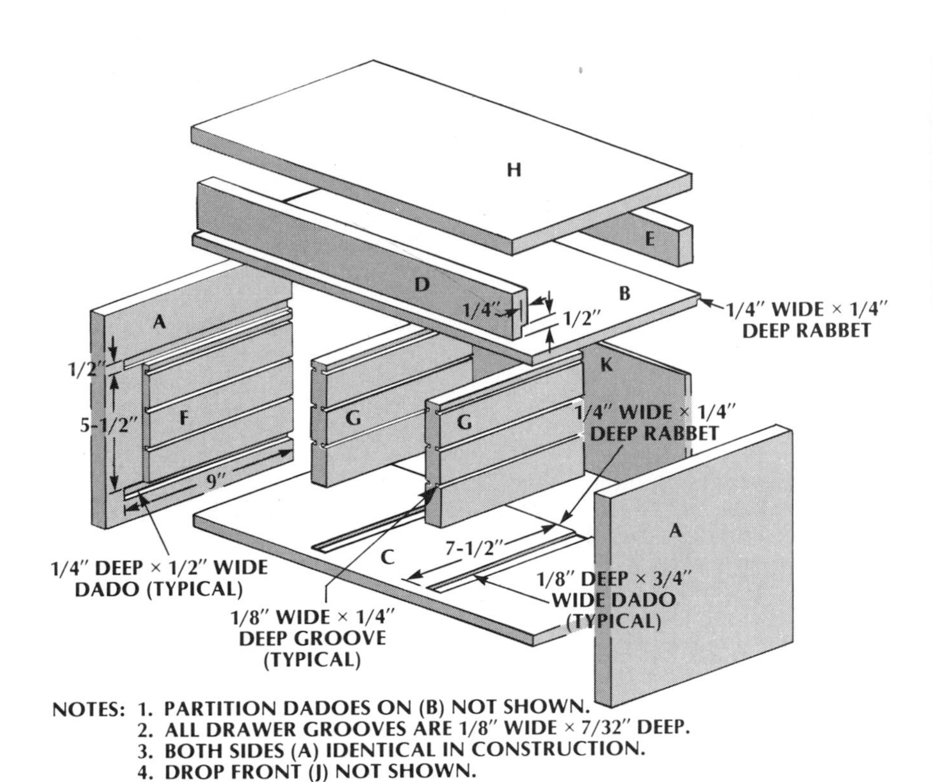

NOTES: 1. PARTITION DADOES ON (B) NOT SHOWN.
2. ALL DRAWER GROOVES ARE 1/8" WIDE × 7/32" DEEP.
3. BOTH SIDES (A) IDENTICAL IN CONSTRUCTION.
4. DROP FRONT (J) NOT SHOWN.

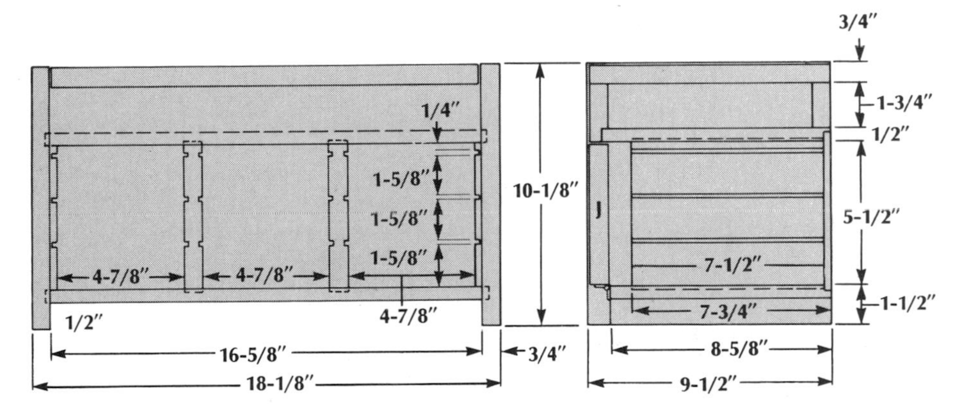

LIST OF MATERIALS

(finished dimensions in inches)

A	Sides (2)	3/4 × 9-1/2 × 10-1/8
B	Compartment bottom	1/2 × 8-15/16 × 17-1/8
C	Bottom	1/2 × 8-11/16 × 17-1/8
D	Front rail	3/4 × 2-1/4 × 16-5/8
E	Back rail	3/4 × 1-3/4 × 16-5/8
F	Drawer supports (2)	1/4 × 5-1/2 × 7-1/2
G	Drawer partitions (2)	3/4 × 7-1/2 × 5-3/4
H	Lid	3/4 × 9-1/2 × 16-5/8
J	Drop front	3/4 × 6 × 16-5/8
K	Back	1/4 × 6 × 16-5/8
	Butt hinges (4)	1-1/2 × 1
	Brass knob	5/8
	Friction lid support	
	Wide hasp	3/4
	Small organizer drawers (9)	1-5/8 × 4-7/8 × 7-1/2

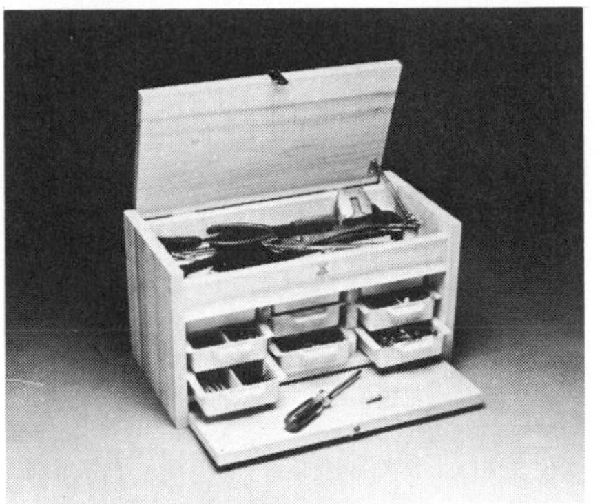

Ample storage space is a necessity for any craftsperson or do-it-yourselfer. Here's a very versatile storage box plan that is suitable for shop or home, depending upon the material used.

One particular benefit of the cabinet is the use of readily available drawers. Because of the seamless drawer construction, this chest is ideal for sewing supplies, art supplies...even a rock collection!

1. Cut parts (A,B,C,D,E,F,G) to size according to the List of Materials.
2. Lay out and cut the 1/2" wide stop dadoes in the sides (A) for parts (B,C). Next form the 3/4" wide stop dadoes in parts (B,C) for the partitions (G). Square all dadoes with a chisel.
3. Cut the 1/4" × 1/4" rabbets in parts (B,C) for the back (K).
4. Attach drawer supports (F) to the sides with glue and clamp. Set the supports (F) 1/4" in from the back edges of sides (A).
5. Lay out the drawer grooves on the partitions (G) and supports (F), then cut these with a carbide-tipped saw blade set at a 7/32" cutting depth. Check drawers for fit.
6. Glue and clamp parts (A,B,C) together. Check for squareness as you apply clamping pressure. Reinforce the joints with countersunk #8 × 1-1/2" flathead wood screws.
7. Cut parts (D,E) to final length and glue and clamp these into place.
8. Attach the back (K) with 2d nails.
9. Cut the lid (H) and drop front (J) to finished dimensions, and attach to the chest with the hinges.
10. Apply the finish of your choice.

ODDS AND ENDS STORAGE CHEST

From *HANDS ON* Nov/Dec 83

Here's a great piece of furniture that solves a big storage problem—where to put those decks of cards, cassette tapes, scissors, needlepoint supplies, and dozens of other odds and ends. Designed to look like the kind of chest used in old-time drugstores, this apothecary chest has sixteen drawers to accommodate lots of things.

This apothecary chest is built out of #2 common pine throughout, except for the hardboard back and the drawer bottoms. You can save money by using particleboard for the partitions and plywood for the drawers.

1. Cut out the top (B), sides (A), drawer fronts (K), and base pieces (G,H) first. This allows you to select the best wood for visible parts. Cut the drawer fronts (K) about 1/8" oversize since the finished drawer sides and bottoms are sanded flush after final assembly.

2. Cut the remaining stock to size according to the List of Materials. We glued up the 14" wide partitions (C) using solid pine. You can also make these partitions out of 13-1/4" wide particleboard, then glue and nail a 3/4" × 3/4" strip of pine facing to the exposed edge.

3. Form the 1/4" deep × 3/8" wide rabbet in the back edges of the sides (A) for the back (J).

4. Attach the drawer guides (E) to the partitions (C) with 4d finish nails and glue. Mount the guides flush with back edges of the partitions and with a 6-1/16" spacing between each. Attach the 3/4" × 3/4" filler strip (D) to the top partition.

5. Assemble sides (A) and partitions (C) with glue and 8d finish nails. Double-check your spacing to make sure that there is a 6-1/16" vertical space between each partition. Glue the drawer dividers (F) into place.

6. Shape the edges of the top (B) and the drawer fronts (K) with a 1/4" quarter round shaper cutter, or use a hand-held router with a rounding-over bit. Shape just the sides and front edge of the top.

7. Attach the top (B) to the case with 8d finish nails and attach the back (J) with 2d common nails.

8. Miter the corners of the base pieces (G,H). Cut the scrollwork using bandsaw or jigsaw and sand the parts on a drum sander. Attach the base pieces with 4d finish nails and glue.

9. Drawer construction. With 16 drawers, you'll need to use a few production techniques. Rip all drawer stock to proper widths, and then crosscut the pieces to equal lengths (use a miter gauge stop rod or a stop block clamped to the rip fence for this operation). Use a dado assembly or a saw blade with a 1/8" kerf to form the grooves in the drawer sides (L). Glue and nail the drawers together, and glue and clamp the fronts (K) into the ends (M). Flush-sand the drawer bottoms and sides using a disc or belt sander. Slide the bottoms (N) in and tack in place with 2d nails.

10. Finishing touches: Final-sand the chest and remove all dust with a tack rag. Finish as desired and attach the knobs.

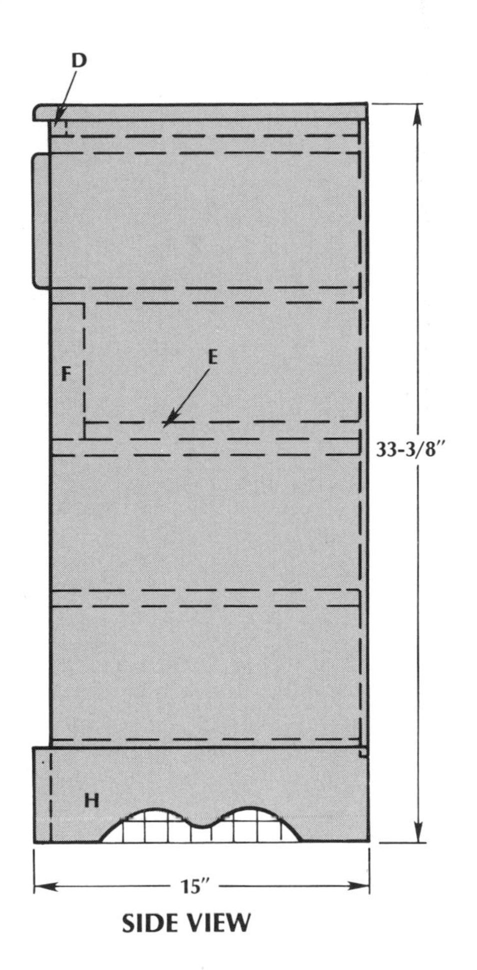

SIDE VIEW

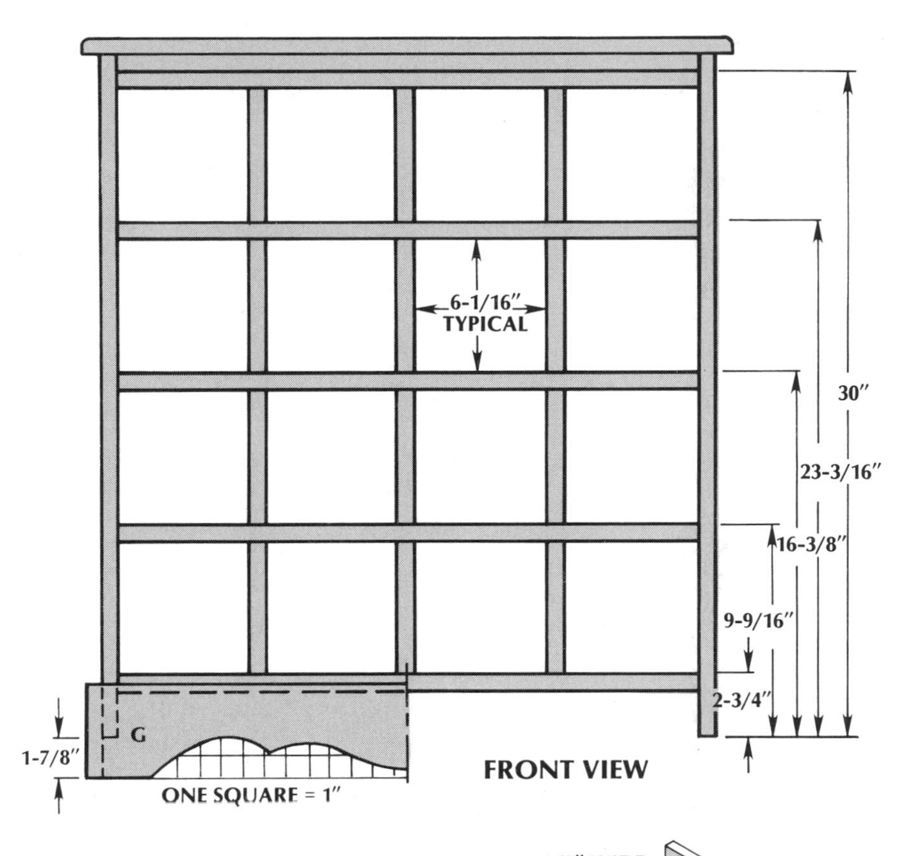

FRONT VIEW

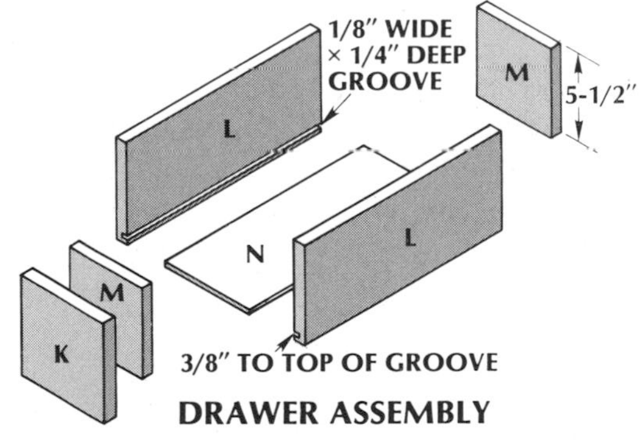

DRAWER ASSEMBLY

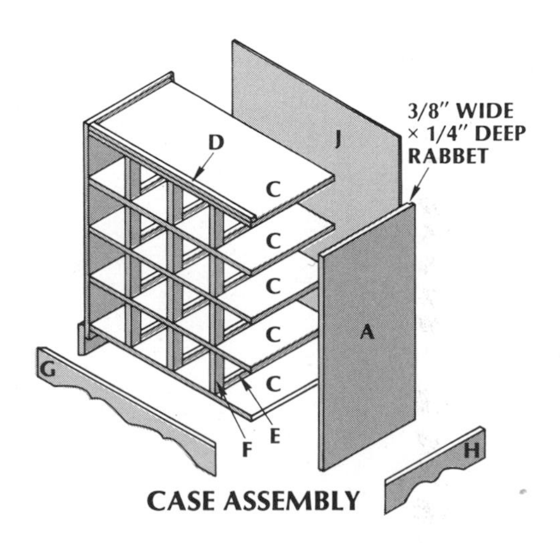

CASE ASSEMBLY

LIST OF MATERIALS

(finished dimensions in inches)

A	Sides (2)	3/4 × 14-1/4 × 30-3/4
B	Top	3/4 × 15 × 31
C	Partitions (5)	3/4 × 14 × 28
D	Filler strip	3/4 × 3/4 × 28
E	Drawer guides (12)	3/4 × 3/4 × 12-1/2
F	Drawer dividers (12)	3/4 × 1-1/2 × 6-1/16
G	Base front	3/4 × 4-1/4 × 31
H	Base sides (2)	3/4 × 4-1/4 × 15
J	Back	1/4 × 28-3/4 × 28-3/4
K	Drawer fronts (16)	3/4 × 6 × 6
L	Drawer sides (32)	1/2 × 5-7/8 × 13-3/4
M	Drawer ends (32)	1/2 × 5-1/2 × 5
N	Drawer bottoms (16)	1/8 × 5-3/8 × 13-3/4
	White porcelain knobs (16)	

Home Improvement

Many people work very hard at making their home cozy and inviting as well as functional. Oftentimes, this involves adding the right finishing touches. The twelve projects here contain many options and suggestions for you to obtain the best utilization of space and convey the mood you wish to create. These projects can be applied as facelifts for an older home or incorporated when building a new home.

DOOR AND WINDOW MOLDINGS

From *HANDS ON* July/Aug 83

Windows and doors are like pictures on the wall. As such, the same considerations that go into picture frames should also go into the moldings around these doors and windows. Dress them up with some fancy or unusual moldings, but don't stop with the selection available from the local lumberyard. Select the design and wood you want by creating your own moldings. Here's how:

1. Plan your trim. Decide what kind of trim you want. Window trim that meets with the stool is called conventional framing. Choose between mitered corners at the top or use corner blocks. Corner blocks allow you to butt-join the trim. This is an easy way to add a decorative treatment to the framing. Around the doors the trim goes to the floor or joins with a block of wood (plinth) at the baseboard. The method of treating windows with no stools is called picture framing. Remember: When measuring for mitered framing, add twice the width of the stock to the length of each frame member.

2. Design the contours. Use molding knives from the molding attachment as templates to draw the contours you want. Then, move knives into various positions to get different contours. Keep in mind that the contours on the knives are slightly longer than the actual cut. Remember that the table saw can be used for bevels and chamfers, and the lathe can be used for turning the corner blocks on screw centers. Plan on making extra trim to avoid duplicating machine setups.

3. Prepare stock. First, rip all stock to width. Use only straight, true and clear stock for your moldings. Ponderosa pine, fir, poplar, walnut, oak, cherry, mahogany, and butternut have all been used extensively in finish carpentry work.

After ripping the stock to width, cut the 1/8" deep relief in the back using the 1" blank knife set of the molding attachment or use the dado attachment. This relief will allow you to adjust to inconsistencies between the wall and the door or window jamb.

4. Mold the trim. Use scrap stock to locate the proper settings for your table and fence. Use a molding jig to make this operation easier and safer. For narrow trim, mold the edge of a wide board, and then saw-off the part that you want. Be sure to use push stick, push blocks, and feather boards at all times on these operations.

5. Install the trim. Use a miter saw. Use finish nails to attach the molding and use a nail set to countersink the nails. Fill the nail holes with wood putty and apply the finish of your choice.

STYLE A—BULL'S-EYE PATTERN

STYLE B—BULL'S-EYE PATTERN

STYLE C—BULL'S-EYE PATTERN

1/8" DEEP RECESS
FIRST CUTS—A & B
RANCH STYLE MOLDING CUTS
BEAD CUTTER
SAW CUT AT 10° TO REMOVE WASTE
QUARTER ROUND CUTTERS
SECOND CUTS—A
SECOND CUTS—B
STYLE C
FLUTE CUTTERS
FLUTE & COVE CUTTERS
3-BEAD CUTTER

BASEBOARD MOLDINGS

From *HANDS ON* Sept/Oct 83

Baseboard moldings play several important roles in any room. Applied where the floor meets the wall, they form a visual foundation for the eye while covering the unsightly floor and wall seam. And they also protect the walls from kicks, bumps, furniture, and cleaning tools.

Baseboard molding has to be installed after the door trim is in place since the length of the baseboard is determined by the width of the door trim.

Here's how you can create baseboard molding for your room.

1. Plan your molding. Baseboard moldings consist usually of either one, two, or three parts. The *base molding* is the wide piece that protects the wall. It can carry a decorative molding itself. *Base shoe*, a trim piece of molding that looks like (but is *not* the same as) quarter-round molding, hides any unevenness between the bottom of the base and the floor. Base shoe is an optional trim with wall-to-wall carpet. A *base cap* is added to the top of an unmolded base to hide gaps between the wall and the base top.

Make a full-scale design of the molding you want using your selection of molding knives as templates, then measure the walls. Be sure to add 20% to the total length for mitering, errors in cutting, and other waste.

2. Make the molding. One of the advantages of making your own molding is that you can select the type of wood you want. In order to make the job of molding and installation easier, select stock that's straight and free of defects.

For the base molding, cut a 1/8" deep relief in the back side with the 1" blank molding knives. This relief allows the molding to fit the wall without gaps.

Make the base shoe and base cap moldings efficiently and safely by cutting the profiles on the edge of a wide board, then sawing off the profiled edge. This method allows the stock to be supported while it's being molded.

3. Installation: The first step to installation is to mark the locations of the wall studs. Use a magnetic or electronic stud finder; or tap lightly along the wall with your hammer and listen for the hollow sounds between the studs; or measure from any known stud locations.

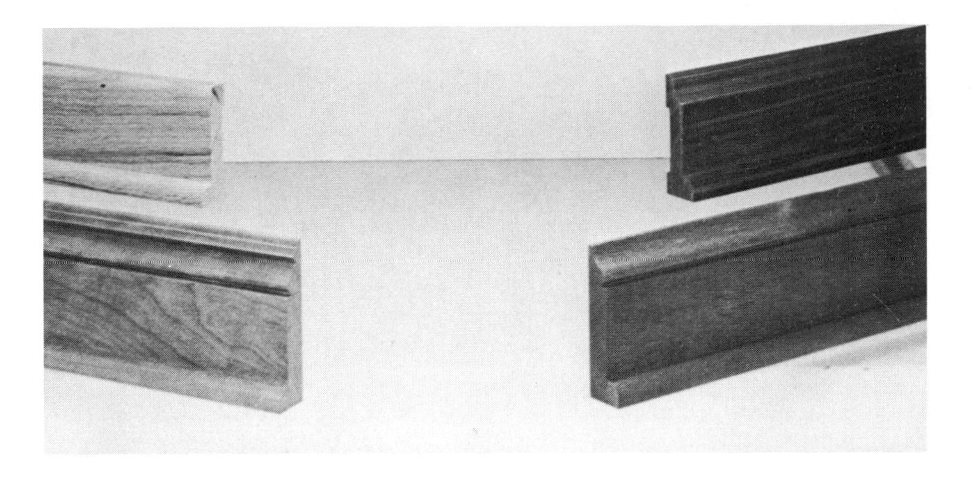

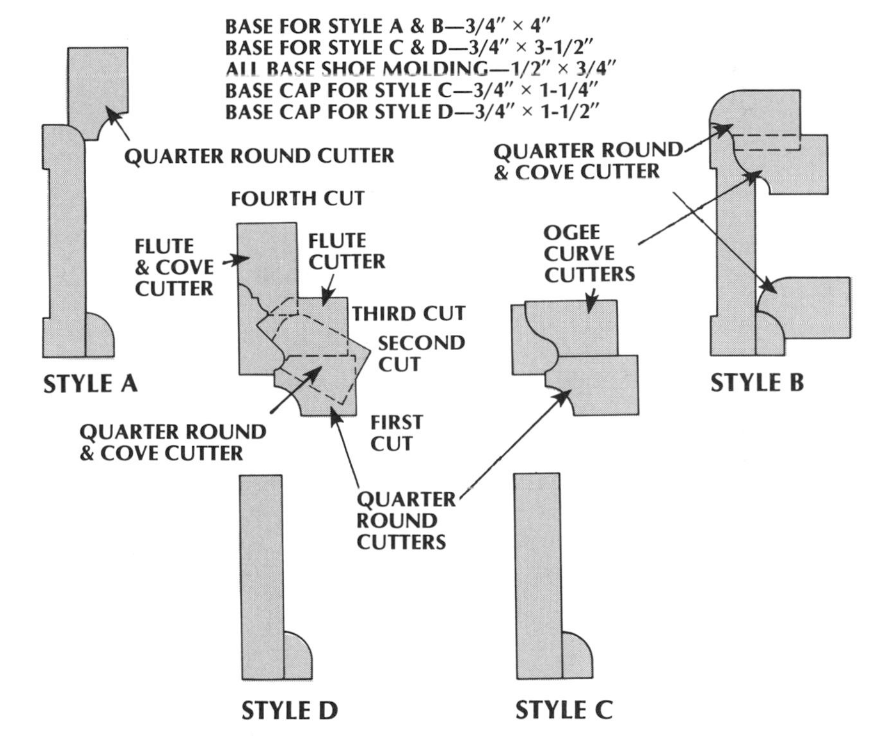

Start by installing the base on the longest walls first. Sink two 8d finish nails at each stud—drilling pilot holes first with a 7/64" twist drill. It helps to cut the base just a trifle long so that it can be "sprung" into place. Too long, though, and you'll punch holes in the wall or cause cracks in the corners. If your molding is not long enough, use a miter lap joint to join two shorter pieces at a stud and nail through the joint.

Next, install the base to the remaining walls with butt joints at the inside corners and 45° miter joints at the outside corners. If the base is molded, you will need to miter or cope the inside corners. After installing the base, follow the same procedure for the base shoe and base cap.

4. Finishing touches: Countersink the nail holes and apply a clear finish such as polyurethane varnish. Fill the nail holes with a wood filler that matches the color of your stock. If you paint the molding, countersink and fill the nail holes before applying the paint.

CEILING MOLDINGS

From *HANDS ON* July/Aug 83

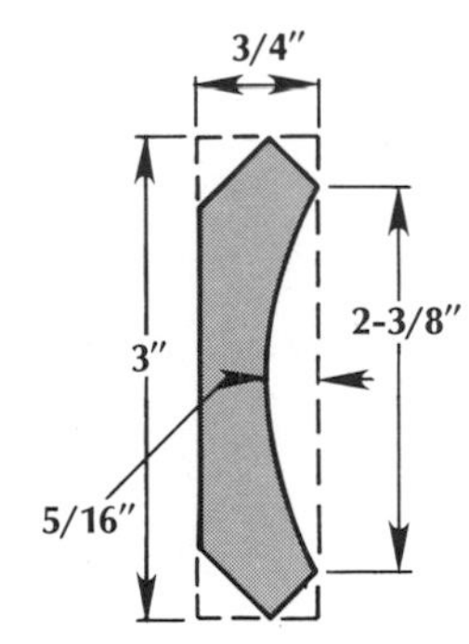

COVE MOLDING

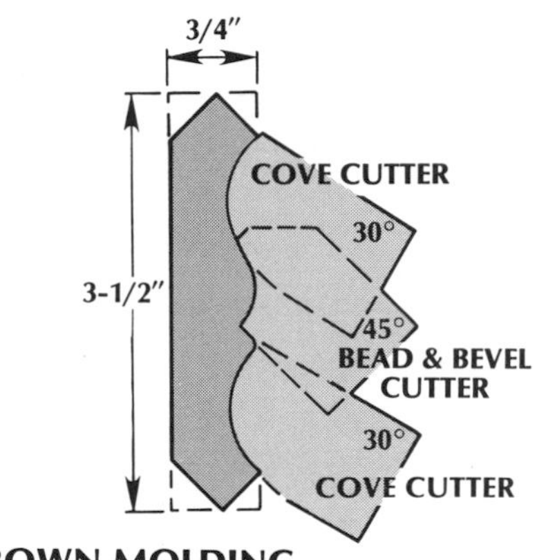

CROWN MOLDING

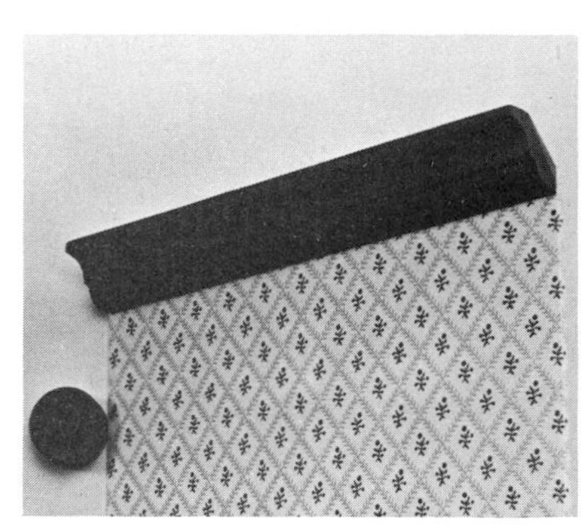

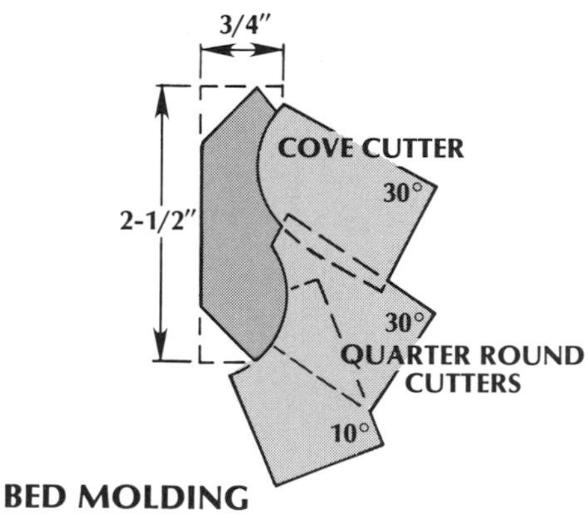

BED MOLDING

Doing your own room remodeling offers tremendous satisfaction for several reasons. Most importantly, you know you're doing it yourself, and you can take pride in seeing the fruits of your labor—a room that's fresh and different. Another cause for satisfaction is saving money by doing it yourself, using your own time and resources. But, the real pleasure of room remodeling discussed in this series is knowing that what you have done is unique—that you have made woodwork that's simply not available to the average homeowner.

Designed to cover the seams where the ceiling meets the walls, ceiling moldings do double duty by also providing an eye-pleasing transition from one surface to another. Again, as with other moldings, the design and type of wood allow you to add personality to your room.

Here's how to create ceiling moldings for your room:

1. Plan your molding. There are three kinds of ceiling moldings you can make—*crown, bed,* and *cove.* An example of each is illustrated below. Crown and cove moldings are always "sprung," meaning that they have beveled edges that rest on the ceiling and wall, thereby spanning the ceiling wall joint. This spanning allows the molding to readily adjust to minor irregularities and provide a clean line where it meets the ceiling or wall. Bed molding can be either sprung or plain—the latter type fitting snug into the joint.

Use one of the designs illustrated at left, or create the profile you want by applying the molding cutters in various positions.

2. Prepare stock. It is necessary to use straight, true, and clear stock for your molding. For our examples we used walnut, cherry, and oak. Rip stock to required widths. Prepare extra stock to allow for cutting errors.

3. Cut the profiles. As you can see by the crown and bed moldings we feature, using just a few cutters can yield many attractive profiles. The cove molding, on the other hand, requires no shaper work; rather, it's done entirely on the table saw. Always be sure to use push blocks, push sticks, feather boards, and a roller stand for safety.

4. Bevel the molding. After you have completed the profiles, bevel the edges of the molding on the table saw. Tilt the table 45°, mount the rip fence below the blade, and use a feather board to help guide the stock.

5. Install the molding. Start installing the ceiling molding on the longest wall first. Drill 7/64″ pilot holes for 8d finish nails and nail the molding through the plaster or drywall into the upper wall plate. For large moldings, nail through to the ceiling joist. Cut the molding just a trifle long so it can be lightly sprung into place. If the molding isn't long enough, use a miter lap joint to join two shorter pieces. Install the remaining molding by mitering the outside corners and coping or mitering the inside corners.

6. Add finishing touches. Countersink the nails and apply the finish of your choice. Fill the nail holes with wood putty that matches the color of your finished molding.

THE WINDOW GREENHOUSE

From *HANDS ON* May/June 80

This window greenhouse is perfect for growing house plants, garden seedlings, flowers, or even a miniature vegetable garden. It's easy to build and can be attached directly to a window frame with screws, or installed in the window cavity like an air conditioner. The window greenhouse should be 12" to 18" deep, depending on its overall size; the larger it is, the deeper it should be. The dimensions may be lengthened or shortened to fit the windows in your home.

NOTE: If the greenhouse will be mounted permanently, its inside rear dimensions, where it meets the window frame, should be the same as the inside dimensions of the window frame. If, on the other hand, the greenhouse will simply rest in the window cavity, the outside dimensions of the greenhouse, where it will enter the window cavity, should be 1/8" smaller than the inside dimensions of the window cavity.

1. Cut all pieces to size according to the List of Materials.

2. To make the top portion of the greenhouse, first cut grooves in both ends of the horizontal pieces. To do this, bolt a large scrap of wood to the miter gauge; this extension should reach to within 1/8" of the rip fence and be perfectly square with the fence and table. Hold the pieces firmly against the extension in order to cut the grooves accurately.

3. Because the top rests on the greenhouse at a 25° angle, cut the upper horizontal piece at 25°. Machine 1/4" off the top of the lower horizontal piece to allow rain to run off the greenhouse without soaking into the wood.

4. To make the front of the greenhouse, cut the upper edge at 25°. Cut a 1/4" wide × 3/8" deep groove on the inside of the lower horizontal piece, and a 1/4" wide × 1/4" deep groove in the edges of the vertical pieces.

5. To make the sides, cut the upper edge at 25°. Cut a 1/4" wide × 3/8" deep groove in the lower horizontal pieces. In addition, cut a 1/4" wide × 1/4" deep groove in the inside of the front vertical pieces. The upper pieces are right triangles with their longest sides slanted at 25° to the horizontal.

6. To make the bottom of the greenhouse, cut a 3/8" wide × 1/4" thick tongue in the right, left and front edges of the redwood boards. To do this, use a dado blade and stack the knives to cut a 3/8" kerf. Set the table and rip fence so that the dado cuts a 1/4" deep × 3/8" wide rabbet. With the fence and table properly adjusted, cut a rabbet in one edge of the boards, then turn the boards over, end for end, and cut more rabbets in the same edges from the opposite side.

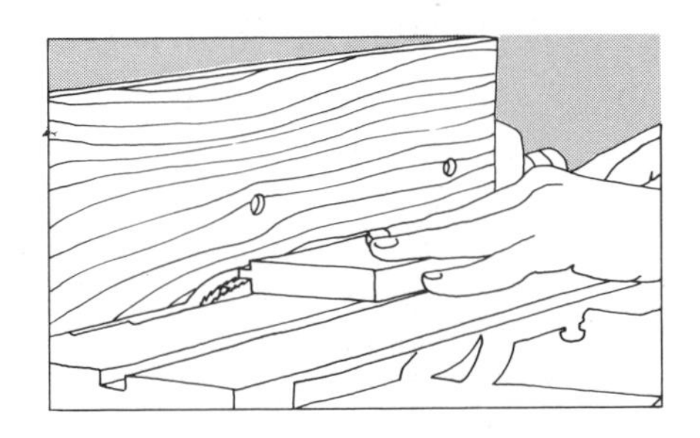

Making a tongue with a dado blade.

Fit the bottom pieces together with tongues and grooves, making sure that their combined width, when joined, matches the length of the front and back pieces.

7. Attach the front to the side with a 1/2" × 1/4" spline in the grooves of the vertical pieces. Slide the bottom into the grooves of the lower front and side pieces.

8. Attach a board of the same width as the back vertical side pieces to the tops of the back vertical side pieces with wood screws. Hinge the top to this board.

9. Using 3/4" × 3/4" redwood strips, make a lip around the front and side edges of the top. Drill a small hole through the greenhouse frame from the inside and partially through the lip. Insert a nail in the hole to lock the top closed; the nail can be removed and the top propped open when ventilation is needed.

10. Install another lip around the back of the greenhouse to help mount it or fit it to the window.

11. Cut or purchase glass panes of correct dimensions, to fit the top, sides, and front. Hold the glass in place with glazier's points while you apply glazing compound around the edges.

12. Insert two or three brass screws in the lower edge of the top piece to keep the pane of glass from sliding off. Extrude a bead of silicone caulk along the lower edge of the top, then position the glass on the bead. The silicone will prevent the entry of moisture along the lower edge.

NOTE: If the greenhouse will be permanently mounted, wait until it has been attached to the window frame before installing the panes.

13. To mount the greenhouse permanently, use the back lip to screw it to the window frame, then apply a durable adhesive caulk around the joint to keep out moisture and cold air. To set the greenhouse in an open window, remove the top and slide it in until the back lip butts up against the sash, then reattach the top. Put weatherstripping around any cracks.

14. Finally, attach a strip of flashing to the greenhouse or window so that the hinges are covered. This material will help to prevent leaks.

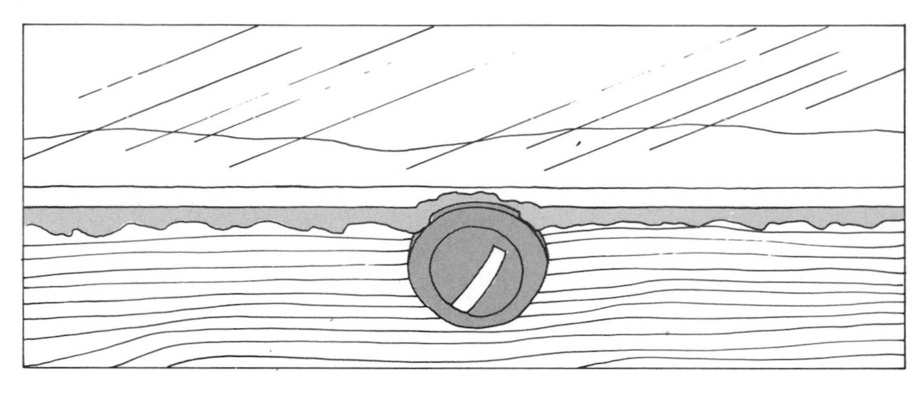

Brass screws and washers keep glass from sliding off top; silicone seal keeps moisture from seeping underneath.

LIST OF MATERIALS

(finished dimensions in inches)

A	Top horizontal pieces (2)	3/4 × 1-1/2 × 18
B	Top vertical pieces (2)	3/4 × 1-1/2 × 12
C	Front horizontal pieces (2)	3/4 × 1-1/2 × 18
D	Front vertical pieces (2)	3/4 × 3/4 × 10
E	Side horizontal pieces (2)	3/4 × 1-1/2 × 8
F	Triangular side board (2)	3/4 × 6 × 8 × 10
G	Side vertical pieces (2)	3/4 × 1-1/2 × 10
H	Side vertical pieces (2)	3/4 × 1-1/2 × 12
J	Bottom pieces (2)	3/4 × 8 × 10 redwood boards
K	Lips (2)	3/4 × 3/4 × 18 redwood strips
L	Lips (2)	3/4 × 3/4 × 12 redwood strips
M	Hinge board	3/4 × 3/4 × 18

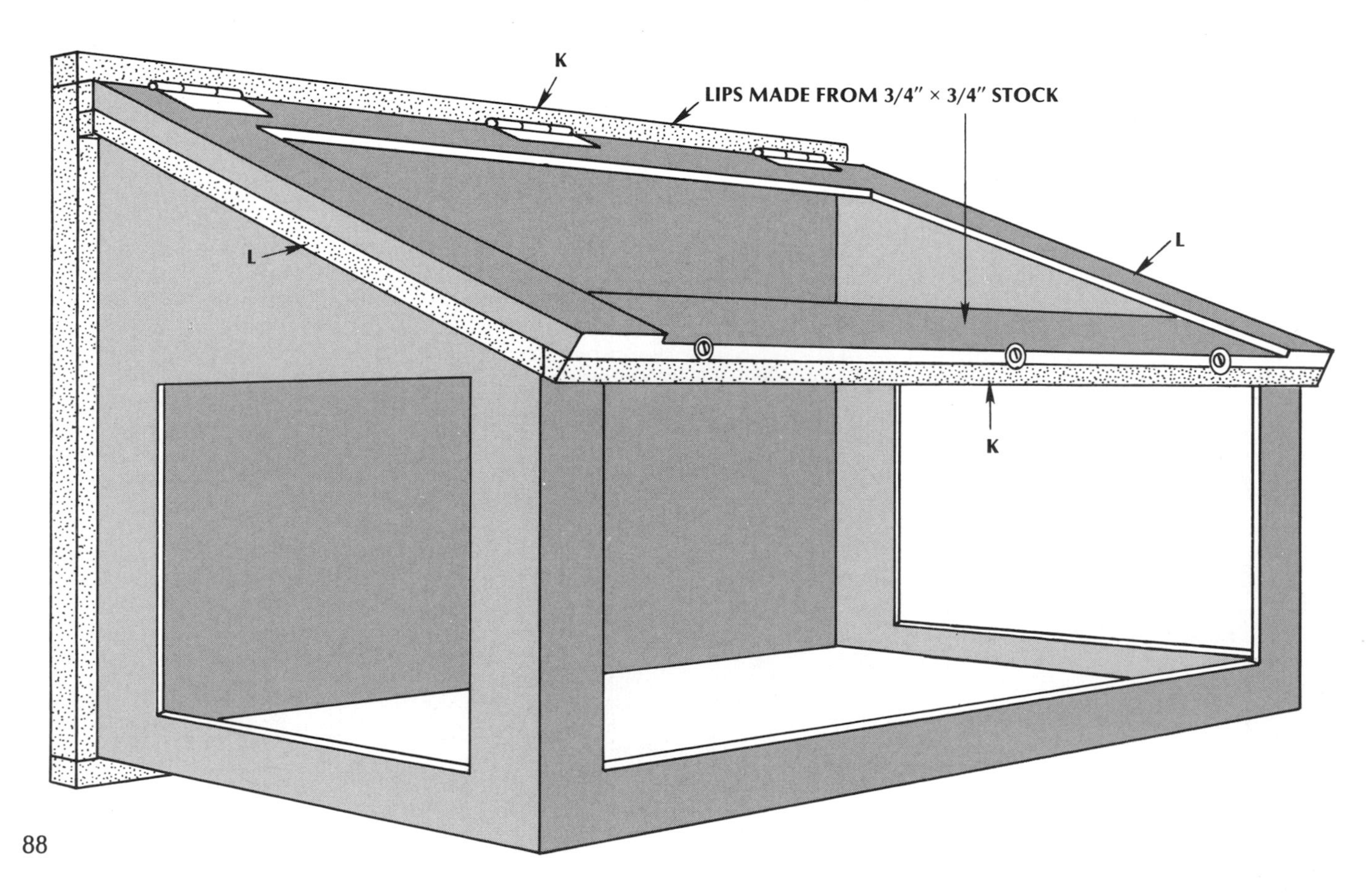

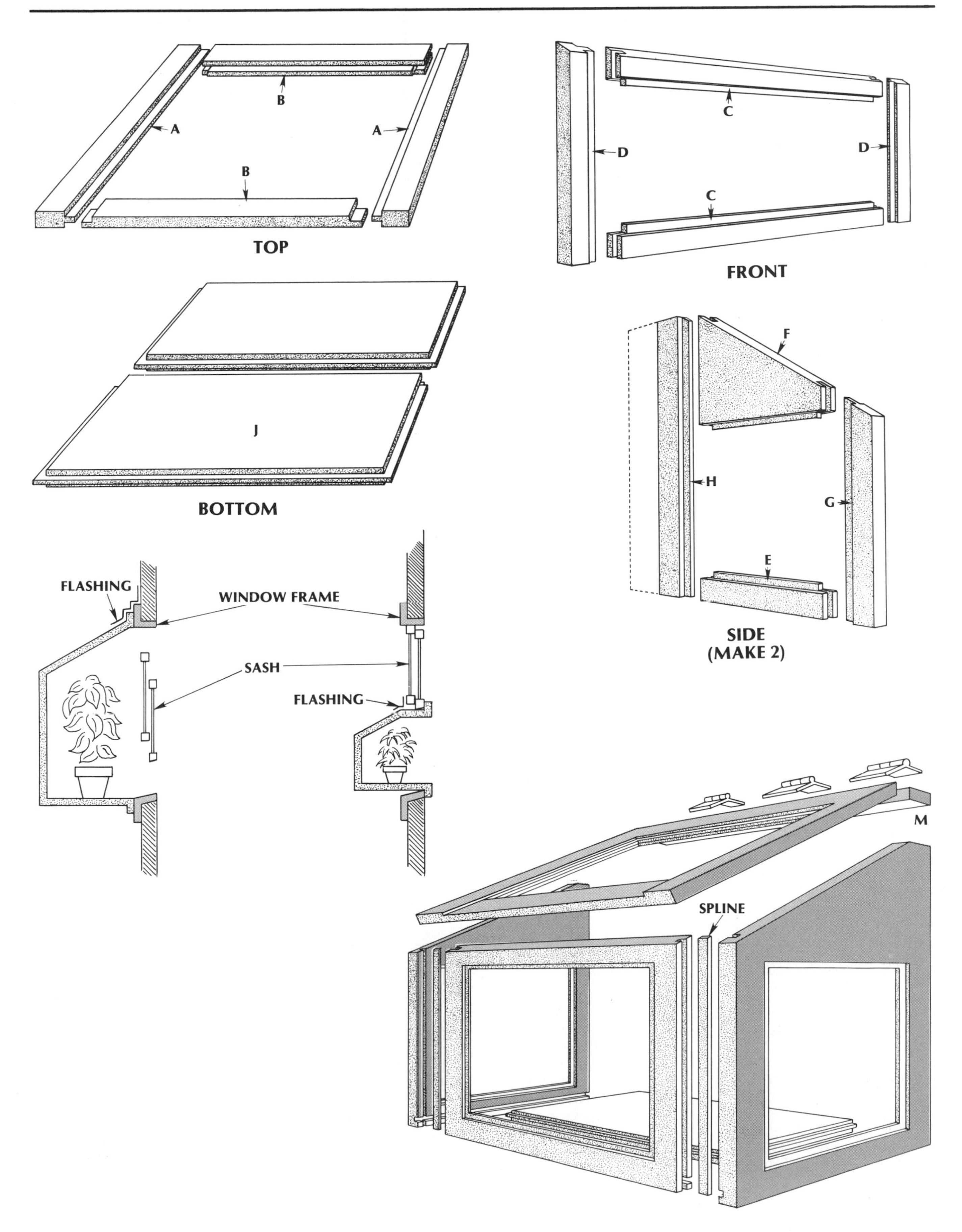

B
A
A
B
TOP
C
D
D
C
FRONT
J
BOTTOM
F
H
G
E
SIDE
(MAKE 2)
FLASHING
WINDOW FRAME
SASH
FLASHING
M
SPLINE

POT AND PAN ORGANIZER

From *HANDS ON* Nov/Dec 80

There must be a law somewhere that decrees that no matter which pot or pan you want to use, it will *always* be at the bottom of the stack. How many times have you had to get down on your hands and knees, reach into the darkest recesses of your cabinets, and move half your cooking utensils just to find the one you wanted?

There is a way around this dilemma. Instead of stacking your pans vertically on a shelf, one on top of the other, file them horizontally in a drawer! A deep drawer with moveable dividers will organize your utensils. And it gives you the versatility to add new items and discard old ones. Just rearrange the dividers to accommodate new pots and pans.

But you don't want to do away with shelves completely. Some items, like small appliances, are most efficiently stored on shelves. But you can convert some of your shelves so they pull out like drawers, eliminating the need to get down on all fours and rummage around. Drawers and sliding shelves put the utensils you need within convenient reach.

MEASURING AND MATERIALS

Most under-the-counter cabinets have room for one deep drawer and one pull-out shelf. The depth of the drawer is determined by the diameter of your largest pans—usually 10″ to 11″.

The length of the drawer and shelf should be 1/8″ to 1/4″ less than the depth of your cabinet. This will give you room to close the cabinet doors when the drawers and shelves are retracted. The width should be a hair less than the width of the door opening.

For the most part, these drawers can be built from inexpensive materials—we used #2 pine and 1/4″ masonite. But make the runners and guides from hardwood.

MAKING THE DRAWERS

The drawers are made from seven pieces—front, back, bottom, two sides, and two runners. Most of the pieces are joined to each other using simple dadoes except for the joinery between the sides and the front. This joint has to stand the strain each time you open and close the drawer. One of the strongest joints you can use at stress points like this is a sliding dovetail.

Using a router accessory and 9/16″ dovetail cutter, rout two vertical slots in the drawer front. The center of these slots should be 7/8″ from either side.

To make the mating dovetails in the sides, use a horizontal router. Adjust the table height so that the dovetail cutter bites into the wood just enough to cut half the dovetail, 3/8″ in from the end. Using a miter gauge and safety grip, pass the sides under the router, against the rotation of the cutter. Flip the board and repeat the operation to cut the other half of the dovetail.

The other joinery is cut using either straight router bits or dado blades.

Cut additional 1/4″ wide × 3/8″ deep dadoes in the insides of the sides, perpendicular to the length and spaced every 2″. These will accommodate the spacers you'll need to organize your utensils.

Rout a handle in the front of the drawer 5″ long, 1-1/2″ wide, and 1-1/2″ below the top edge.

Assemble the front, sides, back, and bottom with glue and wood screws. With a sander, slightly crown the bottom edge of the runners—this will help reduce the friction, making the drawer easier to pull in and out. Attach the runners to the drawer with glue and screws.

MAKING THE SHELF

Cut four boards, 3/4″ thick × 3″ wide to make a shelf frame. Cut a 1/4″ wide, 3/8″ deep dado down the middle of the inside edges of the frame members, using either a 1/4″ straight bit or dado blades. Then cut a 1/4″ thick × 3/8″ long tenon in the ends of the front and back frame members. On the bottom side of the front frame member, rout or dado a groove 3/4″ wide, 1/2″ deep, and 5″ long. This groove will serve as a pull for the sliding shelf.

Cut a piece of 1/4″ masonite to fit inside the frame and assemble the pieces with glue.

INSTALLATION

To install a drawer and a shelf in your cabinets, make two simple guides out of a piece of 1-1/4″ thick × 5″ wide hardwood. Cut two dadoes 1/2″ deep down the length of the board. The dado for the shelf should be 13/16″ wide, for the drawer, 1-1/2″, spaced as shown. Cut the board in half to make your two guides. (*Note:* As described, these guides can be used to mount a shelf above a drawer, as our pictures show. If you want to mount the shelf below the drawer or mount several shelves or drawers, you'll have to make more than one set of guides.)

Using brad point bits, drill two 1" holes, 3/4" deep in each of the guides and centered 5/16" below the dado for the drawer. These holes should be positioned 3" back from the front edge of the guides and 3" back from the center. They will form a recess in which you can mount shower stall rollers. These rollers make excellent glides for heavy drawers.

Purchase four rollers 3/4" in diameter. Mount them with #8 × 1-1/4" roundhead screws in the recesses you've just drilled. (You may have to ream the centers of the rollers out a bit if the #8 screws won't pass through.) Use the pilot hole left by the brad point bit to center the rollers in the recesses. When mounted, they should protrude into the dado slot 1/16".

Mount the finished guides to your cabinet frame. Just tack or clamp them in at first, to make sure you've got them level and that your drawers and shelves slide easily. (There should be about 1/16" of play for both the drawer and the shelf, if you use the measurements we've given you. If you want a tighter fit, adjust these measurements accordingly.) Once the guides are properly placed, mark them for position and attach them to the cabinet frame with glue and wood screws.

Slide the drawers and shelves into place. Cut as many spacers as you need (2 to 4 per drawer) from 1/4" masonite and put them in place.

And that's it, except for putting away your pots and pans; then standing back and admiring how organized they look.

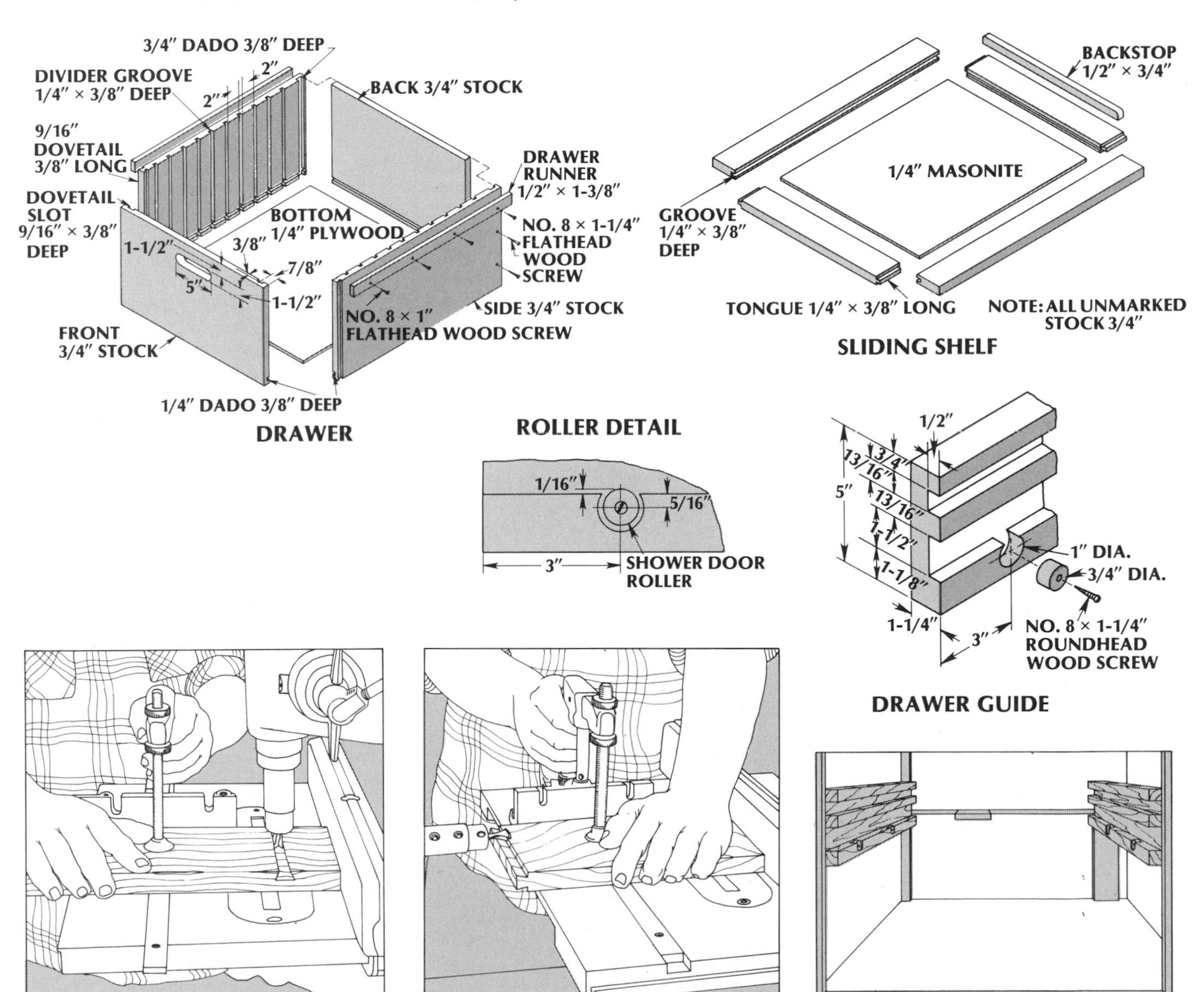

Routing a dovetail groove in a drawer front.

Horizontal routing—making the mating dovetail.

Mount the guides in the cabinet.

WORKBENCH-ON-THE-WALL

From *HANDS ON* Jan/Feb 84

Working with wood is a hobby that can consume a lot of space in a home. A woodcarver who carves miniatures may need only a kitchen tabletop, but other woodworkers seem to need an entire basement and a two-car garage. For the average woodworker, space must be shared—next to the laundry room or side-by-side with the family car. Here's a compact workbench-on-the-wall that serves the needs of the space-conscious woodworker as well as the needs of the rest of the family.

This workbench-on-the-wall is easy to build and quite versatile. When not in use, it folds up and out of the way to permit dust-free storage of tools and easy access to the floor for cleaning. And, because of the compact size and low cost, it's feasible to build several—one for each of your D-I-Y activities.

For instance: three benches in a row would give you over 12′ of workbench surface, plus individual space for your tools. But don't stop there. Consider this handy bench for a...

- sewing center
- potting/garden bench
- electronics bench
- finishing bench
- mechanic's bench
- child's desk

To build this bench you will need to:

1. Cut all stock to size according to the cutting diagram and the List of Materials. Remember: Measure twice, cut once.

2. Cut the dadoes in the legs (M) for the stretcher (K) using the dado attachment. Attach the stretcher to the legs using glue and screws.

3. Make the bench top (A) by first laminating the plywood with glue and screws. Apply the facing pieces (E,F) with glue and 6d finish nails.

4. Assemble the case by first attaching the shelves (C) and bottom (P) to the sides (B) with glue and screws. Check for squareness as you progress. Next, attach the upper and lower cleat strips (G) with glue and screws (the lower cleat strip is fastened with longer screws). These strips need to be secure since they will be used for mounting the bench to the wall. The side cleat strips (H) are attached with glue and nails. Attach the pegboard (R) with screws, and then glue and nail the stop (L) into place.

5. Attach the gusset (D) with glue and screws to the case and then attach a 5″ strap hinge to the gusset.

6. Form the mortises with a chisel in the bench top (A) and the bottom (P) for the hinges.

7. Attach the bench top assembly to the case with the butt hinges. Then attach the leg assembly with the strap hinges.

8. Leg brace. Cut a 45° bevel on the end of the leg brace (J) and glue and clamp the back-up block (N) to the beveled end. With the bench propped open, locate the position of the leg brace and attach it to the gusset strap hinge.

Clamp the brace to the stretcher (K) and drill the 3/8″ bolt hole through the stretcher, brace and block.

9. Attach the screw hook and eye to the lower shelf, and to the back-up block.

10. Mount the workbench on steel shelf brackets that are fastened to wall studs. Steel shelf brackets are available at hardware stores and home centers. Fasten the case to the wall with 3-1/2″ lag screws through the upper and lower cleats. After the workbench is attached to the wall, tack the hardboard top (Q) in place with 4d nails.

This workbench folds up and out of the way when not in use.

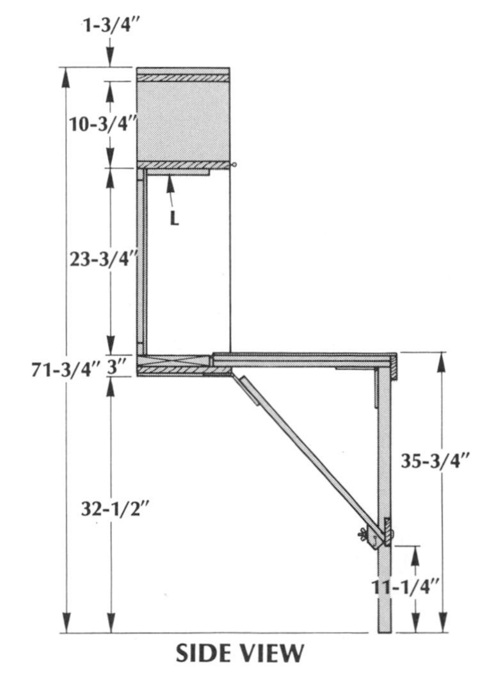

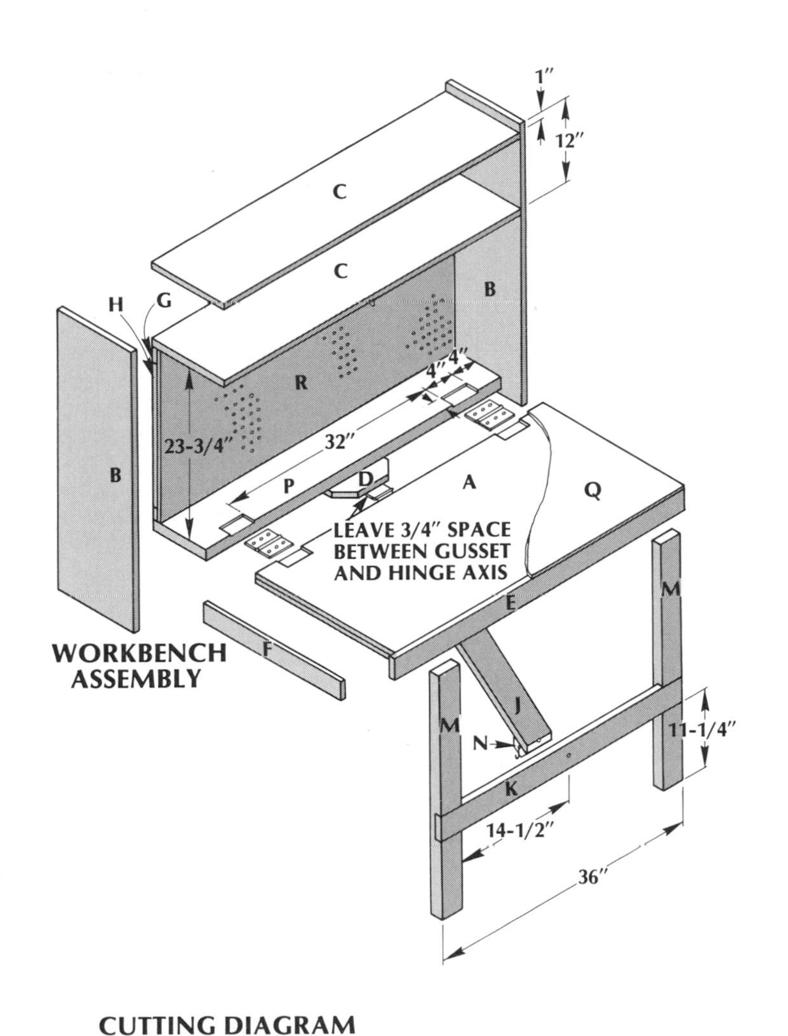

WORKBENCH ASSEMBLY

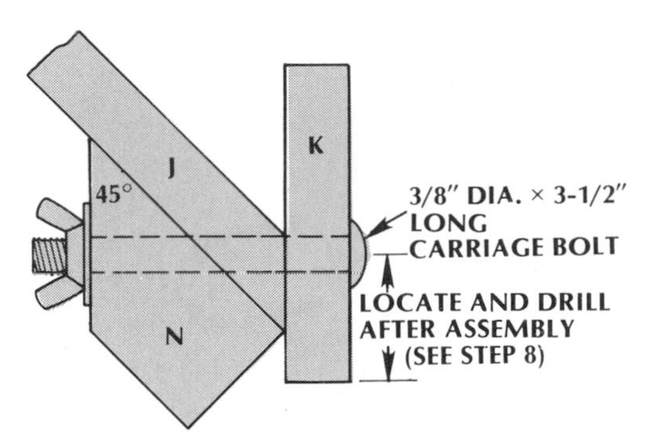

BRACE AND LEG DETAIL

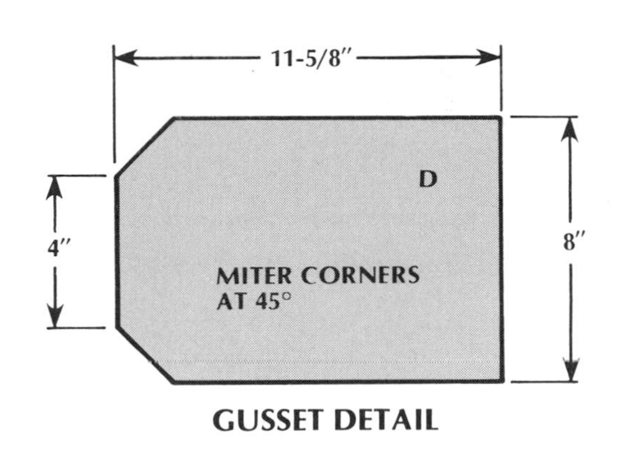

GUSSET DETAIL

CUTTING DIAGRAM

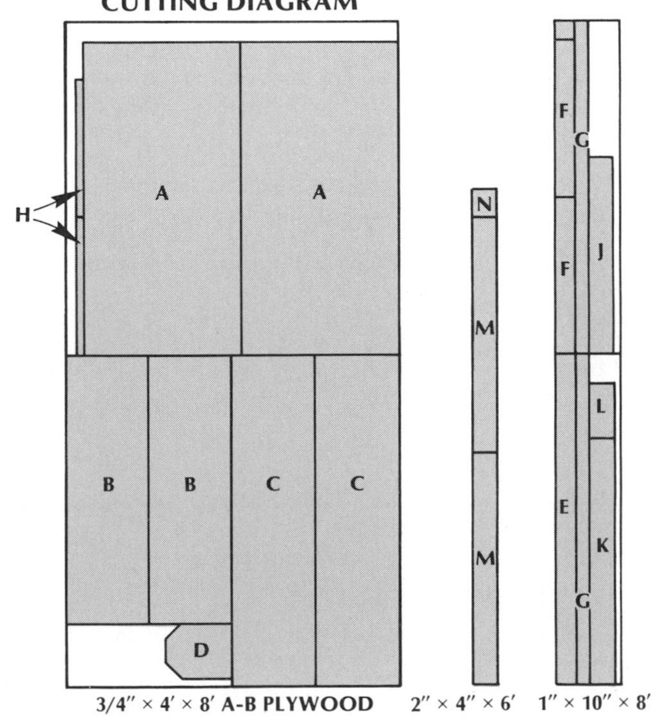

3/4″ × 4′ × 8′ A-B PLYWOOD 2″ × 4″ × 6′ 1″ × 10″ × 8′

LIST OF MATERIALS

(finished dimensions in inches)

A	Bench top (2)	3/4 × 22-3/4 × 46-1/4
B	Sides (2)	3/4 × 12 × 39-1/4
C	Shelves (2)	3/4 × 12 × 48
D	Gusset	3/4 × 8 × 11-5/8
E	Front facing	3/4 × 3 × 47-3/4
F	Side facing (2)	3/4 × 3 × 22-3/4
G	Upper and lower cleat strips (2)	3/4 × 2 × 48
H	Side cleat strips	3/4 × 3/4 × 19-3/4
J	Leg brace	3/4 × 3-1/2 × 27-3/4
K	Stretcher	3/4 × 3-1/2 × 36
L	Stop	3/4 × 3-1/2 × 7-5/8
M	Legs (2)	1-1/2 × 3-1/2 × 34
N	Back-up block	1-1/2 × 3-1/2 × 3
P	Bottom	1-1/2 × 8-5/8 × 48
Q	Hardboard top	1/4 × 23-1/2 × 47-3/4
R	Pegboard	1/4 × 23-3/4 × 48
	Hardware	
	Door hinges (2)	4 × 4
	Strap hinges (3)	5 × 5
	Screws and nails as required	
	Screw hook and eye	
	Carriage bolt, washer, and wing nut	3/8 × 4
	Shelf brackets (2)	

SHELTERED SWING

From *HANDS ON* July/Aug 82

On those lazy summer afternoons, you can't beat the simple enjoyment you get from this sheltered swing. With its own built-in "mini-porch," it offers protection from the sun's rays while letting in all the fresh air.

1. First, cut all parts to size according to the List of Materials.

2. Use your bandsaw or jigsaw to form the contours on the seat supports and arm rests, as well as the angle in the bottom of the back supports.

3. Assemble the five seat supports and the front and rear rails to form the rectangular base of the swing.

4. Attach seven slats, spaced at 1/4" intervals, to the rectangular base. Secure the slats with 3d galvanized nails, drilling pilot holes for each of them.

5. Secure the arm rest supports with carriage bolts, nuts, and washers. The bolts and washers also act as anchors for the swing chain.

6. Drill holes in the arm rests for the chain to pass through. Attach the arm rests to the arm rest supports with 6d galvanized nails.

7. Assemble the back of the swing and attach five slats, spaced at 2" intervals, to it. Place the final slat on the top of the back assembly to cap it.

8. Using 6d galvanized nails, attach the back assembly to the rear seat rail; drive the nails through the bottom of the back supports. Insert carriage bolts through each of the armrests at the spot where they adjoin the back supports.

9. Sand the entire swing thoroughly. Finish (if desired) with polyurethane or spar varnish.

10. The shelter assembly is made from the pressure-treated posts and beam. Bolt the rectangular frame of the roof assembly to the posts.

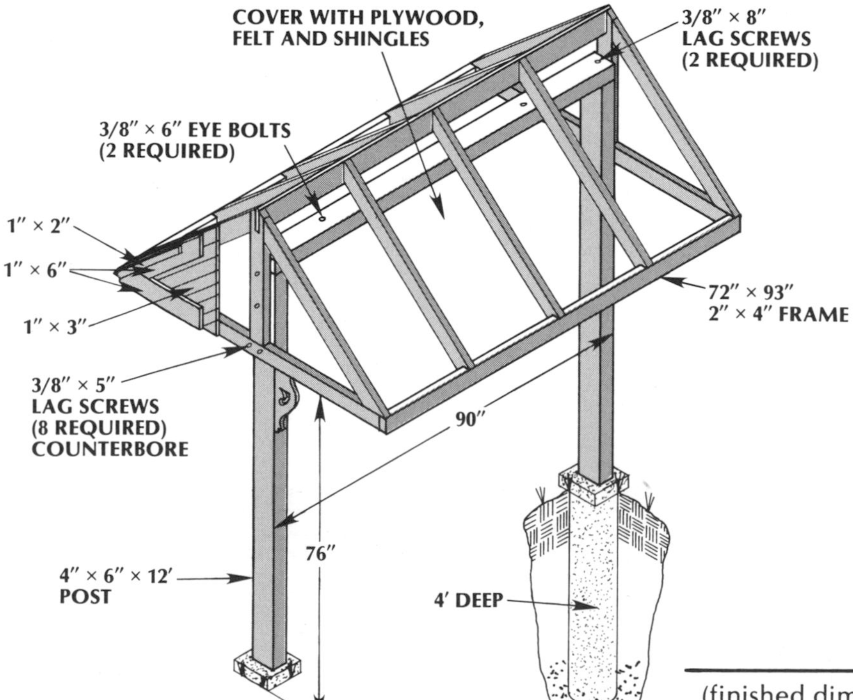

SHELTER ASSEMBLY

LIST OF MATERIALS

(finished dimensions in inches)

A	Slats (13)	1/4 × 1-3/4 × 55-1/2
B	Seat supports (5)	3/4 × 2-1/4 × 14-1/2
C	Front and rear rails (2)	3/4 × 2-1/4 × 60
D	Armrests (2)	3/4 × 2-1/4 × 17-3/4
E	Armrest supports (4)	3/4 × 2 × 8-3/4
F	Back supports (5)	3/4 × 1-1/2 × 22

11. Use a slotted 2 × 4 to extend the ridge board; this will allow the roof rafters to clear the crossbeam.
12. For roof decking, use two full sheets of exterior plywood covered with 15 lb. felt. Three-tab shingles are recommended.
13. Cover the gable ends with 3″ strips of cedar. The fascia boards should be made from 1 × 6 cedar; 1 × 2 cedar furring strips are then attached to the fascia boards to support the metal drip edge.
14. Use an 18′ length of chain to attach the swing to the shelter.

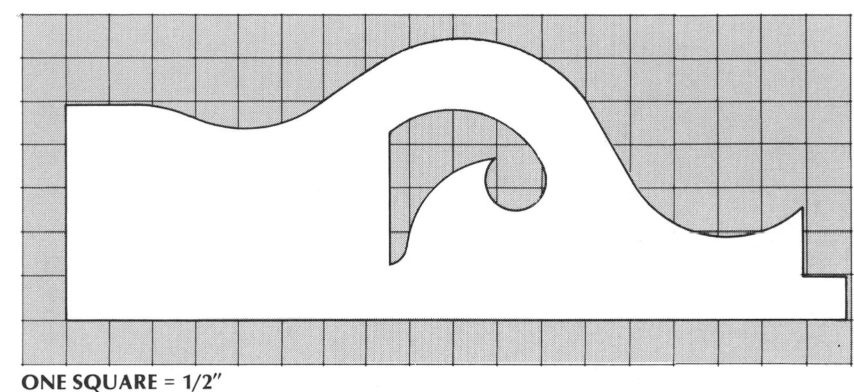

DECORATIVE SCALLOP LAYOUT

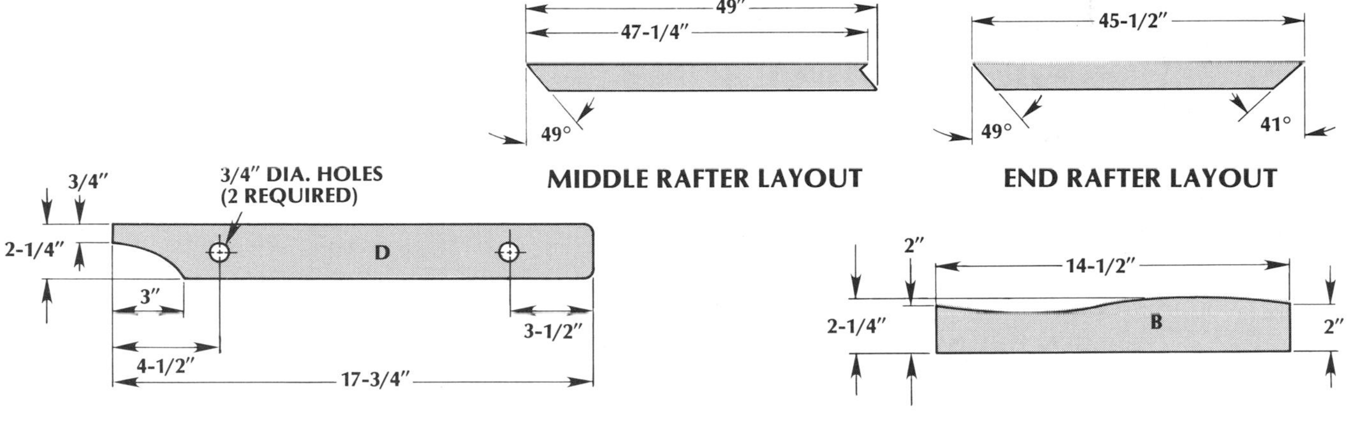

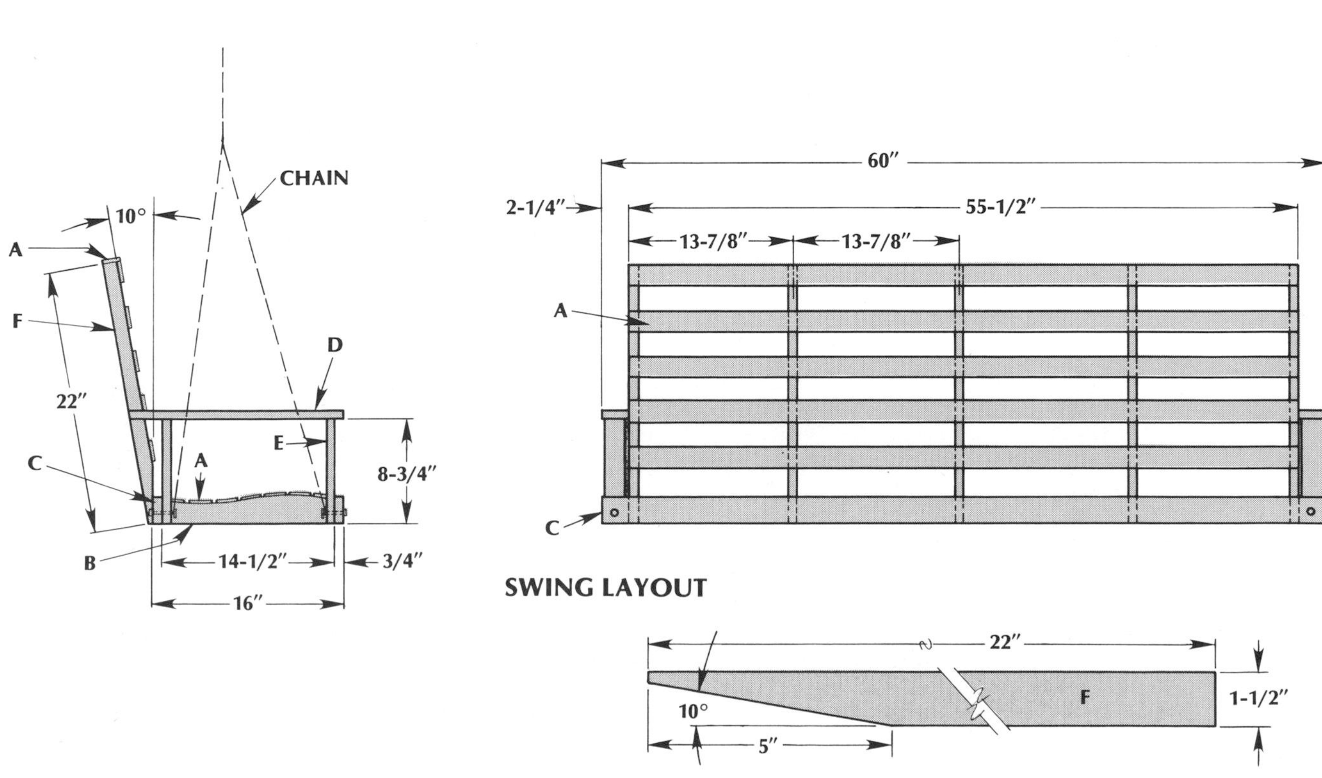

SWING LAYOUT

Index

Many thanks to the following *HANDS ON* readers who contributed to this book: SVEN ABRAHAMSEN, CHERYL BARNETT, JAMES CURTIS, MARK DI SALVO, DALE EBY, JAMES FILLENWARTH, JACK FISHER, PAUL HERMON, R. M. HOUSELY, BILL HOWELL, OREON KEESLAR, CLARK PATTON, RUDE OSOLNIK, PAUL RASANEN, DAVE STRUBLE, YOSH SUGIYAMA, BOB THOMPSON, TOM THOMPSON, STEVE WILSON, and ROGER ZIEGLER.